NEVERENDING Parenting

BE A MATURE PARENT FOR YOUR ADULT CHILD

Aaron Auerbach, PhD

DEVORA
PUBLISHING
JERUSALEM ◆ NEW YORK

Neverending Parenting: Be a Mature Parent for Your Adult Child
Published by Devora Publishing Company
Copyright © 2008 by Aaron Auerbach. All rights reserved.

COVER DESIGN: Benjie Herskowitz
TYPESETTING & BOOK DESIGN: Koren Publishing Services
EDITOR: Shirley Zauer
EDITORIAL & PRODUCTION MANAGER: Daniella Barak

Conversations and events in this book are all true. Some names and identities have been changed to protect privacy.

Hard cover ISBN: 978-1-934440-22-3

E-MAIL: sales@devorapublishing.com
WEB SITE: www.devorapublishing.com

Printed in the United States of America

AUG 2 0 2008

This book is dedicated to

my maternal grandfather,
Nissan (Albert) Selipsky,

and to
David Frank.

Both are neverending parents.

Contents

Preface

When does one become an adult? Many parents in their mature years feel that their children still behave like kids. This book is intended for parents who are concerned that their grown-up children have never really left the nest emotionally or financially.

The underlying assumption of this book is that parenting is a neverending role in life, a role that does not end when the children have left home to build their own families. Parenting assumes special forms at different stages in life, and the principles that hold true for parents in their golden years differ from those that apply to parents of toddlers or teenagers.

Where can one find literature on these principles? There is no shortage of titles in the "parenting" section of every bookstore on how to take care of your baby, survive the "terrible twos," cope with the problems of early childhood or contend with troubled adolescents. But mature parenting – by parents whose ages range from the forties to the late eighties – has been sorely neglected and only begun to be addressed in recent years. This is an issue that is becoming increasingly important with the significant growth in life span over the past few generations and the fact that many young people are delaying leaving the nest.

Each chapter of this book is a story that describes a dilemma and provides a possible solution based on the reasoning of a mature parent, followed by a discussion of a number of tangential issues of a psychological or philosophical nature. This format, with a synopsis at the beginning of each chapter to highlight its contents, is designed to enable readers to focus on the situations and dilemmas most relevant to their lives.

My philosophical and ethical foundation of becoming a mature parent is rooted in over forty years of experience as a developmental psychologist. Over the years I have had many encounters with parents of adult children seeking guidance for dealing with the perplexing issues of parenting in the golden years. This book has grown out of these encounters.

Acknowledgments

No book of any interest is a monologue. *Neverending Parenting* was born out of the dialogue with my former editor Barbara Grancell-Frank in the realms of philosophy, religion, the art of writing, and most of all, neverending parenting. The dialogue continued and developed in new directions with my next editor, Tsipi-Kuper Blau.

I would like to extend thanks to Willy Waks for his continuous support of this project. My cousin Alan Auerbach, my college classmates Max and Devorah Primack, and my childhood friend Florence Rafael Cheifetz provided invaluable commentary. Floyd Horowitz, Joe Marcus, Charlie Greenbaum, Avraham Greenbaum, David Shipler, Sarah Meron, Martin Elton, Robert Cooper and Alice Cooper each provided valuable insights.

I am grateful for the constant emotional support of my partner in life, Irena Gefter, and her son Moshe. Finally, I owe a debt of gratitude to my many clients who have taught and continue to teach me the importance of becoming a mature parent.

Introduction

Your child is all grown up, earning a living, bringing up a family. You're approaching the golden years, looking forward to doing all those things you never had time for. Life is good. But then, something happens that you didn't bargain for. Your adult child is in crisis – perhaps getting a divorce or losing a job – and suddenly you find your offspring back on your doorstep, turning to you for help.

This book deals with the dilemmas experienced by parents of adult children who are either on the verge of coming back home or who have never really left home emotionally (even if they live miles away). The problem has become more widespread in recent decades. A number of factors contribute to this: the significant increase in life span over the past few generations, the fact that people remain productive later in life, and the tendency of many young people to delay leaving the parental home with all its attendant comforts and amenities.

Of all animals, humans are unique in their relatively long developmental period in which the child is dependent upon its parents. With each passing generation, the period of adolescence grows longer. Young adults are in no hurry to leave the parental nest, frequently continuing to live at home for financial reasons. Moreover, even when they do leave home they may return to the parents at the first sign of any difficulty. It is becoming increasingly difficult for young people to be independent at an early stage, as their parents and their grandparents were. Living alone has become a luxury few young people can afford.

Humans continue to lead productive lives for many decades after ceasing to be active parents. This period of healthy old age grows longer with each passing generation. As stated in *The New York Times* (July 20, 2003), there is "a huge wave of 76 million baby boom retirees just over the horizon." As the baby boomers of the 1940s and 1950s reach retirement age, the percentage of retirees in the population – those aged sixty-five years and over – will grow rapidly. According to the U.S. Census Bureau, 12.6 percent of the population in North America were sixty-five years or older in 2002, and it is projected that by 2030, this age group will constitute 20.3 percent of the population.

All cultures maintain conventions for relationships among generations. The general model is that parents take care of their offspring when they are young and that the offspring take care of their parents in their old age. In many cultures the elderly are totally dependent upon their children to take care of them, lest they starve. In more affluent cultures – with elaborate systems of government and workplace pensions for the retired – this is not the case. But in these cultures we now sometimes see a reversal of the previous rule. Elderly parents often find themselves continuing to take care of their adult children for much longer than they expected.

Further, the parents of today whose children are "all grown up" may be experiencing a wealth of problems that their own parents did not have to face. Somewhere along the way the rules of the game change (as they are prone to do at various stages of the parenting process), and parents of adult children often find themselves in the perplexing position of muddling along, not having quite figured out the new rules. Delayed independence can intensify any pre-existing emotional problems in both generations and fan the flames of "unfinished family business." The problems are exacerbated when adult children undergo severe disruptions, such as being fired or getting divorced.

THE PURPOSE OF THE BOOK

Neverending Parenting provides a set of guidelines to help parents deal with their adult offsprings' crises, crises that in extreme cases lead to the offsprings' return to parental care. While such disruptions are generally perceived as troublesome, the advantage is that they provide one final opportunity to "raise" their adult, or even middle-aged, children. The underlying assumption is that even though children grow up, leave home and get married, they will always require some form of parenting. Mature parents – from their early forties to their late eighties – should be *selfless* in resolving their adult children's problems, yet *selfish* in resolving their own issues. According to this double-edged principle of selflessness and selfishness, mature parents should always help their adult children to attain or regain autonomy, but should be committed to maintaining their own autonomy as well.

Raising adult children is a challenge that puts parents back in touch with the youthful enthusiasm of the initial parenting experience. The possibility of "correcting the past" may provide an opportunity for the mature parent to overcome flaws of personality induced by factors previously beyond control. Having to get one's children back on track can be seen as a chance – perhaps the final one – for the parent to grow in ways that were inconceivable in previous generations.

At what age or stage of one's life and one's children's lives does the pattern of always giving end? Are parents eternally committed to loving their children, no matter what they do? Are they committed to paying for education throughout the child's life, or is there an acceptable level beyond which this is no longer healthy? Should they pay for their children's follies in choosing a mate, choosing the wrong job or career, and bear responsibility for the vagaries of the market-place? When one's children are constantly getting into debt, always choosing the wrong mate, or never finding gainful employment, the mature parent faces complex choices about how to help.

As mentioned above, the rules of the game change when one's children can no longer be perceived as children. Being mature parents now means providing conditional love, rather than the unconditional love parents were expected to give when their children were young. If the purpose of mature parents is to help their offspring solve problems and regain autonomy or grow up, then the help and love they extend to their offspring must be conditional. *The conditional love of mature parents has boundaries and obligations* appropriate to the adult child's age.

Where do we locate the road map to find the right course of action? One source, of course, is common sense and practicality. Another is the wellspring of ethical precepts found in the writings of the great sages of our culture, in particular the Jewish philosopher Maimonides (1135–1204). This book provides the reader with a new way of looking at relations between parents and their adult children of all ages and explores the underlying feelings and emotions. It is hoped that this approach will help parents deal with moments of crises. The psychology presented in the book is conservative, and the discussions deal with issues of belief, faith and skepticism, as well as with more pragmatic matters. Thus, *Neverending Parenting* presents a mode of being and relating rooted in ancient wisdom and based on modern knowledge.

THE ORGANIZATION OF THE BOOK

Each chapter begins with a story that highlights a dilemma facing mature parents. This is followed by a section on the reasoning underlying the suggested course of action, demonstrating the two guiding principles of the mature parent – selfishness and selflessness – and by a discussion of various issues that arise in the story, some of a practical nature and others of a more philosophical bent. The reader is assumed to be an independent thinker who can extrapolate from the story and discussion to his or her own circumstances.

The purpose of the stories in each chapter is to clarify the characteristics that mature parents must cultivate in order to be good parents to their adult children. If people are given a choice between a short lecture with direct answers about becoming a mature parent, or reading and hearing complex stories with characters with whom they can directly or peripherally identify, they are likely to choose stories and characters. People learn more through stories or models and characters than through direct tuition. That apparently is human nature, and that is why the stories and characters have been developed in the book, so that you may partially insert yourself into a particular story or character that touches your imagination and allows you to become a better and more mature parent. I hope that one of the stories or characters helps you become the best parent you can be.

Most of the chapters deal with the psychological underpinnings of a parent-child interaction requiring a family financial decision. A few of the chapters deal with often-overlooked issues of learning-disabled adults (who are estimated to constitute 18–20 percent of the population) and are based on my practical and academic experience since 1963. A few chapters deal with exceptional – and hopefully rare – family circumstances: a terrorist attack, a near-death experience, and cult membership. The final chapter deals with mental illness.

I have attempted to maintain my professional distance and objectivity as much as possible. Most of the stories are based on composites of patients seen over several decades; the biographical details in these are fictional. My personal involvement was greater in two stories, and in these I found it impossible to remain detached. One of these is Chapter 14 (Amazing Grace), which is based upon my professional and research experience with the mentally ill. The other is Chapter 6 (Losing a Child), which follows from my real-life experience of working with victims of terror. Living in Israel, where every bus ride could be one's last, I cannot shake the feeling that the only thing that separates myself from the victims of bombings with whom I work is pure chance. While I was in the course of writing these pages, a former colleague, Dr. David Applebaum, who was director of the Emergency Room in Shaare Zedek Hospital and had treated dozens of victims of terror, was himself killed with his daughter in a café in Jerusalem in a terrorist attack on the eve of her wedding.

Mature parents can achieve change for their adult children by searching deeply within themselves for their own truths and projecting them upon the situation facing their children. Mature parents can utilize their experience in areas not familiar to the next generation. Mature parents can learn from parents facing similar issues, or even by reading a good book. For all of us, parenting is neverending because children will always need their parents to some extent, and parents will always feel the need to give of themselves to their children. This book is designed to help parents distinguish between giving as a neverending parent and giving as a neverending sacrifice.

Chapter One

NEVERENDING PARENTING

Synopsis

Elizabeth, the mother of an aging, increasingly moody single son, gets a wake-up call about Howard's "moodiness" and must decide what to do about his inability to make a living. How is she to encourage her dependent son, who at fifty-eight is already set in his ways, to change his lifestyle and develop new patterns of interaction with others? How is she to help him develop a healthier attitude toward productive work? Elizabeth, at an advanced age, must come to terms with her own role in encouraging her son's dependency and must have the courage to find new ways of interacting with him.

THE DILEMMA

Elizabeth refuses to divulge her exact age, although if pressed, admits that she'll "never see eighty again." In relatively good health, despite a tendency towards high blood pressure controlled by medication, she enjoys an ongoing love affair with chocolate, which has rendered her slightly overweight and, when climbing stairs, a little short of breath.

Elizabeth is a generous woman, the kind who would give her friends whatever they asked for. She had a few boyfriends in her youth, but she and her lifelong companion Phyllis, a nursery school teacher, enjoyed raising Elizabeth's son together. Elizabeth remained loyal to Phyllis until the latter died of natural causes. She gives openhandedly now, as she has in the past, to her moody fifty-eight-year-old son, Howard. Elizabeth has been channeling a considerable portion of her income to him throughout his life. During the many years she worked as a real-estate agent, Elizabeth earned high commissions, especially when the housing market in New England was booming. She routinely divided her earnings, maintaining herself on one half of her income and giving the other half to her son. Although Howard's salary as a shoe salesman was steady, it did not quite cover his rent and food bills. With the additional cash he received on a regular basis from his mother he managed to meet all his basic expenses, as well as one expense that was clearly an extravagance. Every winter, until his "sad moods" went from acute to ever more chronic, Howard spent two weeks on a cruise ship in the Caribbean. Elizabeth thought the cruises would cheer him up and give him an opportunity "to meet a nice girl."

After the housing boom ended, Elizabeth's commissions diminished considerably and she eventually retired from the real-estate business. She sold her spacious home in a Boston suburb and purchased a small condominium in the downtown area, about half an hour's drive from her son. The move reduced her own living expenses and enabled her to continue subsidizing Howard's. Her savings and social security benefits allowed her to remain in her small condo and keep running her car, but her income was no longer sufficient to cover Howard's allowance as well.

To complicate matters further, Howard's moody spells began to occur more frequently, exacerbated by the gradual reduction of his mother's funding. He started to miss workdays, and Elizabeth discovered that he was spending those days at home in bed. At her sister's suggestion, Elizabeth arranged an appointment for her reluctant son with a mental health-care professional for a psychological evaluation. Howard underwent a series of interviews and formal testing. When these were completed the psychologist informed Elizabeth that her son was clinically depressed. Elizabeth snapped at the psychologist, "Labels like that are only good for government categories. What I want to know is what can be done for my Howard." After delineating the possible courses of treatment – different medications and extensive psychotherapy, for example – he explained to Elizabeth that "people who are depressed often have difficulty working. In my experience," he added, "those who can work, do work. When they don't, there is usually something wrong."

In order to alleviate the financial difficulties stemming from Howard's inability to work, the psychologist suggested that Howard might be eligible for Social Security Disability Insurance. "On the other hand," he said, "maybe your son would like to retrain in another area through a rehabilitation program?" Elizabeth drove straight from the psychologist's office to her son's apartment and announced that he was either going to enter a rehabilitation program or apply for SSDI.

Howard, more than willing never to set foot in a shoe store again, nevertheless angrily rejected both options. When his puzzled mother asked why, he retorted, "I don't want people to think I have a disability. Why should I enter a program for retards? And I certainly don't want to go on the dole." Elizabeth, who could see fiscal ruin looming on the horizon, telephoned her sister as soon as she got home, frantic with worry and close to tears. "I'm sending you a ticket to Florida," the sister informed her. "Come and stay with me for a week. It's time you had a vacation, too."

When Elizabeth boarded the plane, she stared out of the window until she heard the stewardess begin to lecture about safety procedures in the event of a plane crash. Part of her almost hoped the plane would crash. At least the flight insurance would solve Howard's financial problems. She banished the self-destructive thought from her mind and watched as the use of the oxygen mask was being demonstrated. Mothers traveling with young children were instructed first to affix the oxygen mask to their own face and only afterwards to their children. "If you are unconscious," the stewardess cheerfully reminded her listeners, "you won't be able to save your child."

THE REASONING

Elizabeth has only two options. She can either continue to provide for her son financially, as she has always done, until she drowns in a sea of red ink and debt, taking her son down with her, or she can, for the first time in her life, check her impulse to give completely of herself to her son. If she takes the latter option and refrains from sharing her money with her son, she will be able to maintain her own modest but sufficient standard of living for the duration of her lifetime. Both alternatives are distasteful for Elizabeth. She has been accustomed to giving, and she has always derived pleasure from providing for her son. She must now forego that pleasure. This is an enormous and painful adjustment for a mother. But Elizabeth must change for the sake of her own financial well-being. She must also deal with the negative emotions her son may direct towards her as a result of having to apply for a form of public assistance. Howard will have to deal with his image of himself and with how he will be viewed by others. This, however, is Howard's problem and not his mother's.

Withholding funds from her son and withstanding his anger will be difficult, but there are no other viable options here. Elizabeth has to acknowledge these difficulties. Only when she does so can she change her behavior in order to retain her autonomy and to enable her son to achieve some form of independence at the age of fifty-eight.

Many parents simply do not wish to see the real implications of growing older on a fixed income. Their emotional lack of preparedness can lead them to make poor choices about a dependent adult offspring. By ignoring Howard's obvious dilemma, Elizabeth has slipped into a potentially catastrophic situation for herself as well, for *the greater one's age and fiscal limitations, the fewer the available solutions to problems.* Whereas Howard suffers from depression, Elizabeth suffers from the curse of endless procrastination in coming to grips with her son's limitations.

Somewhere along the way, Elizabeth has forgotten the fundamental goal of parenting, the original purpose underlying the parenting of children. *The principle job of parents is to help their children become independent adults,* insofar as this end is physically, emotionally and financially possible. Achieving this goal is generally feasible in most families. But an overgenerous parent guilty of giving too much or giving inappropriately does not permit a child to develop autonomy.

Elizabeth's generosity in sharing her wealth with Howard has proven, in the final analysis, to constitute poor parenting. It has fostered financial and emotional dependence on both sides. Howard has never learned to live within his means, and Elizabeth has never learned to "just say no" to inappropriate demands on her finances. Elizabeth may have equated opening her pocketbook with loving her son. Sadly, her son may have done the same. When reality, in the form of old age, decreasing health and insufficient monetary resources intruded into their lives, mother and son were ill prepared to handle the consequences.

Elizabeth should try not to feel guilty about her inability to continue giving money to Howard. She should constantly remind herself that if she destroys herself financially now, she will have nothing to leave her son in his old age. As with the oxygen mask on the plane, the mother must survive so that her son can survive. She can also console herself with the fact that she has become, admittedly at the eleventh hour, a good role model of autonomy for her son. It would have been better for all concerned if, rather than having to dispense "tough love" to her son so late in the game, she had encouraged him to manage his money more prudently years earlier. As it is, Elizabeth will undoubtedly pay a price for not having done so. And so will Howard.

If Elizabeth suffers qualms because of what she must now do, she will simply have to live with her guilt. Similarly, Howard will have to adapt to a different life style and overcome his shame at having to take money from the government. The physical and economic circumstances of mother and son give them little room in which to maneuver. The mechanisms of giving and receiving in their family must finally be dealt with realistically. It is never too late to let go.

THE ROOTS OF GIVING AND RECEIVING

Giving and receiving are not separate modalities, but an expression of a healthy relationship between two intertwined entities. Each modality by itself is insufficient to develop a whole human being, for a generous spirit like Elizabeth cannot give endlessly and a dependent soul like Howard cannot continue to take eternally from his mother.

The paradigm of giving and receiving begins with the mother and child relationship and extends soon thereafter into the family and the emotional environment. Children are legitimately seen as justified in receiving from the parent the gifts of love, education and money. The generally agreed-upon rules on how to raise infants and toddlers are found in a wealth of how-to books. There are rules for what to do when they are teenagers and young adults up to thirty, such as those found in the widely read books of Erik Erikson.

But what are the rules for caring for adult children? At what age or stage of the child's life and the life of a mature parent does this paradigm end? Are parents eternally committed to loving their children no matter what? Are parents committed to paying for education throughout their children's lives, or is there an acceptable level beyond which it is no longer reasonable? Must parents pay for their children's follies in choosing a mate or the wrong job or career? After a certain age the child is acknowledged by all to be an adult. After this age, the responsibility for their well-being no longer resides solely with the parent, as it did in the child's youth. Lest we forget, Howard is fifty-eight.

The rules of relating to grown-up children should be addressed in the context of dialogue between the two generations. Responsibility for the adult child's well-being should be allocated according to the age and the circumstances that each generation brings to the discourse. The paradigm of normative giving and receiving has broken down in the case of Elizabeth and Howard. When one member of a family is eternally needy, the other member often becomes eternally giving. This constitutes a life sentence for a blameless individual. Elizabeth may indeed be guilty of loving too much and needing to control her son, but does this oblige her to take care of him forever? She was forced to examine a situation of illness and unemployment not, as expected, of herself, but of Howard. The balance between giving and receiving has finally broken down.

A precondition of fostering a loving relationship between mature parents and adult children is the ability to set limits. This is a concept fundamental to parenting at any level of the child's maturation. After all, whereas the bonds of affection between parents and adult children constitute the emotional core of decision-making, it is the relative physical, intellectual and financial resources available to each that are crucial to translating that emotional bond into reality. Elizabeth and Howard should recognize each other's strengths if a solution is to be achieved. Elizabeth is in a strong position with regard to her beloved son. The sub-agenda of decision-making is that the strong are expected to do what they can, while the weak are expected to do what they must, in order to enable both parties to reach a compromise in the gap between necessity and desire.

PARENTAL POWER

A child at any age, including Howard at fifty-eight, wants to be independent but also thrives on limits. Even though children know that being independent means doing certain things by themselves, they assume that their parents will always be there for them. In many instances the assumption of dependency is so strongly rooted that the gestures made towards independence are down-right amusing. Many college students in major East Coast cities in the fifties and sixties lived at home, but considered themselves to be independent because they had scholarships and worked at odd jobs on weekends. Today they view their adult children, aged twenty-five to thirty-five, as dependent, but wonder if that dependency is still temporary.

Does the financial well-being of many mature parents mean that their adult heirs are automatically entitled to all of the accoutrements of wealth, despite the fact that they have not earned them themselves? The answer is a resounding "no." The discrepancy in power between the generations may be in the parents' favor in areas such as ego strength, financial means and coping with tough situations, but this same discrepancy may engender emotional booby traps. Parents may project their own ego strength onto their children, expecting them to "just do it" as they did at that age. "I went to work at fourteen. What do you mean you're too young to work?" Such an attitude gives children a negative message about their strengths, implying worthlessness.

The opposite situation – the parents giving their child all the good things that life has to offer because "we can afford it" – is no less fraught with problems. "Hell, no child of mine will have to go through what I went through. Only the best for my child – Nikes, Levis, BMWs, whatever." This kind of attitude may undermine the offspring's will to struggle and make it on his own. After all, he receives everything he needs – and a lot that he doesn't – on the basis of entitlement alone. A careless parent may turn a child into a trust-fund case, a rich recipient of welfare who is dependent on the parent's "dole money." After all, why work towards a financial goal when one is already entitled to it through a parent's material achievements? *Money may weaken the adult offspring and not serve as a spur to independence.* This argument may not ring true to any parent who would have been grateful for assistance at critical moments and who cannot conceive of money being a weakening factor. Nevertheless, look around and draw your own conclusion. The adult child with a trust fund may not be a fulfilled, hard-working individual.

The parent whose working life began much earlier than that of his or her child may view an adult offspring as an eternal student. After all, the child started going to school at an early age and, unlike the parent, never stopped. Such a child often continues school well into his or her late twenties and frequently into the early thirties. A grown-up child habituated to learning postpones entry into the world of work. Apparently there is more prestige in scholarships than in paychecks. Scholarships are proof that one has brains; getting a job, on the other hand, means overcoming certain fears and anxieties about one's sense of worth. One student – an excellent scholar – reports that when she went to her first job interview she was actually scared of getting the job. After she had obtained the approval of her professors, a job could not provide satisfaction to the soul. Ultimately, however, it was her stomach that convinced her that the soul needed to eat as well.

When adult offspring want concrete help from their parents in the form of money, food and a place to sleep, more intangible help, such as emotional support, understanding, sympathy, security and acceptance, is also sought. A mature parent assumes that no one ever outgrows the need for maternal or paternal love. Troubled adults are no exception. They are, in effect, asking to be re-parented. They want their parents to listen to their problems, to share their distress and to help them figure out what to do. Howard's unpleasant immaturity may appear as anger or disappointment at feeling no longer needed or wanted at the shoe store. The parent's initial job is to listen and be patient and to refrain from making suggestions not likely to be heard. Listening, rather than speaking hastily, is the key activity at this point, and Elizabeth was wise to keep quiet and to take "time out" visiting her sister in Florida in order to contemplate her predicament.

When parents fulfill the adult child's financial needs straight away they are encouraging the child's fiscal dependence. After all, most adults who turn to their parents for financial help tend to do so repeatedly. Howard's failure to achieve emotional and financial independence stems from his inability to prioritize debt, obligations and feelings. Elizabeth's examination of Howard's debts, in accord with him, can remove the most pressing and threatening of the debts. This simple beginning can create a climate of talking about underlying emotional problems so that the other financial problems become slightly more manageable. Giving a needy son money is a quantitative investment and, as noted above, should be conditional. But a parent is required to make qualitative investments as well. Elizabeth should set aside special time for Howard. She could dig out board games – chess, Monopoly, Risk and Scrabble – and play with him. They could watch videos together or go for walks. When a parent like Elizabeth chooses to spend time in such activities with her offspring, the message that she sends is the one she really feels towards Howard: "I love you. You are valuable to me. I like to be with you."

The parent's initial response to financial problems can lead to the fantasy of a one-time payoff. However, this heroic cutting of the Gordian knot is generally ineffective. It involves overestimating the importance of the financial dilemma, while underestimating the emotional issues. Few financial problems are one-time events; instead, they are often the result of accumulated financial and emotional miscalculations. Therefore, systematically addressing the emotional problems as one is dealing with the financial issues will provide a better chance of a long-term solution to future money problems. Often money problems are chronic and due to a lack of capacity, as in Howard's case. The parent has to evaluate the depth and breadth of the problem and, rather than try to provide a one-time money fix, should attempt to improve and alleviate the underlying conditions of financial distress.

In order for change to take place, there has to be some necessity. Elizabeth must impose limits on the use of Howard's credit cards. Going to restaurants on a daily basis is a luxury when one is short of money. Cooking and eating at home is less expensive and can give one more control over eating habits. Big spending has to be confined to necessities. For example, a legally binding debt must be paid on time by adult offspring or their parents to avoid legal consequences. In instances when a man loses his job and cannot pay alimony, for example, the courts may need to periodically intervene and adjust the debt payment schedule. *People change when they have to, not when they want to.*

Howard's Caribbean cruises are a luxury. All the young women on the cruises know Howard by now and wouldn't dream of interfering with his relationship with his mother. They have long ago reached the conclusion that he is a loser. But that's not how Elizabeth sees it. Howard may believe that he is not able to perform tasks or learn certain skills because of past failures, but some inner voice tells him that his critical situation requires obedience to Elizabeth's demands, not discussion of old problems. Elizabeth cuts a deal with Howard. Howard's problem of unemployment or underemployment must be looked at through new eyes by a supportive but firm Elizabeth, whose own work experience is considerably more than her son's. He must read newspapers, look at new jobs, consult an employment counselor, and speak to mature friends. He must submit resumes, go to interviews and follow up as required. Areas of employment alien to Howard should be taken into consideration. A psychologist can deal with the adult child's feelings; the parent's job is to enhance a sense of worth. One way of doing this is to encourage the child to seek independent employment. The paycheck is an external validation of independence.

If a job calls for skills the child does not possess, mature parents should help their children to be re-educated or retrained. Even if Howard is convinced that he "is no good in that area" and that he "just can't do it," the mature parent, who believes that his or her child is capable of handling a challenge, should firmly insist: "Yes, you can do it." The parent, realizing that necessity is the mother of invention, should say, "Forget the past. Stay in the present, and study hard. You can acquire the skills if you try hard. Your life depends on it. I know what that is like." When a person works hard at a seemingly endless difficult task, it can be as painful as hitting a brick wall, as every student knows. Elizabeth would not urge Howard to hit that wall if she didn't have full confidence that he could hit it head on and walk away intact. But most people can do many things with the support and encouragement of a relative, if they are pushed by nurturance and pulled by dire necessity. If you don't do the training or get the job, the consequences are worse than the pain of hitting the wall.

Howard may complain daily for six months or more as he completes a program under his mother's moderate emotional pressure, but he will nevertheless succumb to that pressure. He will keep his part of the deal with Elizabeth because an inner voice has told him a long time ago that none of the women with whom he ever had a drink on a Caribbean cruise would do as much for him as his eternal parent.

Chapter Two

THE BURDENS OF BEREAVEMENT

INTRODUCTION

Elizabeth's son might be seen by others as a "child whom only a mother could love." Everyone recognized his problem and commented on his behavior, but Elizabeth didn't listen to them and procrastinated because the blindness of love overcomes counsel proffered by a friend, the repeated observations of a prudent person or relevant information. The striking inertia of this dependent parent-child relationship ended when the reality of impending poverty showed its dreadful face. Change was forced upon her by external, not internal reasons, due to her life-long blind love. Elizabeth was coerced into growing up herself for her son's sake.

Elizabeth's story is all too common and as simple to understand as her son. By contrast, the following story of Marianne is one of coping with complexity and past unfinished business. Elizabeth changed her approach to her child due to external financial coercion; Marianne is required to develop psychological insight, a mostly internal process, to help her strayed child. Elizabeth's road to help her child had few twists and turns; Marianne's road required her to discover both emotional intelligence and the traditional value of courage. Elizabeth's family system collapsed because of the ill health of her son; Marianne's system collapsed because of the death of her husband, an all too common occurrence for many women. Sometimes external circumstances, as in Elizabeth's case, and sometimes insight into one's inner being, as in Marianne's case, are required to change an unhappy situation with an adult child. Nonetheless, whether a parent's problems are simple or complex, a parent must become mature herself; this is a necessary precursor to helping the adult child grow up.

Synopsis

Marianne, who recently lost her husband, finds herself dealing with the consequences of her son's dilettante attitude toward education and his frivolous business ventures that cost her a bundle. Although she has always come across as a "dumb blonde," Marianne has sound business sense and is irritated by her son's irresponsible behavior. Now, on top of her grief at her husband's death, she has to deal with these issues on her own. What does it take in order to find within oneself the strength to cope with the pain and to emerge from the state of mourning with a fresh lease on life?

THE DILEMMA

Marianne is a stylish blonde in her sixties whose husband made good money as a consulting civil engineer. She raised their two sons, Eddie and Ritchie, largely by herself, as her husband was married first and foremost to his job.

Marianne's pastime, in addition to her duties as an at-home mom, was investing her husband's salary. Having been brought up in a poor family, she knew virtually nothing about the stock market when she began, nor did she have the option of studying for a degree in economics. Instead, she walked into a public library, asked to see the *Morning Star* on the advice of her accountant, and read it from cover to cover. She then took out a subscription to *Barron's* financial newspaper and, over the next five years, proceeded to double the value of her husband's stock and bond portfolio.

Marianne became a widow when Eddie was two-thirds through his first year of studies at an expensive dental school and Ritchie was completing his junior year at a local college. Eddie came home for his father's funeral and decided not to return to his studies. He confessed to his mother that he was feeling overwhelmed by all the information thrown at him and that he wasn't at all sure he wanted to be a dentist. Marianne, who was paying interest on a bank loan of $50,000 to cover Eddie's tuition and dorm fees, grimaced, but didn't force the issue. "Go back and get your stuff," she said. "We'll figure something out." Eddie, relieved at her response, promised, "I'll pay off the loan. I can always go back to my summer job on the ice-cream truck." But $50,000 worth of ice cream, Marianne thought to herself, was a lot of ice cream.

Eddie left school toward the end of the academic year and worked all through the following summer on the truck. He did well. Though he didn't pay off his debt, he did make a significant dent in it. So Marianne was more-or-less prepared for the proposition he put before her in September, when she asked him what he planned to do next. "I'd like to go into the ice-cream business," he answered. "My major expense would be buying the truck. But the mark-up on ice cream is so huge, I can easily make the truck payments out of my profits." "Okay," Marianne replied, privately wondering whether her son wasn't perhaps being overly optimistic. "I'll pay for a down payment on the truck and for the first month's supply of ice-cream. With your profits you can finish paying for the truck. We'll worry about the dental school loan later."

While Eddie was busy selling ice cream, his brother Ritchie finished college. "Are you going to set me up like you did Eddie?" Ritchie asked his mother. Marianne choked. "You want to sell ice cream, too?" she demanded. "No way," replied Ritchie. "I want to sell T-shirts from a cart in the mall, shirts you personalize with iron-on decals. Trust me, Mom, you're getting off cheap. It costs a lot more to buy a truck than it does to buy a cart, stock it with shirts and decals, and get an ironing machine. It's T-shirt weather out here most of the year. I'm going to be minting money." What she had done for her eldest son, despite her better judgment, she could not refuse to do for her youngest. "Go scout locations," Marianne advised Ritchie, privately hoping the mall was not saturated with T-shirt stores.

After Marianne had launched both her sons into the entrepreneurial orbit, she made two discoveries. The first was that the house in which she had lived in comfort and contentment for twenty-three years was too big for her. She surveyed the empty tennis court and swimming pool and realized that, just as Eddie and Ritchie had moved on, so should she. The second discovery was made when she started to look around for a smaller home. The price for a three-bedroom condominium in a full-service retirement community was exorbitant. The sum she would have to come up with, coupled with the college and business loans for which she had signed, came to more than one-quarter of her total net worth. Marianne was not poor. There was no danger that she would fail to keep a roof over her head or know where her next meal was coming from. But she began to wonder whether she would have the kind of life in middle and old age that she had anticipated, one that included travel, without having to worry about money. Her financial portfolio was in excellent shape because the market had been upbeat for some time. But sooner or later that would change, and then what?

As Marianne was making the rounds with her real-estate agent, her first-born was making discoveries of his own. With the start of the school year and the shorter daylight hours, the ice-cream business was becoming less lucrative. There weren't as many children on the streets in the fall, and there were no food concessions available in the various swim clubs that dotted the city, particularly the indoor clubs. Eddie also found out that even a new truck, still under warranty, had to be taken to the dealership for maintenance every so often. In addition, he made the unfortunate discovery that his most profitable business hours on the street coincided with the hours he would have preferred to party or to hang out with his friends at the local coffee shops.

Because business was bad, Eddie figured that taking a day off now and then wouldn't make that much difference to his overall profits. The result, not surprisingly, was that business went from bad to worse, and as fall turned to winter, the occasional day off became the occasional week off. In December he missed his first loan repayment. By the time he had missed three such payments he decided he had better tell his mother what was happening before the bank did. In any event, he wasn't sure the ice-cream business was right for him after all.

Marianne was appalled. She had finally seen two condos she liked, although the asking price for both apartments was much higher than she had bargained for. She was about to make an offer on the one she preferred, when Eddie invited himself to dinner and told her that he was through with the ice-cream business. "I'm thinking about becoming a respiratory therapist," he confided over his Jell-O mold. "Half the kids I sold ice-cream to had small change in one hand and an inhaler in the other. It's only two more years of school, and at least my science background won't be wasted." Marianne mentally computed the monthly truck payments and the interest on the dental school loan and had a hard time swallowing her Jell-O. If Eddie wasn't going to be a dentist or an independent businessman, he would never be able to help her repay his past education debts.

THE REASONING

Marianne and Eddie need to talk. Although Eddie has not behaved in a particularly adult manner until now, Marianne should nevertheless address him as an adult. She needs to listen to his problems, and she should do something she has not done until now:

she should make him understand hers. Marianne has not confided in Eddie regarding her concerns about money, and he is therefore probably unaware of them. She has to explain to him that laying out more money for his new educational goal, while simultaneously paying off his old education loan, means that she will have to downgrade her lifestyle in her old age. Marianne should sit down with a calculator, pencil and paper, and show Eddie where she stands financially. If she is afraid that she may be in dire financial straits later in life, she should tell him so.

The fact that Eddie did not achieve his past academic goals constitutes a serious problem for both of them. Marianne is not only worried about her own finances; she is also concerned about her son's happiness. She wants him to find a job he likes and can do well in, just as his father did, because she believes that the right occupation will make Eddie happy. But she cannot simply write another check to cover Eddie's latest adventure.

Marianne feels obligated to continue to pay off the dental school loan because that was her decision prior to her husband's death, and she has told Eddie that she will take responsibility for part of his financial obligations. Marianne should convey the message that he should assume responsibility for paying off the truck, even if this takes a year or two. Eddie should stay in the ice-cream business and take the responsibility of trying to make a go of it. Once he does own the truck, he can sell it and put the sale money toward tuition for the program in respiratory therapy – if, at that time, that's what he still wants to do.

Marianne and Eddie will need to engage in a lengthy dialogue about the manner in which he makes his vocational decisions and choices, for it appears that he makes them in a haphazard way. His track record suggests that he stumbles into different occupations. He doesn't pursue them on the basis of interest, which, where Eddie is concerned, has been fleeting. Nor are his decisions based on where his abilities lie. Deciding what to do for a living is not easy, and Marianne can certainly be empathetic toward her son while he is confronting his vocational dilemma. She may even want to suggest counseling. What she cannot do is allow her son to keep striking out and remain at bat.

THE IMPACT OF BEREAVEMENT

The underlying emotional thread of their relationship is that both Marianne and Eddie are still in mourning for the man who was Marianne's husband and Eddie's father. Their ongoing bereavement has put them in a weakened state, one in which decision-making is best avoided. Most religions and cultures observe a mourning period where the mourners are given "time out" from decision-making. It is only natural to make poor judgments when in mourning, a time of extreme vulnerability. *Major mistakes* on the professional, financial or personal level *are often made in the first year after the death of a loved one.* Marrying in order to fill the void, selling the house to get away from the memories, changing profession in an effort to become closer to someone who is no longer there, making financial investments that are not evaluated with a clear head: these are the pitfalls of hasty decision-making while still in bereavement.

Neither Marianne nor Eddie is up to a much-needed discussion of the family's financial affairs. The myriad ways in which the death of a loved one affects the various family members cannot be underestimated. Had his father been alive when he was in dental school, Eddie would probably have at least finished his first year. This would have been a real achievement, because it would have given him some sense of closure with respect to his aspirations of becoming a dentist. Instead, he regressed to the comfort level of his youth, selling ice cream and attempting to grow up by owning a truck.

Eddie is paying a heavy emotional price by failing to work out his feelings toward his father. He did not take stock of his new position in life. But it is even more costly to jump from one activity to another, without the satisfaction of completing anything. Eddie, who was not born to fail, has established a pattern of failure by not coming to grips with the loss of his father and not understanding its impact on other areas of his life.

If Eddie is paying an emotional price, Marianne is paying a heavy price financially. Marianne's decision-making in the aftermath of her husband's death was flawed. She readily acceded to her son's request to come home, partly because she sensed his unhappiness and lack of contentment at dental school, but also for her own "selfish" reasons; simply stated, she was sad and needed him to be close to her. Her support of the ice-cream truck venture stemmed from an attempt on her part to serve as both mother and father – to be emotionally supportive of her son, while at the same time providing the practical aid necessary to help him achieve the goal of financial independence, as his father would have done.

To rectify the situation and put them back on track, Marianne should become aware of her vulnerabilities and postpone any critical life decisions until she feels stronger. Only then will she be able to advise her son adequately. She should begin to strengthen herself by saying "no" to Eddie's requests for money and "yes" to talking about how much she still misses her husband.

The major issues will become clearer for her and her sons at some future point in time. By rejecting Eddie's latest scheme for self-improvement, while explaining her reasons to him in a clear, thought-out manner, she is helping him to grow up. She is not "juvenilizing" him with her refusal; on the contrary, by confiding in him about her financial situation and needs, she is establishing a grown-up relationship with Eddie, a relationship of equals.

Marianne felt emotionally abandoned by her husband's death, as did her sons. The abandonment was not only emotional but also financial. Now, almost one year later, it is time for them to move forward as an emotional and fiscal unit. Refusal to acquiesce to Eddie's whims in this instance does not constitute an abandonment of Eddie or an emotional withdrawal. Quite the opposite is true: by reaffirming her own judgment and refusing to go along with Eddie's new scheme, Marianne is reestablishing her original status as a sound economic investor, a status that was diverted by her husband's death. Her eldest son's professional and personal difficulties will not be resolved by throwing money at him.

MONEY PAST AND MONEY PRESENT

Marianne started off parenting with a desire that she shared with many of her generation – to make sure that her children had it easier than her family of origin, who had to struggle with poverty. She may have been indulgent to her children because times were good when her husband was alive, but she can no longer indulge them as adults. Even if she was a good parent to Eddie and Ritchie when they were children, she needs to parent them in a different way now, because they are different people under different circumstances. Essentially, they need to be re-parented by learning how to deal with their own painful problems of loss and economic instability. They can do so with parental help, but they are required to pay their own dues.

Eddie's return home was triggered by tragedy, as well as by Marianne's need to have him nearby. She all too willingly accepted his tale of difficulties in dental school and empathized with his regression to the ice-cream truck. Eddie's dropping out of school is proving to be hard on him and painful to Marianne as she is called upon to provide endless safety nets for his failure to make it financially.

Marianne's status as a parent has grown in importance: she is now the sole parent and a "giver," but she should keep Eddie in touch with the harshness of reality. The reality is that Eddie is an unemployed son with few real prospects. He might consider retraining in a field that would make use of his scientific background, but if he feels that the ensuing job is beneath him, he is unlikely to keep it for much longer than the ice-cream truck. Marianne should keep him in touch with reality. If the only jobs available are those that Eddie feels are not good enough for him, then Marianne will have to make it plain that his options are either retraining or unemployment. Eddie possesses a full set of defense mechanisms, such as denial, avoidance and clever shortcuts to circumvent the difficulties and boredom of the ice-cream business. But Marianne knows that the abundance of energy channeled into defense mechanisms could be better deployed. She hopes to help him refocus his energy to achieve the desired goal: recovery of the economic position that he enjoyed prior to his father's death.

Marianne should insist that Eddie seek vocational counseling. This would provide him with objective tools to make an important life-changing decision, separate from the emotional issues generated by his father's demise. Ultimately, vocational counseling may guide him into an occupation similar to his father's. This would be a healthy and productive way for Eddie to feel close to his father again, as distinct from the unhealthy patterns of decision-making that he has been pursuing for the past year.

By insisting that Eddie share the financial burden of his future education and/or vocational training, Marianne is helping her son attain autonomy and is changing the unrealistic, non-pragmatic character of their relationship. She is finally teaching him that there is a penalty for failure. At the same time, she is re-establishing her own autonomy. Eddie should learn that Mom's cookie jar does not contain an endless supply. When he finally understands that he cannot reach for more cookies every time his supply runs out, he will have traveled a long way toward independence and adulthood. Marianne's conviction that he can cover this ground once he knows and accepts her financial constraints will probably bring her closer to her son and increase their mutual respect – one of the side benefits of being a parent.

PAIN – A SOURCE OF COURAGE

To continue to educate and strengthen her children, particularly Eddie, Marianne must deal with feelings of frustration as she attempts to bring clarity to the complex situation created by her husband's death. When everything in her life was going smoothly, her straightforward answers to problems presented by her sons were effective. Eddie needs money for football? "Sure, mow the lawn for me, and I'll give you the twenty bucks." Ritchie wants to upgrade his bike? "No problem, take over a paper route, and I'll pay you double for Sundays." This approach to problems would have continued to stand her in good stead after her husband died had she continued in her pre-bereavement state of mind.

The new widow had two options: to deal with the raw pain of her loss or to take a tranquilizer to deaden the existential pain. She chose to confront the pain head-on, to "go through it" and not sidestep around it. Ultimately this decision will ensure that she transcends the pain and moves ahead with her life. However, the emotional and financial complexity in which she now finds herself – a consequence of that courageous decision – means that she must delve into herself and her past experience once again and find the inner strength necessary to carry her through. By choosing not to avoid or numb the pain, Marianne is enabling the healing process to take place within herself.

An analogy to American football seems in place here. A ball carrier encounters direct pain by running straight into the opposing line. Running directly into the line defines the player as a courageous one. Nevertheless, the smart thing to do would seem to be running around the line or making short or long passes to gain more ground – rather than running directly into a burly linebacker intent on stopping you in your tracks, a move which has got to be painful. Nonetheless, tackling physical pain head-on is less painful psychologically for the whole team when compared to the desperation of the "Hail Mary" pass of a last-ditch effort to save the game. Losing the game hurts more than going into the line. Like the ball carrier who will absorb the painful tackle of the linebacker and do anything to prevent his team from losing the game, Marianne does not want to lose her remaining family – losing her husband was painful enough.

Should Marianne acquiesce to her adult child's views on schooling and business opportunities because they share a common loss and are in no mood for conflict, however minor? The answer is a resounding "no." Marianne should not avoid her own profound pain or try to protect Eddie from his. Marianne, like all adults, has had to deal with pain in the past and has, undoubtedly, had previous experience in dealing with Eddie's pain. Minor manageable pain is an inevitable part of growing up. Sports injuries and other childhood injuries establish thresholds that train youngsters to deal with pain. Many children fall off their bicycles often while learning to ride. Falling off a bike hurts, but it establishes the inevitability of pain.

Wise parents are there when their children fall, armed with sympathy and a bandage – and as soon as possible, they put their children back on the bike. In this manner children learn that although pain is inevitable, it is not the end of the world. By mustering some courage children can face whatever pain might come along and not collapse under physical – or later, psychic – pain. The most important lesson children learn is that getting back on the bike and not avoiding pain is what makes them big boys or girls. Learning hurts. But let's not forget the joy of finally being able to ride a bike. The greatest lesson of all for both Marianne and Eddie is to get back on the bike, despite the pain.

The hardest step in resolving any crisis is the first one. It requires Marianne to summon up her internal resources and courage and to confront the mental meanderings of her son. A clear distinction should be made between the legitimate period of inactivity and solitude – the "time out" – necessary for the mourning process to take its course, and time wasted in procrastination. That first step requires that Marianne overcome the devil she knows – the heavy inertia of mourning for her husband – to deal with the devil she doesn't know, namely, how to raise troubled grown-up children who lack a father. Profound courage is required for Marianne to plunge into the unknown to change her current unhappy reality. The purpose of procrastination is the avoidance of pain, whereas the purpose of mourning is to work through the pain. Avoidance may be effective as an immediate palliative, but the dulling of pain may carry the side effect of institutionalizing the chronic pain of mourning. Unchecked, the wound may fester. Putting things off does not solve problems.

Marianne should be using the year spent in a state of mourning to plan her next moves, to prepare herself for the critical decisions ahead. The mourning period is a legitimate "time out" from the ongoing issues of life, but a temporary respite cannot be allowed to develop into full-fledged procrastination. *Problems not dealt with immediately can become more complicated.* Just thinking about them "doth make cowards of us all," as the Bard noted. Marianne should provide a warm welcome and a sympathetic ear before putting Eddie "back on the bike" and preferably off the truck. People admire courageous people of all ages, and what is required from Marianne is the courage to become the mature parent she needs to be. While, as already discussed, one should not make rash life-shattering decisions immediately after the death of a loved one, *there is a thin line between prudence and procrastination.*

Our ancestors viewed pain as being far more prevalent than joy. They would have been astounded at the notion, ubiquitous today, that happiness is our birthright. Maimonides, whose mother had died at his birth, once said that he had never had a happy day in his life and did not know what people were talking about when they said that they were happy. Our predecessors knew – an awareness born out of necessity – that the chances of achieving any happiness in this life is best enhanced by dealing with the ongoing problems of daily existence without procrastination.

Apparently, pain has some healthy function because it is part of the reality of life. One need not praise pain to note its inevitability in normal growth. Whereas a parent like Marianne would never be cruel or abusive to her children, the reality beyond the control of parents sometimes entails pain, be it in the form of a callous teacher or the everyday cruelty of school children. Children who have not felt the pain of normal living have not paid their dues as children, and as adults lack the experience of dealing with pain. It has been said that pain that does not break you makes you capable of coping with life's troubles. Eddie needs to move forward with his life.

A PERSONAL SENSE OF INADEQUACY

Eddie's sense of inadequacy – one of the factors that led to his dropping out of dental school – had begun to develop in high school. As a teenager, Eddie had been a football player who couldn't be bothered to study much and consequently devised endless ways of cheating. He had a dubious talent for coming up with different ways of concealing "ponies" or "trots," interlinear English translations of difficult French sentences. The pupil was required to stand up next to his seat and do a sight translation of a French sentence. With an interlinear translation concealed in his book he could read the English slowly, stammering as if trying to master the intricacies of French grammar. He may have fooled his teachers, but he never managed to fool his classmates. As soon as he sat down someone would always yelp, "Hi-Yo Silver!" in acknowledgement of this Lone Ranger needing a "pony" to "trot" through French class. When he was accepted at a well-known college in his senior year on a football scholarship, he was sure that he now had confirmation that he really must be smart – the confirmation that he needed in order to mitigate his underlying sense of inferiority. But of course, he wasn't really smart. At best, Eddie was an average guy with average intelligence who, with hard work, would be an average grade student.

But Eddie was prepared to work. He came to college armed with good intentions: he would work hard, do all his assignments diligently, and not go searching for shortcuts, as he had in high school. But his high-school infamy came back to haunt him in the form of one classmate – a bright young man who didn't hesitate to set the record straight. "You ain't smart, Eddie. You had to use a 'trot' to get through French class. You got a scholarship because you're strong enough to play tackle in college. But that won't help you in graduate school. Yeah, you're a nice kid, but if I were you, I'd forget about becoming a medical doctor or a surgeon. Me, I'm going to be a surgeon. You? Well, maybe you should settle for being a dentist."

Eddie's self-confidence was undermined by his peer, and he began to feel like a second-rate person who was not good enough to make it in medicine. He thought about a career with status and prestige rather than having an inherent interest in science or medicine. He was reminded of his inadequacies every time he heard the William Tell overture, which used to play in the *Lone Ranger* adventure radio and TV program. The cry, "Hi-Yo Silver," haunted him in dental school, where he struggled to keep up with his high-school classmate who was taking many similar courses as precursors for the medical program.

The loss of his father was the excuse Eddie needed in order to extricate himself from his sense of inadequacy and a humiliating peer relationship. Eddie presents himself as an innocent victim of his father's death, blaming everyone and everything for his troubles – the weather, the truck, the cost of coffee – and, as he finally acknowledged, his relationship with his classmate. But most of all Eddie blames himself for being distracted by his peer's apparent sense of security and self-confidence and his unmitigated harsh judgment of Eddie. Eddie may blame the malevolent gods of fate for his troubles, but his mother should help him understand that the gods had nothing to do with it.

Eddie must learn to take responsibility for his past failures and to deal with his mortifying relationship with his criticizing peer. The peer may be totally unaware of the hurt he has caused his classmate and might very well be sympathetic to Eddie's feelings if he knew about them – after all, it is rare to find a high-achieving student who does not have some feelings of inadequacy. It may be that neither understands the problems between them and perhaps Marianne can find it within herself to understand how Eddie feels. No one party is ever wholly innocent with respect to interpersonal problems. Marianne has to find out who is to blame for the problem between Eddie and his classmate. She may be able to help him develop a reality map to check whether his classmate is the major source of his feelings of inadequacy.

Marianne herself experienced difficulty in school when her major was English literature, but she went on to start an MBA program anyway. Eventually she dropped out and felt that she had failed in some way. Even though she later became a relatively successful businesswoman, she could identify with Eddie's feelings of inadequacy in stopping short of his goal of a higher degree. One is often defined by one's unfulfilled academic or professional goals more than by one's actual skills and achievements. Waiters who yearn to be actors and actresses often do not feel truly good about themselves; this may be reflected in the discourteous service they provide "in between" acting jobs.

As Marianne's dialogue with Eddie progressed beyond his requests for money for a business and they began to discuss the issue of his classmate, she was able to perceive that his sense of inadequacy in dental school was not the only problem. He was narrating an additional source of woe. This one dealt with love.

SEXUAL BLACKMAIL

Marianne realized that Eddie's feelings of inadequacy stemmed from the high-school putdown of his classmate. Having entered dentistry by default could make him feel "not good" about himself, but the vehemence of his negative reaction to her advice to talk to his peer about his feelings stunned Marianne. Sensing that something or somebody was responsible for Eddie's moodiness, she kept asking questions. Eddie responded, "As long as we're on the subject, Mom, there's something else I feel not so good about, but I don't know if I can talk about it." Marianne followed the timeworn trail of any young man's unhappiness and bluntly asked, "Who is she?"

Eddie's narrative was high drama rendered in the style of *National Enquirer* headlines. Shortly after entering dental school Eddie had met a woman, moved into her apartment, and studied her instead of dentistry. Eve, an intellectually intense, somewhat neurotic and over-possessive person, would endlessly question the scientific facts that Eddie was expected to memorize as axioms, thereby confusing him immensely. She expected Eddie to be there for her all the time and regarded his studying as a threat to their relationship. In addition, she was too involved with her own issues with her mother to have any resources left over for Eddie.

Marianne groaned as she heard the tale and reflected that she had once been told that life would become easier as one matures. What a crock! Woody Allen's famous mantra about infidelity came to her mind: "My wife ran away with another woman." The French phrase "Cherchez la femme" could, Marianne supposed, be used to refer to Eve's over-involvement with her mother – a relationship, which she, having maintained a proper emotional involvement with her sons, could only see as twisted. Who would have thought that life could be so complicated?

Marianne realized that Eve was probably not available emotionally for Eddie at the time of his greatest need, when his father had died. How was Marianne to deal with her son's romantic involvement? She hadn't dated in forty years and had no recollection of an experience with conflict about sexuality. Moreover, her husband was her first – and only – sexual partner. She had never experienced anything remotely close to what Eddie must have been experiencing. Or had she? Marianne suddenly had a flashback to the one pre-marital sexual experience that she had done such a good job in burying so many years ago. The memories came sweeping back over her and she felt that all-too-familiar choking feeling in her throat. Shocked, she realized that Eve's emotional manipulation of Eddie – peppered with a heavy dose of sex, which was bestowed upon him or withheld at her whim – was tantamount to sexual blackmail.

Marianne had experienced once in her life what she called a "triple whammy" that had made her feel as though her whole world was disintegrating around her. She was considered a "dumb blonde" in her youth because she believed that the purpose of life was to marry and have children and that everything else would work itself out. She had been told that a girl as pretty as herself didn't have to think and that she would be fine if she went along with whatever came along. The middle-level boss who liked to fondle her breasts near the copy machine once said to her when she objected, "Don't be dumb. It's no big deal. Besides, no one will believe you anyway. You're a good-looking fox. Smarten up." Confused, she went into an extended depression, dropped out of college, and became a recluse, rarely leaving her apartment. She vividly recalled assuming the "witness state" of observing herself at the copy machine with someone touching her in a way that made her feel uncomfortable and saying to herself at that moment: "This is not really happening to me. I'm not the sort of girl that this happens to. It didn't happen." Marianne had thought at the time that this "out-of-body" experience marked her as being a little crazy, so she decided not to mention it to anybody.

Because of Marianne's sinking so low at that long-ago point in time, she was able to understand how bad Eddie felt about himself with his girlfriend. Marianne's dissociative reaction to the sexual harassment she had undergone made her realize how Eddie could be so out of touch with himself as to get involved with Eve in this manner. Marianne's delayed reaction to the forty-year-old incident was a key to her understanding of Eddie's powerlessness in the face of sexual blackmail, making it impossible for him to get on with his studies.

Thinking back over the events that followed the incident in her own life, Marianne realized that it had been her mother who had solved the immediate problem and snapped her out of a dangerous slump. Despite years of arguments and a well-established love/hate relationship, when Marianne's mother came knocking on her door with chicken soup in one hand and want ads in the other, Marianne was only too glad to let her come in and "take charge." Marianne had difficulty taking advice from her mother when in emotional pain. Nevertheless, a mother and her offspring continue to bond at a primal level despite serious alienation that takes place over extended periods of time. Marianne didn't tell her mother about the incidents at the copy machine because she wouldn't have believed her and would have criticized her instead.

She had taught Marianne not to get involved with "men like that" and, instead of becoming indignant, would have thought Marianne dumb for not having listened to her.

"My daughter's life will be ruined if she doesn't smile at men," thought her mother. "After all, her face is all she's got going for her. Maybe I should teach her how to make cakes. Men like that, too." Her mother arranged to meet Marianne a couple of times at the supermarket where they both liked to shop. Although not much of a cook, Marianne's mother was extremely knowledgeable about cake mixes. The two women stood in front of the cake mixes at the supermarket and Marianne was privileged to receive a lecture in her mother's area of expertise. They "dated" for a few weeks at the cake section until Marianne invited her mother to her home to try out the tasty cake she had baked. By then Marianne had regained her independent functioning and was strengthening her sense of adequacy by taking what her mother had to give.

In her mind, her father was no better in the respect department. Even now, years later, Marianne grimaces when she remembers his response to her request for a girl's bike for her birthday, an expression of her girlhood. He had his own old bike, the one he had received from his father. He proceeded to rebuild this old bike at a cost higher than that of a new girl's bike. Thus, her father expressed his affection for her in the only way he could, rather than in the way she would have liked. She had learned a valuable lesson in economics that birthday, no less significant than reading the financial journals. Still, he was her dad and he loved her, and she learned to accept his affection in the way it actually came.

Reflecting on her childhood, Marianne realized that she had learned the cost of being a lady more directly at her high school prom. She had only been able to afford a homemade dress. Both the quality and cost of the cloth served as an indicator of her family's economic status. Later in her life every time she bought a dress, she checked out her economic standing: that is an invaluable lesson, given the ease with which credit-card discipline can be breached.

The loss of control, her failing in school, and being harassed had forced Marianne to put herself in the hands of someone close to her, her mother, despite her feelings of alienation toward her. She discarded her depression as soon as she was prodded into taking control of her life again. Her mother decided that enough was enough. In short order Marianne had been fed, dressed and hustled off to a job interview. She began to feel better almost at once. The interview resulted in her first "real" employment. Ironically, since the position turned out to be the kind that rewarded her for her performance and not her looks, something good came out of her depression and her internship. As her mother had taught her, Marianne promptly forgot about "those incidents" and put on a happy face. Still, she reasoned, dragging her thoughts back to her present concerns, if her disrespectful mother could have done that for her, surely she could do at least as much for Eddie.

THE DEVELOPMENT OF THE DUMB BLONDE

"Maybe I really am dumb," Marianne thought to herself, "like the guy at the copy machine told me." She was in no frame of mind to grapple with issues of the ultimate meaning of life, with weighty questions such as whether the mother-child relationship was stronger and more vital than the male-female relationship in some greater scheme of life forces. She was not seeking some grandiose answer, but was merely trying to prevent further tragedy in her child's life. She was concerned about Eddie's relationship with Eve, but the girl herself was of no vital interest to her. The source of the girl's problems – perhaps her relationship with her own mother and her problems of trust – were simply not relevant to the issue at hand. Maybe being dumb meant being focused. Marianne could live with that.

She mused about the pleasurable moments she had spent bathing Eddie in the kitchen sink, but now that he was a big boy she couldn't simply wash the problems away. Marianne should listen long and hard to Eddie to learn if anything is being withheld, such as, for example, an unwanted pregnancy. Fortunately, this is not the case. Confessing to the affair relieves Eddie's guilt to some extent and frees up energy for growth. As exhausting as it may be, Marianne has to listen patiently until Eddie finishes draining his emotions about his girlfriend, and she should hold herself back from passing judgment.

Marianne discusses the issue of sexual harassment with Eddie and tells him that she understands his confusion. Things are not always what they seem, she says. She isn't liberated enough to confide in him about the incidents at the copy machine; nevertheless, Eddie senses that her understanding of what he is going through comes from a very deep place. Marianne feels somewhat better about herself after hearing Eddie's story. She knows that the sins of the fathers are visited upon the children, according to her vague recollection of the Bible, but she thought that the sins of the mothers were exempt. She's not sure about that one. She'll have to look it up somewhere. A light flickers in Marianne's head. Things were finally beginning to make sense for this "dumb blonde."

Now that the whole truth is out, Marianne can help channel the energy that Eddie spent concealing the affair into growth and an effort to resolve his identity problem. While he gives lengthy expositions on his girlfriend's problems – expositions that may be accurate factually, analytically and emotionally – he is physically and emotionally drained by the mourning process. This exhaustion has been exacerbated by his need to conceal a relationship that he knew was not good for him just at a time when he and his mother needed each other the most. Marianne may be disapproving or discouraged after Eddie's disclosure, but she should not condemn him. Her attitude should be non-judgmental; she should focus her energies on helping him discover the underlying reason for his poor choice of partner. In addition, she should let him know that his girlfriend is no longer only his problem, but a common family issue. In short, he is not alone.

Marianne seeks the underlying source of Eddie's unhappiness, utilizing the road map provided by what she knows about his sense of inadequacy in the past. Much perseverance from

Marianne is required to help Eddie maintain his focus. She realizes that his affair is an indication of some deep lack of intellectual self-respect, possibly triggered by his having to study dentistry instead of having the choice to decide whether he really wanted to become a doctor. After all, if he wasn't good enough to be a doctor, perhaps he might as well choose a girl who is second-best – just like himself. Marianne is terrified at the prospect of having Eve as a daughter-in-law, who could control her access to any grandchildren that might result. She is glad that Eddie finally had a good sexual affair, but at what price? Does he sound happy about the relationship, or is it mostly anger that Marianne hears?

Marianne should listen carefully to the anger to ascertain whether it stems from obvious reasons or from causes unconsidered. If she succeeds in unraveling the source of Eddie's anger and pain, she should try to bring him to the same understanding. Knowing the real reasons for the anger may not immediately dissolve the negative feelings, but *truth provides a platform from which parents and children can act constructively.* Eddie brought with him a "shopping list" of anger, sadness, depression, an unrealized dream and insecurity about his abilities. This nightmare scenario was so overwhelming that he sunk into the infantile stupor of the ice-cream truck with the passive expectation that his remaining parent would now take care of him.

Eddie had not had much sexual intimacy prior to his relationship with Eve – which he regarded almost like a marriage – although he had been sexually active since the end of high school. On what basis can Marianne respond to her son's misadventure? "My own sexual experience is so limited," she thought, "how can I possibly give my son any advice about such matters?" But Marianne has both maturity and wisdom to use in confronting her son about his immature behavior in an inappropriate sexual relationship. Marianne can draw upon her own long-term marriage and its intimacies, sexual and otherwise, in guiding him. It is clear to Marianne that while her son somehow grew in this relationship, the girl was a case of arrested development. She was so immature that she was still in need of a mother instead of a man. Maybe Eddie is similar, still needing his mother instead of a suitable woman. Marianne should make sure that Eddie doesn't follow in his girlfriend's footsteps and doesn't remain immature and return emotionally and permanently to his mother. *Emotional immaturity is an all-too-common cause of collapsing relationships*; one of the parties may grow while the other doesn't. It is Marianne's job to make sure that Eddie is the one who grows up.

In addition to her personal experiences in marriage and parenting, Marianne has a broad database of her peer group's stable relationships from which to draw inferences. The older generation of parents has observed their peer group for a longer time and can make reasonable assumptions about whether a marriage is headed for divorce or separation. The younger generation is frequently characterized by living together for various periods prior to an often short-term marriage. *Marianne's age group sees the new generation as having more sex with more partners, but with less ease in social relationships and less spirituality.* Why do these sexual relationships seem superficially appealing, but unattractive upon closer examination of the social and spiritual sub-structure?

Marianne knows from experience that the underpinnings of marriage are unusually complex and continue to be viable despite the problems besetting the relationship. Parents of married children generally tend to stay out of their children's personal business as long as the marriage works. Parental intervention is only called for when one person abandons the framework of the marriage or the long-term relationship. *Parents are equipped to help their adult offspring when marital problems surface because of their own previous experience in navigating the children through the turbulence of adolescence.*

Inevitably, such marital problems and their consequences cause the involved parties to regress to an adolescent state, even when the marriage failure occurs in middle age. Marianne should be prepared to raise her child through his adolescent and immature relationship with Eve. She cannot assume that just because

Eddie has achieved chronological maturity, he has reached the requisite level of social and emotional maturity. Marianne's making sure that Eddie attains maturity is an act of love and of concern for his well-being.

THE CONSEQUENCES OF A SENSE OF INADEQUACY

Marianne should begin to consider the possibility that Eddie will live out his self-image of being only second-best and will spend his life as an unskilled or semi-skilled worker, with all its physical, emotional and economic fragility. This potential dentist is now facing unemployment. He may call his sense of inadequacy into play in the future as well, whenever facing a challenge. "I'm not good with numbers, so how could I possibly do well in a computer course?" Eddie may be headed toward further emotional injury.

The shock of impending harsh endings may chip away at an undeveloped identity such as Eddie's. The anticipation of serious consequences to behavior can protect an immature personality from going into shock. Getting that dreaded pink slip that gives you two weeks' notice, the slam of the door heralding the end of the marriage, the court's decision to question your authority as a parent – all these and other crises often drive men back to their parents' home, seeking a connection to the source of authority in their pre-marital life. Is this the fate that awaits Eddie in the future sequences of his life? If his already existing state of emotional dependency might become institutionalized through a regular allowance from his mother, the money would probably serve to reinforce his sense of emotional inadequacy. Eddie is in a perpetual state of being only one paycheck away from financial insolvency; he therefore turns to whatever support is available. The support he chooses is what will make him or break him. He displayed sound judgment when turning to his mother and not-so-sound judgment previously, when he turned to his girlfriend. The outcome of the next crisis is therefore one of the luck of the draw.

The death of Marianne's husband has served as a reminder that she won't be around forever, either. Marianne is petrified by what might happen to Eddie if she were to abandon him by dying unexpectedly. *The quintessential fear of abandonment has sent many an adult back to the parents.* If Eddie is hurting at any future time, and his girlfriend or spouse is unable to respond adequately to his pain, he may again attempt to turn to his mother. This is a common reaction, shared by most hurting children – even if the parents are no longer among the living. Marianne is terrified that she will have to go through this kind of crisis yet again in her lifetime – or worse, that Eddie will have to go through it alone.

True parental love requires whatever it takes to raise an adult child. Marianne should let go of her old habits of dealing with Eddie, such as supporting his half-baked economic ventures, but she need not let go of her continuous love for her son. Eddie, like all children at any age, will require some form of appropriate parenting. Cultivating the essence of continuous love can eventually transform a good parent into a mature one. Therefore, her task as a caring mother is to find a better way to parent Eddie.

Marianne was in the habit of consulting her dead husband about things that were on her mind. As long as she was evaluating her relationship with Eddie, she wanted to share the problem with her spouse. She was aware that it was a one-way communication. Still, she could fill in the gaps in the conversation because she knew from experience what he usually thought under these circumstances.

Eddie, Marianne thought, is a thinker, a contemplator, rather than a doer. Are thinkers weaklings, as her husband had often stated? Marianne disagreed with her husband then, and she disagrees with him now. Contemplation and courage are the tools of life's trade. Marianne took the initial step of identifying the heart of the problem by being honest about Eddie's sense of inadequacy in many areas of activity. This courageous step can lead to the psychological truth. The truth exists to be discovered, not to remain eternally hidden, and the conspiracy of silence not to articulate the family secrets is generally broken if the welfare of the family is at stake. Eddie needed the kind of help that her husband had been unable to provide. Marianne, reminiscing about her husband with nostalgia, realized that in this case she was right and he had been wrong.

It crossed Marianne's mind that her husband had died at an opportune moment in Eddie's life – if there is ever an opportune moment for death. Eddie had returned home not, as she had originally assumed, to help her through the mourning process, but out of his own need to extricate himself from a catastrophic relationship. She silently mouthed thanks to her late husband for having come through for her one final time. Life goes on. Marianne was starting to heal.

Chapter Three

CHAMPAGNE TASTES ON A BEER BUDGET

INTRODUCTION

Marianne's road to becoming a mature parent was an emotionally stressful trip that required her to deal with unresolved past issues in addition to the current problems with her son. She was ill prepared for the task at hand because parents can't have expertise in all areas. Yet she found the resources within herself to do what it takes to become a neverending parent to her son.

Like Marianne, Helen was unprepared for her daughter's overt request for money and had to explore the emotional underpinnings of the relationship. Helen had not given money much thought until forced by circumstances to contemplate her own diminishing income and her daughter's limitations. She seeks advice to help her muddle through her financial and emotional relationship with her daughter but finally has to use the personality resources available to her. She uses her gentle but firm disposition and her parental superiority for micro-management to strike a balance between selfishness and selflessness.

Synopsis

Helen, a retired widow, visits her divorced daughter in California. A minor medical mishap highlights their different approaches to money. Helen, who has always been price conscious and level-headed, is dismayed by her head-in-the-clouds daughter who seems blissfully unaware of her mother's financial limitations. Can they reconcile their different expectations? Their weekly lunches provide the framework for negotiations, and Helen slowly leads her offspring into an emotional "comfort zone." Helen's suggestions for micro-management of the budget enable them to reach a financial solution, ultimately leading to personal autonomy for mother and daughter.

THE DILEMMA

Helen is a thin woman with wispy hair that used to be blonde. Although her back is bent by her seventy-six years, her eyes behind gold-rimmed glasses sparkle with intelligence and goodwill. Neatly dressed and well-groomed, she walks every other day to an open-air market two blocks from her apartment building to buy the fruits and vegetables she loves out of the pension earned during the years she worked as a nurse. In her youth she had dropped out of a pre-med program when she had mononucleosis. Instead of her mother nursing her back to health, she had the responsibility of caring for her mother's mental condition for years, thereby becoming a nurse instead of a doctor. She found her profession emotionally satisfying and enjoyed relating to her patients much the same way as she had to her mother.

Helen looks exactly like what she is – a prosperous widow who enjoys her life. She owes nothing to anyone. A modest inheritance from her father, a pension from her work, insurance payments from her late husband's estate, and a paid-off apartment in Manhattan all contribute to her current financial independence.

Helen has an only child, Margaret, who lives in Sacramento, California. Margaret is a forty-nine-year-old childless divorcee for whom "things have just not gone right." Things started not going right for Margaret in her twenties, after the man she had quit college to marry told her he wanted a divorce. Margaret granted her husband the divorce but did not return to school. She began to weave and sporadically sell specialty carpets and wall hangings, and has been doing this ever since.

After her divorce Margaret moved to California and found a two-bedroom walk-up on the outskirts of Sacramento. Her father did not urge her to return to college and develop professional skills, instead supporting her with a monthly allowance of $1,500. Helen has always felt uncomfortable about the allowance, but after Margaret's father died she felt even less comfortable about going against her late husband's wishes. Thus, Margaret continued to enjoy – and rely upon – her monthly stipend.

The week before her birthday, Helen flew to the West Coast to celebrate with Margaret. The trip was uneventful until Helen disembarked from the plane. Coming down the steps of the moving escalators, she tripped and fell, suffering a hairline fracture of her ankle. Margaret was waiting at the airport. She managed, with the help of airline officials, to get her mother to a local hospital, where x-rays were taken. Helen was fitted with a cast and told to keep off her feet for at least a week. Although she didn't require hospitalization, she couldn't stay at her daughter's third floor walk-up. "Don't worry, Mom," said Margaret. "I'll take care of you." Helen's daughter proceeded to book a room in a luxury hotel a five-minute drive from her own apartment. "Nothing but the best for you," she told her mother. The price of the room was $300 a night, but Helen, shaken and still in considerable pain, agreed to check in anyway. Before the week was half over, the budget Helen had allotted for her ten-day stay in California was all but depleted. "Book me into a cheaper hotel," Helen instructed her daughter, "or book me a ticket to New York today."

A genuinely surprised Margaret found a less expensive room the same day, and her mother remained in Sacramento for another week. Helen's flight back home, although not as eventful as the incoming voyage, was marred by her concerns about her only child. Margaret either had an inflated idea of what her mother could afford to spend, or, if she had a reasonable awareness of Helen's financial circumstances, she lacked the ability to allocate money wisely for unanticipated expenses.

Not long after Helen's return to New York she received a telephone call from her daughter. Margaret, too, had been worrying about the future and had come up with an idea. She told her mother that she had decided to have an engineering evaluation of her apartment building with the goal of installing an elevator in her rent-controlled apartment or to buy a condominium in the same area, but in a building with an elevator and doorman. "That way, the next time you visit you can feel comfortable and safe," she explained. Helen asked Margaret the price of the condo. "It's a bargain," Margaret informed her, "only $275,000."

Helen gasped. The amount constituted more than half of what she held in liquid assets, the interest from which she used for her day-to-day expenses. Complying with her daughter's request for improved housing would mean drastically lowering her own standard of living. Trying to keep the panic out of her voice, Helen told her daughter, "I'll have to think about it" and hung up.

Helen did some serious thinking about her financial relationship with her daughter. She was in the habit of giving Margaret substantial presents on holidays and birthdays, as well as annual insurance payments for the car and money known in California as "life-style enhancement." Helen's late husband had always considered such presents an elegant way to help Margaret out. Helen had at first thought that this well-established pattern was positive for their relationship. Now she wasn't so sure, for she could see that Margaret took these gifts for granted. Moreover, the money was a disincentive to work; after all, Margaret's financial needs were taken care of. Margaret had not internalized any financial boundary between her mother and herself, and here she was, dunning Helen for money for an engineering evaluation of the structural safety of the house and for the future installation of an elevator.

Pondering the matter, Helen realized that she didn't really know what her daughter's needs actually were. Worse still, she realized, *meeting vague needs leads not to satisfaction, but to increasing demands and*, worst of all for the relationship, *recriminations.*

Over the next few weeks, Helen continued to worry and fret. She took a long-term friend into her confidence and asked for advice. "Your daughter's a grown woman," retorted the friend. "Isn't it about time she took care of herself?" Helen then turned to her general practitioner, a kind man who had attended her and her husband for over three decades. "That's a tough one, Helen," he responded. "What do you think you should do?" A family friend, when broached on the subject, answered, "Your daughter wants a nice apartment? Give it to her. Bring her here so she can live in yours." The more people she turned to for advice, the more possibilities she had to consider, and none of the solutions Helen received were satisfactory. She felt that she had drawn her wagons in a circle and was fighting off her daughter as a hostile marauder who was threatening her water hole of emotional and financial security. Was she becoming paranoid in her old age?

THE REASONING

Helen cannot and should not abandon Margaret financially or emotionally. Buying an apartment is a worthy goal in principle, one that Helen's late husband, who didn't approve of renting, would have supported. Helen has never been entirely happy about the free-flowing presents and money, because deep down she believes that money should not be given freely, as if it fell out of the pocket on the sofa for a child. But her late husband used to do that with Margaret, and it was easier to continue the well-established tradition than break it. Helen would prefer a negotiated relationship between two adults that should result in a verbal or written contract. As in all negotiations, the stronger side should be firm and gentle in ensuring conformity to the contract.

Parents should always consider the context of the problem. Clearly, due to the mother's limited income, Margaret's lifestyle cannot be subsidized to the extent she would wish. Nor should it be, even if Helen were much better off financially. In Helen's present circumstances continued subsidizing might even lead to her losing her own fiscal independence, another circumstance her late husband would never have countenanced.

It could be argued that Helen's accident, although an unfortunate occurrence, was a wake-up call. First, it made her aware of her own physical vulnerability and, by extension, of her mortality. Second, she was forced to confront her daughter's incompetence in making financial decisions. When Margaret said, "Nothing but the best for you, Mom," ushering her into a five-star hotel, the subtext was, "Nothing but the best for me, too."

When Margaret asked for money for an engineering evaluation and suggested that Helen consider installing an elevator or buying a condo, Helen took time to mull over the issues. She decided that she should help Margaret in a manner that accords with her ability to give financially and emotionally, as well as with Margaret's ability to adjust her expectations and adapt to a new fiscal reality. That way Helen could retain her own standard of living and fiscal autonomy and not feel as if she were in a financial jail filled only with innocents.

Helen should carefully examine her living expenses – and that includes the monthly $1,500 allotted to her daughter. She should determine how much money she needs in order to maintain her own lifestyle and then work out how much she can spare for her daughter. Margaret has to scrutinize her living expenses as well and decide which expenses are essential and which she can do without. The two women have to arrive at a middle ground so that they can achieve their ends while both maintain a decent standard of living, as well as their independence. *"Dialogue" and "compromise" are two vital implements in the parents' toolbox.*

Helen needs to take into account both the financial and emotional issues. Financially there will be no additional sources of income either for her daughter or for herself. At this stage in their lives the pie is not going to grow any bigger. Helen needs to come to terms with the evidence that her daughter is not only monetarily dependent upon her, but does not demonstrate good judgment in money matters. Emotionally the crunch will come when Helen goes against her late husband's desire to provide a permanent generous monthly subsidy. Initiated soon after Margaret's divorce, the monthly payments symbolized the father's perception of Margaret as being incompetent in her relationships with the opposite sex. Ironically, it was the same subsidy that locked her into the role of incompetent woman. Helen should no longer accommodate her daughter's "champagne tastes."

On the positive side, Margaret's housing crisis presents Helen with an opportunity to resolve the problem of granting an allowance she has always believed to be somehow wrong. By changing the unhealthy paradigm of giving and receiving, Helen and Margaret now have the opportunity to resolve the issue and, in the process, to develop a new pattern of mutual respect. Resolution of the issue will thus be internally satisfying to both parties, as it will forge a new bond between the only surviving members of the family.

Because this way of thinking and behaving was not part of her education, Margaret will probably be unprepared for the action her mother should take. Helen should state, simply and unequivocally, that Margaret will have to compromise. After all, Helen's squandering so much money would mean putting herself at financial risk.

Margaret may of course counter with: "What risk? If you can't make ends meet, you could always move in with me." Helen has to reject this line of reasoning categorically. She could respond with: "We haven't lived under the same roof in over thirty years. What makes you think we could live together now without driving each other crazy?" Or she could simply say: "I'd rather live alone. I can afford it and I prefer it that way." If Margaret acquiesces, the stage will be set for dialogue and an eventual compromise that is crucial in parenting. If Margaret does not accept Helen's viewpoint she should be given time to come to terms with her mother's decision.

The only way this can be accomplished is for Helen to stand by her decision and not back down.

One suggestion would be for Helen to fly back to California and spend a brief period looking at apartments in the neighborhood in which Margaret wants to live. Since the condo her daughter has chosen is too expensive, other options should be investigated. Alternatively, Helen could hire a local real-estate agent and send him into the neighborhood with her daughter, providing both her daughter and the agent with clear financial guidelines. Margaret and the agent will find a suitable dwelling if they are persistent. It might be an apartment in an older building, or it might turn out to be smaller than the apartment originally chosen. Margaret may be less than thrilled, but Helen, even if she feels a bit guilty about insisting on boundaries, should hold out. The only alternative for Margaret, if she cannot find something she likes, is to remain in rental housing.

Margaret will also be unhappy when she learns from her mother that her allowance is to be drastically reduced. But Helen must remain resolute. Finally, she should gently suggest to her daughter that she start looking around for alternative employment. This would enable Margaret to maintain herself in the style to which her parents' over-generous allowance has accustomed her.

Only after both women produce their pared-down budgets can Helen make a decision about how much money to give her daughter and what demands she should make upon her in return. For Margaret the difficulty will lie in coming to terms with the fact that she no longer lives on a one-way street. If she wants something – in this case, money – she will have to be more realistic about her options and assume responsibility for her own life.

Helen decided to invite Margaret to babysit an absent friend's apartment in New York as this would give mother and daughter the chance to resolve their differences. Margaret was only too happy to comply. Once Margaret was settled in, Helen asked her out to lunch with the request to receive a list of her daughter's financial requirements. Margaret picked a restaurant up-scale from Helen's modest tastes, but Helen decided to go along with her daughter's culinary choice so that Margaret could feel in a "comfort zone" – an emotional space that encourages one to make personal statements only when one feels comfortable. Margaret didn't bring a list, and she obsessed the same old way about the engineer, the elevator and the estimate. Helen stood her ground. First the list, then a consideration of the issues. "No money until I get the list."

That same evening Margaret called her mother and accused her of not respecting her independence, not trusting her with her requests, and behaving like a spoiled child herself with her stupid request for a list of Margaret's needs. After all, if she didn't really need something she wouldn't be asking for it, would she? Helen thanked Margaret for sharing her feelings with her, said how much she had enjoyed dining with her and was looking forward to eating out with her again next week. And, by the way, could she bring along that list of her financial needs so that Helen could take the time to look them over?

The women enjoyed their lunches together on what had now become their weekly rendezvous. The conversations were animated, yet at the same time list-less. Margaret's requests for money were tactfully side stepped by Helen. The lack of a list was mentioned no more than once at each meeting and no discussion about it ensued. They talked of men and fathers and family and of their mutual interests in music and pottery. Admittedly, Margaret's outbursts against Helen continued, but each time with less intensity. Finally, at one of the meetings Helen took out pencil and paper and said: "I'll tell you what, let's make a list together, just like we did when you were in elementary school. I often remember what you were like at that age." It took less than a minute for Margaret to share her financial woes with her mother, who responded: "Now, then, that wasn't so bad, was it? Thank you and now I can look it over and get back to you." A few weeks of lunches went by with Helen telling Margaret that she was thinking about things and that she hadn't come to a decision yet, but that she would be happy to hear anything else that Margaret had to add.

Finally, over brunch, Helen said that she had decided to pay for the engineering examination of the house because of the safety factor, but that she would not pay for the redoing of Margaret's house, which was not on Helen's list of priorities. She would be willing to chip in for an upgraded car when Margaret had made a little more money and had picked out the car, but would not support the purchase of a new car. Margaret calmly thanked her mother for making her feel secure about the house, and said that she'd like to have lunch next week at the same restaurant.

Helen felt that she had redeemed Margaret's sense of security without jeopardizing her financial well-being. She recalled a story that her late husband had once told her about Maimonides in the Middle Ages. Maimonides had had to raise funds to redeem Jewish captives from Mediterranean pirates. He had instructed the negotiators not to appear too anxious to redeem the captives, because then the pirates would raise the price. The negotiators had to pay to guarantee the survival of the captives, but they could not bankrupt the Jewish community's survival in the process. Helen suddenly felt more at peace than she had for a long time.

MICRO-MANAGEMENT OF THE FAMILY BUDGET

The hardest thing parents have to do for their children is to draw a line in the sand. Admittedly, Helen's request for a list was somewhat arbitrary and unreasonable, but it focused all the unreasonableness and lack of clarity into that one point. It was incredibly hard for Helen to stand firm when she herself saw her request as arbitrary. She was not used to being the unreasonable one – after all, that had always been her daughter's role. But Margaret grew ever more reasonable as Helen remained unreasonable. Helen stayed the course because she didn't know any other way of dealing with her daughter's unreasonable requests. She was grateful that the technique was effective.

Margaret entered an emotional comfort zone as the boundaries were drawn for her. She felt good, protected and emotionally supported, and when her mother finally came through with the money for the engineering examination of the house, she experienced a sense of both emotional and financial relief. The mother and daughter's regular long lunches were what made all the difference. They began to get to know one another as adults and developed a respect for one another's strengths and weaknesses.

Parents manage budgets in a way that is simply different from that of adult children. *The micro-management of budgets has become the parents' area of expertise by dint of necessity and history.* Many parents of the previous generation understand the necessity of budgeting better than their children because as children the only money they had was the money in their pocket; and when that was gone it was the end, for their parents generally had no money or resources to give them. For adult children of the next generation, money in the pocket marks only the beginning of expenditure, not the end. But as adult children grow poorer – the outcome of divorce, downsizing or accident – necessity dictates that the parental generation teaches the next generation the importance of organizing a budget. Adult children have to learn that there are limits to their parents' financial capacity. The older generation knows the value of money: running water, electricity, telephones and cars all cost money. The younger generation was born into a world in which running water, electricity, phones and cars are as taken for granted as the existence of free grass or trees. Budgetary organization is a skill that has to be learned, and who better to teach it than one's own parents?

THE ROAD TO RESPECT AND RESPONSIBILITY

There is a general consensus that raising infants, young children, adolescents and even young adults is the responsibility of the parents, but reverse situations are more frequent than we would like to admit. For a variety of reasons some small children, sometimes as young as ten, feel that they are the ones who have to take care of their parents. This responsibility is obvious when one of the parents is blind or deaf or cognitively impaired. Satisfying the parent's needs is not impossible and is akin to a modern youngster's ability to alleviate a parent's relative computer illiteracy by superior knowledge.

Satisfying the parent's needs may, however, be impossible if the need is psychologically hidden. A father who grew up without a father may expect his son to relate to him like his absent father. A mother who lost her younger sister in the Holocaust may expect her oldest daughter to be her missing younger sister as well. A parent who suffered deep poverty may expect the child to make enough money to compensate for the early deprivation and its accompanying insults. Parents who were unable to please their own parents through no fault of their own may expect their child to be so perfect that they would also please their child's parents. The child must eventually learn to distinguish between those needs that can be met and those that cannot. Frequently, they experience many years of anguish, often including therapy, before these children – by then young adults – come to the realization that they are in fact supposed to take care of themselves and not their parents.

Another common assumption is that it is the role of the adult offspring to take care of their parents when they reach old age. However, this conception too is often not borne out by reality and in many cases again the reverse situation occurs. *It is the aging parents who find themselves faced with the responsibility of taking care of their needy adult offspring.* Just like a child who feels that he or she has to take care of his or her parents must find the boundaries of responsibility, a parent taking care of a needy adult child needs to find the boundaries of responsibility.

Helen feels that her daughter's constant neediness creates a paradigm in which she is compelled to be eternally giving. This amounts to a life sentence for a blameless individual who feels obligated to take care of another person in the family forever and for unclear reasons. The bonds of this unexpected and heavy burden on the aging parent's soul can be freed by redistributing the responsibility.

The rules of relationships now have to be negotiated between the two generations, with the responsibilities divided between them according to age and circumstances. At this stage in the game the responsibility no longer rests solely on the parents' shoulders. Whereas children are seen as justified in receiving from their parents the gifts of love, education and money, this legitimate relationship wanes when the adult children are grown up and independent. At what age and at what stage does this pattern come to an end? Are parents eternally committed to loving their children, no matter what? Should parents be expected to pay for their children's follies in choosing inadequate education or the wrong partner, job or career? Should parents bear responsibility for the vagaries of the marketplace just as they bore responsibility for providing a nurturing environment for their young children?

Unexpected burdens weigh more heavily than expected ones. For some reason, when a problem exists for one person, somebody close is often blamed and made to feel guilty for not resolving it. Guilt by association seems to be pervasive. Individuals often feel guilty for being unsuccessful in meeting the unreasonable and irrational needs of another. The family of somebody who is chemically dependent, for example, is often blamed for not being able to get the afflicted relative off drugs. "Bad medication" is blamed for making the person sick, and the responsible family member is urged to turn to the latest cure noted in a popular magazine or during casual conversation at the hairdresser's.

A corollary of this position is that the parents of dependent adult children are made to feel guilty for unresolved problems. Mature parents find themselves in the company of doctors who are blamed for creating illness to make money and mental health professionals who are blamed for inventing the myth of mental illness to justify their earnings. However, bad things happen in life no matter what is done, and it is a waste of time and energy to assign blame instead of coping actively and responsibly without guilt. Feeling guilt and assigning blame, although natural human processes, cannot resolve any problem. Helen may have been burdened with a sense of guilt and blame for over thirty years for failing to help her daughter out of her dilemma of poor education, bachelorhood and inhospitable housing – even though Margaret's problems were of her own making and not the result of any wrongdoing or errors on Helen's part.

Relieving guilt and mitigating blame through an understanding of the situation and often through therapy is a prerequisite to producing a pragmatic solution to the problem. Harkening back to the root of the problem may expose old wounds but does little to heal them. Thinking about what should have been done differently in the past is less than useful and is often an impediment to finding a solution. Rather than seeking to lay blame and hurl accusations, the parties should strive to enter into negotiations in order to uncover a pragmatic solution out of commitment to mutual respect.

The bonds of affection between parents and adult children lie at the emotional core of decision-making, but the physical, intellectual and financial resources available to each of the partners should also be laid on the negotiating table. A deal that is like a quick snack rather than a complete meal is ultimately unsatisfying and leaves one clamoring for more. Both sides should compromise. The parents should help in accordance with their intellectual and financial resources, but should also be able to set limits – a concept fundamental to parenting at all levels of the children's maturation. The adult children should be ready to accept less if necessary. The dialogue conducted is initially inherently unbalanced because parents are in a position of strength vis-à-vis their adult children, but each of the parties should recognize the relative strengths of the resources at hand if a solution is to be achieved through dialogue. The family ideal of a delicate internal balance between giving and receiving is rarely attained – because one party is accustomed to giving, while the other is accustomed to receiving. *The decision-making process should be based on the assumption that the strong will do what they can, while the weak are expected to do what they must.*

For this reason the critical prototype of giving and receiving takes into account the benevolent power of the giver and the frailty of the receiver. This inherent imbalance of giving and receiving is attested to in the tale of a benevolent God giving the Torah to the children of Israel, who are compelled to accept the Torah and to obey its commandments, such as resting one day a week and observing dietary restrictions. Similarly, God is ready to bestow his blessings on all people when they become ready to receive Him (or Jesus, in the case of Christianity) in their hearts, as proven by their behaving in a socially acceptable manner. Thus it is evident that the relationship of giving and receiving lies at the core of religion. The parties complement each other; neither is whole in and of itself. Helen and Margaret should thus be able to reach a resolution of their dilemma in the microcosm of their lives.

As noted above, when one person turns to another for help, the hierarchical issues between giver and receiver should be dealt with gingerly and sensitively and not by dredging up old advice, such as, "I told you not to marry him," or, "You should have taken the other job." The purpose of bringing up such "good advice" seems to be to establish a dominance hierarchy, with the helping party in the right and the needy party in the wrong. But human beings, unlike God, are not omniscient or omnipotent; they have to learn to share by discussion and by a process of give and take, rather than by dictating rules and responses. Care should be taken to prevent hierarchical issues from degenerating into a dominance pattern that carries with it angry outbursts from either the giver or the receiver. The parties to the dispute should not revel in malicious rebuking and criticism of one another, lest hierarchical issues interfere with the healing process.

Civilized discourse and discussion out of respect is of paramount importance. The dialogue between the aging parents and adult children in trouble can expedite the establishment of healthy mutual respect. These parents have been given the opportunity to delve into their souls to become better givers and supporters, even as they give space to their adult children to grow and develop into more independence. If parents keep at it long enough they will eventually feel that their good nature is not being exploited.

In short, they will become the kind of parents their children need. Luckily, adult children in trouble always seem willing to be re-parented. This is the ultimate reward of constant parenting.

Parenting is constantly devalued: everybody is expected to be able to do it, for better or for worse. Anybody can become a parent, without having to prove capability or competence. No legislative ruling or licensing board is required. Despite this devaluation, parenting is typically the most demanding role in one's life. It is the most selfless of activities and is characterized by eternal giving. It is a universal truth that parental love exceeds all other types of love in its inclusiveness and totality. Parents get up in the middle of the night to attend sick children and parental love motivates them to accept sleep deprivation as just "part of the job description." They tolerate their children's kicking, hitting and spitting behavior and accept intrusion into their personal space – intrusion that would never be tolerated in other relationships. Helen recalls that as a young child, Margaret would cling to her leg and ride on her foot as she was preparing dinner. As she was dragging her from table to refrigerator to stove, she suddenly looked down at her and said, "It's a good thing I love you, because otherwise I'd kill you." Parents may be exhausted, over-tired, emotionally eroded by stress, depressed by events in their lives, and disappointed in their relationships, but they are still expected to function well with regard to their children.

But love is not enough. Parents must acquire knowledge in numerous fields to optimize their children's development. What are the child's stages of development, and what kind of behavior is appropriate at what age? Which school is best suited to the child's needs? What kind of orthodontia will ensure that healthy smile? What course of study is preferred for the jobs of the future? The list is endless.

Of course, merely possessing knowledge about good parenting, such as learning the ages and stages of child development, cannot ensure success in raising a properly socialized child and adult. Knowledge is necessary, but often not sufficient. Even professional knowledge of parenting at advanced levels of psychological study seldom suffices in dealing with the pragmatic issues of raising a child. Knowing what to do is not the same as having the capacity to do the task. Effective parenting depends upon factors beyond our control, such as physical stamina, emotional resources and social and financial stability – to mention but a few. Thus, while the possession of theoretical knowledge helps to reduce anxiety and encourages clear thinking, the expectation that this will automatically provide answers to pragmatic problems is unrealistic; it has only a moderate effect because parenting is learned "on the job" under stressful conditions.

Whereas parents' selflessness goes with the territory when the children are young, the same does not hold true when those children reach their twenties and begin to branch out on their own. At this point they are seen as adults and their parents now begin to feel they have a right to a life of their own. If there is one thing that modern psychology has taught us, it is never to underestimate the selfishness of the human being. The same parents who were so willing to renounce sleep in order to nurse a sick child or to give up a good job opportunity in order to spend more time with the family now feel a burning desire to pursue their own personal goals. Despite the fact that selflessness tipped the parental scales throughout childhood and adolescence, when the children formally become adults, parents begin to feel they have a right to develop their own capacities and to explore new horizons in their own areas of interest. The scales begin to wobble in an effort to attain some balanced equilibrium between selflessness and selfishness.

Selfishness is not a dirty word. Growth and development is desirable not only for the children, but also for older people who have worked all their lives and suddenly discover their creativity under conditions of unanticipated leisure. The desire to pursue their own intrinsic interests only intensifies as parents grow older and the burden of child rearing eases. Their selfishness may show in rigid patterns where they put themselves first with little consideration for their adult children. Apparently, *contemplating the end strengthens the will to live what is left of life to the fullest.*

The parents' own aptitudes coupled with empathy for the adult children in trouble are the two prerequisites for teaching the children to handle life's problems competently and humanely. If parents are in touch with their own traditions of child rearing and have clarified their feelings about their own parents, they can draw upon their personal pasts to reconnect through familiar rituals that create a framework for the parent-adult child paradigm to develop. Withdrawal ceases and a balance is achieved through familiar bonding activities that establish a relationship of equals, such as playing a game of cards or checkers, going shopping, having a picnic or going bowling. In turn, the adult children listen to the parents, responding to their information. Helen, for example, should be objective and selfless in scrutinizing Margaret's problem, but emotionally involved and selfish in demanding a change from her daughter.

Adult children in pain are in need of their parents. As children regain the comfort of positive predictable responses from their parents, their primal source of security, the overload of pain is diminished. Other sources – the spouse or the employer, for example – cannot provide that same degree of reassurance. The adult child's first steps toward autonomy are taken by becoming detached from the parents' covert support of the child's dependence. Margaret's first steps to improve her low self-image should be to forge a new relationship with her father, who continues to control her life from the grave. By negotiating with her mother and agreeing to settle for a lower-priced condo, more compatible with her mother's pocketbook, Margaret is establishing equal footing with her mother and is ceasing to be her father's dependent daughter, at least economically. As Margaret begins to feel better, flexibility increases, the pain diminishes, and so does her compulsive need to do it her way. *Turning to a parent, originally a move taken out of desperation, gradually becomes one of a myriad of options.*

Mature parents welcome their adult children's turning to them, recognizing that the goal is to get them to turn away from the painful issues of the immediate past and to use their psychic energy for problem solving. Some adult children spend their energy trying to connect emotionally with their parents, leaving little room for dealing with the crisis at hand. Under the more primitive and harsh conditions of the past, survival depended upon the parents' immediate response to any problem that presented itself. When children become adults, survival depends upon thinking through a problem by utilizing knowledge and emotional awareness. The first rule in a crisis, therefore, is to stop and think about one's adult offspring. No parent anticipates the job of parenting to be infinite: the expectation is that the children will grow up, leave home and become independent, returning perhaps to visit with the grandchildren once a week. Nobody is really geared towards or prepared for all-embracing eternal parenting.

Parenting at a mature age offers one final chance to change the old unhealthy paradigm of giving and receiving. The establishment of a new relationship based on mutual respect is internally satisfying, not only for parents but for children as well. The rewards for such healthy patterns of parenting are internal; no degree is conferred in public and no testimonials are given. Successfully helping their adult children increases the parents' internal sense of worth. The relief of finally being able to communicate with their adult children engenders happiness and generates the security that a solution can be found for any problem facing their children. The reduction in the adult children's stress and anxiety is a great reward for mature parents. Improved communication, instead of avoidance of eye contact, is internally satisfying and makes both parties feel good.

Being in touch with the vulnerabilities of adult children increases the parents' wisdom as their fantasies about what their children might have been are replaced by the reality of what their children are. This painful clarification can make them feel more secure in their dealings with their adult children. The last words that Helen and Margaret say to one another after all these years in their daily late evening phone call is, "Good night, dear." Helen feels better about the reality of Margaret's life and about her own life as a parent. Mother and daughter are doing well.

Chapter Four

MAY YOU HAVE MALE CHILDREN

INTRODUCTION

Mothers like Elizabeth, Marianne and Helen have the inner strength to regain their balance when confronted by a problem child. Their willingness to consult others keeps them from going over the top in their evaluations, but men are different and often less balanced.

The following story is about the academic Karl, a man whose emotional relationship with his son is threatened. Karl's instinctive negative emotional reaction to his daughter-in-law is not unknown; many families do not like a favorite child's spouse imposed by marriage. Karl's objective analysis of his son's choice may be right. He may behave in a witty, charming and funny manner, but this behavior is unlikely to shelter him from unanticipated negative consequences in relation to his son. Karl's analysis of the family situation has rendered him immature and unprepared to parent his adult child in the future. An alternative for Karl is to learn the virtues of listening, refraining from speaking, learning not to mock and becoming impervious to gossip in order to cope with a key relationship in his life.

Synopsis

Karl, who enjoys a strong relationship of affection and trust with his son, Daniel, has an antagonistic reaction to his daughter-in-law. Although he "does the right thing by them" financially, his emotions remain so raw that the barely hidden anger disrupts his ability to pay attention to his wife's advice to hold his tongue. His sardonic and critical attitude suggests that he would welcome a crisis in his son's marriage, and he looks forward to a potential divorce and the inevitable gossip that would ensue. In his mind, this would allow him to re-establish a grown-up relationship with Daniel.

THE DILEMMA

Karl and Rita were both born in Germany, spent much of their childhood and early adolescence in the relative safety of London, and came to America as teenagers in 1948. The two met when their families, hearing that New England was home to many colleges and universities, settled in a working-class neighborhood of Boston.

Karl and Rita attended the same high school. Karl, a handsome and gifted athlete, was the star of the basketball team. He noticed Rita, a blue-eyed cheerleader, right away. They were going steady by the end of the tenth grade, with their parents' approval. The kids had more in common than good looks and athletic ability. Although outwardly no different from their classmates – studying hard, active in various extra-curricular activities, dancing the jitterbug – they were nevertheless more European than American. Their speech patterns reflected this, retaining traces of an English accent and the softer Bavarian tones of the German they heard spoken at home. They were both bright and wanted to be teachers. While in graduate school they decided to get married. Karl continued his studies and obtained a PhD in German literature, eventually becoming a lecturer at a major university. With the accompanying rise in income, he took out a mortgage on a sprawling Victorian-style home in the suburbs.

Rita taught for nine years in the Boston public schools, saving to start a family and buy a house. Rita, with Karl's consent – Karl has some of the German authoritarianism built into him and his wife adapts to being relatively submissive, as expected in a good German hausfrau – taught part-time while devoting herself to their children: two girls and finally, to Karl's great delight, a son. Karl commented irreverently: "You finally got it right." The baby of the family was named Daniel after his paternal grandfather who had perished in the Holocaust. Karl was hands-on with his son in ways he had not been with his daughters, changing diapers on occasion and, as the boy grew, watching him pitch Little League baseball games.

Karl and Rita "did" for their children just as their parents had done for them, subsidizing all three at university. This entailed many sacrifices for them, despite the fact that their offspring received partial scholarships. Tuition fees for higher education had risen drastically since Karl and Rita's college days in the 1950s. The two daughters, almost a decade older than their brother, married and moved away from the Boston area while their brother was still in junior high. Rita returned to teaching full time as soon as Daniel entered elementary school, and, since her entire salary was earmarked for savings, she and Karl were able to provide down payments on starter homes for their girls. They also established a college fund for Daniel. With his daughters no longer at home Karl drew even closer to his son.

Daniel was not the scholar his father had been, but he was good with figures and did reasonably well as an economics major. He graduated and found employment at a stock brokerage firm. Not long after he had begun to work there he began to date Sondra, a young woman slightly older than himself. Sondra, twenty-four, was still completing an undergraduate degree in biology. Her ambition was to be a dentist. Daniel, in love for the first time, was smiling and happy. Rita, who had nothing against her son's girlfriend, was content. Karl was miserable.

When Sondra walked through his door for the first time one Friday night for dinner, Karl took an instant dislike to her. He observed her surreptitiously, listening carefully to her dinner-table chitchat with Daniel and Rita. That evening, after Sondra had departed on Daniel's arm, he confided to his spouse, "She's a phony. And none-too-bright into the bargain. I trust this affair will come to a quick end." It didn't. Over the next six months Daniel stopped dating other women and announced to his parents that he had "found the right one." Rita, knowing her husband's sentiments, offered only tepid encouragement to her son. To Karl she stated flatly, "Accept her. If you try to stop the relationship you will lose your son." Karl stared at Rita and replied, "If he marries her I'll lose him anyway."

The wedding took place the weekend after Sondra received her bachelor's degree. It was a quiet ceremony, followed by a small reception, since family and friends on both sides were few. Karl was devastated, but he hid his emotions and drank more than he should have at the reception. His new daughter-in-law, oblivious to Karl's feelings, was jubilant. She had just received an acceptance letter from a dental school in California. The registrar did not offer her a scholarship. Enclosed with the letter of acceptance was an application for a bank loan.

Daniel was happy for Sondra. He had no desire to leave Boston, but he knew it was a necessary step to take until his wife acquired her professional credentials. His brokerage firm had branch offices on the West Coast, and nobody objected when he put in for a transfer to Los Angeles. He was not so happy when Sondra told him what her tuition fees would be. "My folks can't help much," the bride explained, "but yours can. I know they've set aside money for a house for you, like they did for your sisters. If they added a little something to that, plus what you'll earn while I'm in school, I might be able to get my degree without going into major debt. What do you think?" Daniel, somewhat taken aback by his wife's request, said cautiously, "I'll have to ask my parents."

THE REASONING

Karl and Rita conferred with Sondra's parents. Although the in-laws were not well off, they had some equity in their home that could be used as collateral, but not enough to get Sondra through dental school. Finally, seeing no alternative, Karl and Rita agreed to put up their own home as additional collateral for school fees. Although offering collateral does not require any actual outlay of cash, it does involve risk. Conceivably, something might happen to prevent Sondra from completing her studies, returning her loans or even staying married to Daniel. And even though the prospect of his son getting a divorce might in principle make Karl happy, if his daughter-in-law were to default on a bank loan, Karl and Rita would be seriously putting their only major asset in jeopardy. The rationale of the decision was that if both sets of parents were to provide collateral Sondra would have greater motivation to honor her academic and financial commitments, and the risk of default would be reduced for all concerned. In addition, they stipulated that the newlyweds should take out a bank loan to share the risk. Karl and Rita told their son that if he preferred, he could channel the money designated for his starter home into Sondra's tuition payments – as long as he and his wife made no future demands for housing assistance. Sondra's income from her profession would have to be devoted to getting them a home.

Karl and Rita do not see eye-to-eye about their new daughter-in-law, but Karl should be circumspect to protect Daniel from being torn between his obligations to his wife and his loyalty to his parents. It's not easy to do the right thing when one doesn't like the person concerned. Like all parents, he and Rita should present a united front. Karl should not have to justify or apologize for his reluctance to pay Sondra's tuition. He should not, after all, be required to make sacrifices for a daughter-in-law's education. That responsibility belongs to her parents. Karl can state this matter-of-factly because it is true, and the truth is not likely to alienate Sondra and Daniel. It is also a fairly harmless way for Karl to vent his feelings about being manipulated.

This story focuses on the distribution of emotional and financial resources by mature parents to their potentially vulnerable adult son and emotionally manipulative daughter-in-law. Karl's emotional and financial resources are inevitably limited: there is never enough to go around. As he grows older, his emotional resources may wane faster than his financial resources. *Many parents would be more than willing to give financial aid if they could only unburden themselves of the emotional component.* It is, however, this emotional component that requires most of the focus. The wise investment of financial resources follows from the awareness of the emotional component, which, in turn, restores both the emotional and financial balance to their lives. Even in families in which virtually unlimited resources are available, it is folly to give children everything they ask for because it prevents them from growing up and fending for themselves. Instead, like the continuous feeder of the hungry lion, these parents will have taught their children that their best option is to go after the parental pocketbook and that hunting outside the humble family hearth is a risky and dangerous occupation.

Karl's allergic reaction to Sondra might easily have led him to refuse point blank to help his son with his wife's tuition payments. As previously noted, Karl would have been within his rights to do so. But parents always help because of their emotional involvement, and a curt refusal from Karl and Rita would have been counter-productive as it would have damaged their relationship with their son.

By giving Daniel the option of using the housing money for another purpose, Karl and Rita are conveying the message that their son has some degree of control in the difficult financial straits in which he suddenly finds himself. And because autonomy is inherent in this kind of decision-making, Karl and Rita are responding well. They are promoting Daniel's independence.

The loan option represents a willingness on Karl and Rita's part to share with their son the risk associated with borrowing a large sum of money. It is also, on a certain level, a statement of belief that Sondra will achieve her professional goals and that Daniel's marriage will endure. At the same time it is a warning to their son to keep an eye on the money and not allow love to blind him to the reality of his own limited financial resources. Finally, redirecting the money is a covert acknowledgment of the closeness between Karl, Rita and Daniel, a closeness that will enable Daniel to turn to his parents in good times and bad. *When parents give money to their offspring conditionally, the message is heard more clearly than if they were to extend largess without conditions.*

It is impossible to know whether Karl's assessment of his daughter-in-law's character is accurate. *There is no shortage of parents who believe that their offspring have chosen unworthy spouses.* And Sondra may, indeed, embody the negative attributes Karl ascribes to her. But this does not mean Daniel will be unhappy with his chosen bride. Even if his marriage turns out to be a mistake, it is a mistake Daniel must be allowed to make if he is to grow. Without risk and pain, there is no internal growth. In any event, failed marriages are rarely fatal errors. Experience demonstrates that *people often derive as much* (if not more) *from their failures as from their successes.* So will Daniel, if Sondra is wrong for him.

Moreover, parents cannot continually run interference for their offspring, while at the same time claiming to support their personal autonomy. Karl and Rita are saying to their son, "We accept you as an adult. We may not approve of everything you do, but we love you and will always be there for you." Rita does not perceive her daughter-in-law as a threat, probably because she has invested as much in her daughters as she has in her son. Her approach is therefore more balanced than Karl's. Rita's message to Karl is: "Nobody said raising kids was easy or fair. But whether you're right about Sondra or not, you have to make peace with her if you want to have peace with Daniel."

THE RAWNESS OF EMOTIONS

Unfortunately, Rita's sensible advice does not fall on receptive ears. Karl's raw, visceral emotions about this threat to his son, whom he sees as an extension of himself, far surpass any hardship or stress this immigrant has ever experienced. In an effort to explain to Rita how he feels, Karl reminds her of the time that Daniel, only six months old, had been running a high fever and Rita had been away. At his wits' end, Karl had called the pediatrician late at night. When the doctor said amicably, "Give him a cool bath and two aspirin and call me in the morning," Karl had experienced for the first time in his life a depth of murderous anger towards the doctor, a feeling that he had never had before. "That's how protective I still feel about Daniel," Karl explained.

Karl and Rita should avoid the common strategic error of making one parent the naysayer, while the other retains and strengthens the comfortable position of the ultimate giver within the family. This strategy may be tolerated when dealing with a pre-adolescent child, and may perhaps be permissible in adolescence and young adulthood, but it is clearly self-destructive at later stages when active involvement of both parents is critical to resolving the problems of an adult child. Karl and Rita should use their successful history together to help them to function as a parental unit, regardless of their deep differences of emotions. They operated as a pair when their two daughters were younger, Rita being the disciplinarian while Karl was out working, and they should operate as a pair now, when they anticipate a possible crisis.

Rita sees no distress; Karl is biding his time and just waiting for it to surface. Rita predicts a happy ending for Daniel and his wife Sondra, but Karl is geared for trouble and disaster. Rita sees the launching of her youngest child as similar to throwing a stick forward in their walks through the New England woods. Karl accepts the analogy but sees this last stick as crooked and expects it to return like a boomerang. Despite their differences of opinion, they should maintain a united front vis-à-vis Daniel and not allow him to regress to committing the cardinal error of childhood by playing one parent against the other. Legitimate personal differences of opinion between Karl and Rita should be dealt with calmly and, most important – privately. *The parents' united front may calm the adult child in distress, allowing him to enter a comfort zone.*

Any loud or "leaked" disagreement between them might irritate the adult child considerably and thus might help maintain him in a juvenile mode instead of helping him progress to an adult mode. Furthermore, a united front presented by the parents highlights the fact that all concerned are adults dealing with the presenting problem together. The paramount common goal of the parents in any scenario is to prevent Daniel from sliding into dependency and helplessness under the stress of his impending financial undertaking.

No wonder parents long for an end to the job of child raising. The expectation of children growing up and leaving home is a welcome fantasy for Rita, for it is the fulfillment of her life-long goal of successfully rearing well-socialized children. Her two daughters left home successfully, and her expectation is that Daniel will continue in his sisters' footsteps. Rita is optimistic about her children's future, yet Karl is pessimistic about Daniel's prospects with Sondra. Karl sees Rita's hopes as an illusion. Sometimes children linger at home in a comfort zone, as did Daniel. But even worse, if they do succeed in leaving and establishing themselves independently, they sometimes come back more needy than before. Parenting is an interactive task that is seen by Karl as neverending because of the constant, perpetual, emotional involvement with his son.

Why is the specter of neverending parenting so alarming to parents like Karl and Rita as they contemplate Daniel's potential problems? After all, these parents have solved many of their own and their children's problems throughout their lifetime by themselves. They have been successful in raising their children and sent them to good schools. Everything should have been perfect. They have seen people fail to achieve because of a lack of intelligence, opportunity or psychological competence. But they are the fortunate ones and they are now approaching the green pastures of retirement. They have seen other parents age prematurely, fearing that their children will be the death of them. They have seen their friends divorced or die in accidents. They have witnessed dysfunctional families of their acquaintance. They have seen handicapped children being parented by other members of their family, including grandparents and siblings, and they are grateful that they do not have that burden to carry. *They are survivors by dint of their abilities, devotion and good luck.*

But Karl anticipates not merely a distressed son and an unaffordable daughter-in-law, but a more profound danger, a threat to his very survival. Has misfortune finally caught up with them? Has their life until now been only a temporary reprieve from great hardship? Are they going to share the fate of parents who bear the brunt of serious problems with their children? Will parenting age and impoverish them and siphon the fun out of their golden years, after all the years of work and sacrifice? Karl contemplates being catapulted into catastrophic situations of Daniel's making. *"Why me? Is it now my turn for trouble, despite my successes as a parent?"*

Karl and Rita do not have to live vicariously through their children. Nevertheless, successful parents such as Karl and Rita have earned "bragging rights" about their children's achievements. Any time adults with children congregate, there is the inevitable, unavoidable conversation replete with the handily available family pictures and a reportage of the adult children's areas of study, job prospects and marriage options. One might think from these parents' enthusiasm that they themselves had gone to that school, studied that subject, gotten that job, and were considering getting married.

Parents like Karl and Rita, despite having earned bragging rights, know that they are not solely responsible for educating their offspring. They often acknowledge a particular teacher or psychologist as having been critical in their child's development. *Many educators and therapists are self-selected for the helping professions by natural talent, special training and by having supe-rior role models available to them.* These educators and therapists have assisted in parenting many children. Parents are aware that sharing the burden with a professional can, at times, provide in-valuable help.

Parents need valid and accurate psychological information to help them do the "right thing" as they anticipate a crisis situation. Unfortunately, learning in the real world often takes place through negative illustrations rather than through positive images. Parents are more easily told what not to do rather than what to do. Karl is rejecting and critical of his daughter-in-law, but Rita is accepting and understanding of her. Clearly, therefore, neither can possess the full truth about her. When forced to choose between irrec-oncilable positions, finding a compromise is sometimes recom-mended. Since each of the parents, Karl and Rita, inevitably has an individual path, the middle way is the only sensible choice for parents who function as one unit. *The middle way is the ultimate meeting place of mature parents. By contrast, arrogant approaches lead to family separations, not to a common path.*

MANAGING ANGER

Parents are often selfish people who use the tragic occasion of a family crisis to improve their status as problem solvers by show-ing how much they know and how they would handle the prob-lem. Such hauteur is common to domineering relatives, lawyers and know-it-all saviors who take pride in being able to handle difficult situations, while assuming no real responsibility for the outcome. They revel in the role of a crisis manager who alone can save the situation at the last moment. They have the "buzzer beater" mentality of a basketball player who, with one carefully aimed shot, with a fraction of a second to spare, can win the game. They convey the message to the person in crisis that one is indeed fortunate to have turned to them for salvation.

Conceited people hinder access to real human problem solving by introducing irrelevant and erroneous thinking, thus preventing the emergence of rational crisis management. Superior mothers often use the word "inappropriate" to convey a high moral tone, generally judgmental, to demonstrate the unshakable belief that they know "what's right for you." Their self-image is enhanced and they are respected for standing up for their principles and always being in the right.

Anger on the part of the injured child is generally the reason for lack of implementation of good parental suggestions. Parents should not augment their adult children's anger by adding their own wrath to the fire, regardless of how justified it might be. Modest parents should never explode in rage at the behavior of adult offspring, for *anger shadows the mind, has harmful effects and prevents clarity of thought.* The flow of anger should be controlled by the parent and channeled so as to facilitate a change in thinking. Controlled anger is a vehicle to transport the adult child to a reality with consequences with which the child and parents can live. The control of anger is necessary so that parents don't lose their wisdom or their ability to direct their unwise offspring.

Parents should refrain from reproaching their sensitive and vulnerable children to limit their feeling of being insulted, ashamed or excessively certain about the rightness of their cause. Unfortunately, people in trouble have reached this situation precisely because they are not always right: they have made mistakes and are not feeling good about themselves. The parent must beware of taking an arrogant position lest it generate further anger in the adult child. He should think before speaking, not criticize, condemn or make disparaging comments about the person.

The parent should not utilize acknowledged expertise in one field of specialty to transfer to the immediate crisis situation. For example, a lawyer might give medical advice or an intelligent person might give psychological advice on the assumption that he is smarter than most psychologists anyway. The parent should not introduce and expound "conservative" or "liberal" concepts largely irrelevant to the issue. The compassionate conservative's distillation of "tough love" may trickle down to rejection or a plain "no."

The giving liberal may become accepted as a nice person but disrespected as a role model. In sum, irrelevant self-satisfying arguments are generally not heard. By contrast, modest people listen and feel secure that they will be heard in time.

Anger generally increases when money is involved, as in a pending divorce. Sequencing issues for discussion can avoid or postpone the interfering effects of anger. By discussing separately the issue of whether the grandchildren should go to a public or private school prior to discussing school fees, the issues of values and money can be sequenced. When money is tight, school fees can raise the temperature of the discussion to a boiling point, as absolute values meet financial limitations. Whether the father should leave the house in a divorce situation should precede a discussion of family support, lest the father's anger at being forced to support two households puts him in a legally untenable situation. The individual wealth of the mother and the father prior to divorce, as well as the wealth of their respective families of origin, should precede resorting to the law of the state. When considering the retraining or education program to be pursued in order to return to the job market, one should first focus on the expected financial outcome before complaining about the cost of the training program. In sum, managing money and managing anger are intimately related.

LISTENING

Parents should be modest, quiet and not talkative, and should make a conscious effort to listen to their offspring. This seems on the surface to be sensible advice that is easy to follow. In many cases, however, it just doesn't happen. Karl and Rita have very different listening modes. Rita listened to Daniel and her daughters in a calm, sensible manner, and she assumed that this mode of listening would suffice for them in their adulthood. Karl listened to his son in childhood in an instinctive manner based on an inner sense of what was best for him as a child. Like Rita, he presumed that his mode of listening would suffice in Daniel's adulthood.

Even if there is no history in the family of the elder generation listening to the younger, parents should make a conscious and concerted effort to do so, lest the lack of parents who listen become an insurmountable handicap for the adult child.

Friends listen. Friends who feel free to air their feelings to other friends because they know that someone is listening intently come away feeling better, even if nothing external has changed. The knowledge that they have been listened to intently has changed them internally and is frequently the reason that they can begin to resolve their own problems. The act of listening with one's whole consciousness gives one better insight into a problem, and such insight is likely to result in the resolution of the problem.

Rita has a family history of listening. She was the only one of the grandchildren who had the patience to listen to her great-grandmother, who reigned over her extensive brood of descendant with an iron hand, dispensing financial security to those who followed her dictums. Rita's grandfather listened to her after she had earned her name as a polite listener herself. She had learned that it is normal for children to listen to their elders before they speak and she was invariably surrounded by politeness. Her good manners served as the basis of listening prior to the reciprocity of her own speaking. She had been blessed with being listened to as a child and as an adult and was able to reciprocate this gift with the ability to listen carefully to teachers and later to students. As a student, she heard a different drum beat in class sessions because of her well-developed listening capacity. Her above-average student grades were a by-product of her habit of close listening. Rita was able to remember almost to the letter the lectures of a beloved college professor more than forty years later.

Listening in good times and in times of crisis *is not a passive process*: it is an active one, which often provides the key to resolving the presented problem. In the same way that thoughts cannot be separated from words, active listening in times of crisis cannot be distinguished from problem solving. A history of being listened to is incredibly helpful if one is to listen to others, and it does not matter whether it comes from parents, friends, teachers or other significant people in one's life. Most people have had someone in their past – a teacher, a doctor or perhaps a friend – who, at some point, listened deeply and made a difference in their lives. Rita listened dutifully to Karl's driven speech about Daniel and Sondra. But, try as she might, she could not make head or tail of what he was talking about.

SPEAKING, MOCKING AND CRITICIZING

Parents should avoid excessive criticism of their grown-up off-spring when presented with age- or stage-inappropriate problems. Parents may feel worn out with rage when presented with problems that they would have handled differently had they been in the child's situation. For example, when confronted with the prospect of having to meet their offspring's mortgage payments at this point in their lives, the parent might articulate to a divorcing child about having bought too big a house. This annoyance, however, does not deal with the real issue.

The real question regarding housing is the parents' willingness to pay in order to keep their descendant from living in a hovel. A modest home or apartment in a safe neighborhood with good schools for the grandchildren is not an unreasonable expectation. If the young couple previously lived in poor accommodation, the parent can empathize with their need to have a large house. Criticism of what might have been and what should have been has little meaning in a new economic reality. The best response to the offspring's changed circumstances is to find a way to ensure stability while postponing major decisions regarding the living space that will be required in the new circumstances. For example, offering to pay the mortgage for a while could satisfy the adult child's need for support and help establish trust.

As teachers, both Karl and Rita have been encouraged and rewarded for verbal behavior. If, God forbid, Karl's prophecies come true, they will probably deal with the personal misfortune befalling their son with a well-preserved silence that will allow them to recoup their psychological forces. Parents should at first say little, and should speak only when it is essential. They may lose influence and be disrespected by their adult children as a result of unnecessary verbosity. *Silence guards wisdom not by speaking, but by listening.* The effectiveness of silence is highlighted by a consideration of its extreme opposite.

Shouting, yelling or speaking in a loud voice turns people off and distracts their attention – leading to their concentrating on the yelling and the style of speech instead of on the content. *People who shout do not get heard.* This, in turn, only stimulates them to speak louder. Eventually, they sound like a foghorn looking for a receptive audience in the haze of speech.

Instead of wasting energy deciding whether they are correct in interfering with their adult children, parents should focus on what to say or not to say in times of crisis. Parents should behave like "good soldiers" and prevent a situation from deteriorating by keeping their mouths shut until deliberately deciding to speak. They should try to recall talking to other adults of a similar age as their offspring. If they do this, their endeavors will surely be worthwhile. If the parents have the bad habit of always talking in a crisis they should acknowledge that, although old habits are hard to change, the effort must be made.

If they want to be listened to by adult children in times of trouble, parents should speak their own emotional truth, for what comes from the mouth must come from the heart as well. *Gestures such as providing money upon request, paying trip expenses or tuition fees should come simultaneously from the heart and the mind in order to demonstrate emotional support,* otherwise the parents will be seen merely as clever people trying to seduce their children with grown-up goodies.

Wise parents resist the temptation to mock their children in times of woe. The parent should be aware that while wisecracks may be witty and amusing, the wise guy eventually loses his credibility. Once, while waiting with Daniel for the doctor, Karl made fun of the way pediatricians talk to children and their families. Three of the seven people present in the waiting room fell off their chairs with laughter, clutching their bellies. The other four laughed and said that it was all right to think that way, but that it was not all right to say it out aloud in public. Karl eventually accepted the majority opinion.

Laughing at or mocking the situations that adult children can get into is a great temptation because these situations may be inherently hilarious. Resisting the temptation to be a wise guy is not easy, especially in emotionally sensitive situations. Karl stopped being a wise guy and grew more mature as a parent; he wasn't as funny, but he was far more effective. He understood, as he rehearsed in his head the worst-case scenarios for Daniel, that *down-and-out offspring don't like wise guys and can't stand being mocked.* Karl anticipates Daniel's emotional return to him. He expects him to be in an angry and petty mood and disrespectful toward the architect of his personal disaster. Karl has learned from his prior experiences as a wise guy that neither mocking Daniel nor joining him in the depths of his despair is emotionally effective.

The most effective thing parents can do is to just listen to their adult offspring's pain of disappointment in marriage. And there may be yet another scenario based on the rule of trouble coming in bunches. If Daniel leaves Sondra in the future, he may eventually lose his job as well, as a consequence of complications coming from his bad moods. If this comes to pass he might be bitter at having been "down-sized" at his job. Daniel is a healthy adult with a good work history and is therefore likely to feel resentful that his employer or supervisor didn't fight to keep his job and may harbor a sense of betrayal. His perceptions of his fate in the job area may be heavily influenced by his feelings about the marriage breaking up. Although it is the parents' obligation to rebuke their offspring for bad judgment in an effort to ground them in reality, parents should take care not to juvenilize their children by speaking in a disrespectful or harsh way.. People are not always defined by what they do, especially when they are in crisis. *People behave inappropriately in the grip of strong emotions and even smart people may behave stupidly.* Emotions are not logical and often do not receive high grades in the school of hard knocks.

ANTICIPATING RETURN

When a child like Daniel grows up and leaves home he automatically expects the world to be as accepting of him as his parents were. Then reality hits. When in the throes of a life crisis, he might consider returning to his parents, assuring himself that it will be a temporary move as he strives to regain that sense of acceptance provided by the family. He should not settle back into the world of eternal adolescence. When adult children are in the process of leaving home they are likely to see their horizons expanding, but when getting divorced or getting fired they are likely to feel their horizons contracting. *Parents should not let the adult child regress into adolescence.* A return home ought to carry with it the concept of transience: it should be clearly established that the return is a temporary situation until the returnee can regroup and leave home once again in order to regain his independence. The return home is part of a deal or a contract that carries certain obligations on both sides. Returnees simply do not have the rights to parental support that they had as children. They are, after all, no longer children. The demands of adult reality should take precedence over extended adolescence, when the teenage Daniel anticipated getting the Mustang, the stylish sneakers and the Harvard education to which so many of his peers aspired. Returning adults may want to acquire the status symbols of their peers but cannot be allowed to slip back into the former emotional state of adolescent anticipation. The rules are now different.

Setting limits focuses energy and generates a healthy apprehension, driving home the message that the parent means business. Returning children should drive the car they can afford, wear clothes they already own, and perhaps retrain without depleting their parents' bank account. Moreover, all of this should be done with the clear understanding that the dependent status of the returnee is temporary. Adult offspring, unlike children and teenagers, cannot "hang out" with their parents indefinitely. Both the parent and the adult offspring should realize that dependency in adults has a starting point – when the child returns to lick his wounds and to gain comfort – and an end point.

Karl is secure in his relationship with Daniel despite Rita's warnings that he should be accepting of Sondra, or at least come to terms with the new situation. Karl knows that the bond of trust between parents and adult offspring may become deeply frayed by stressful situations, but he is also confident that the tie rarely breaks or disappears completely. Karl anticipates Daniel's returning home in crisis and grasping at that frayed rope. Karl's hanging on to that trust by his fingernails bears witness to the strength of the bond. Parents are obliged to act as though their relations with their offspring had never deteriorated because of the offspring's marital relations.

Karl believes that Sondra is cheating Daniel. He is convinced in his heart that Daniel will make the right decision about Sondra in the fullness of time. He is a parent who has taught his adult child both trust and distrust through a game of cards. Card players know that they should only play cards with people they trust so that they can relax and feel comfortable. Even so, one must cut the deck before playing. Karl believes that Sondra is playing the card game of life unfairly and that Daniel will, in due course, realize that she has stacked the deck in her favor; eventually Daniel will start to feel uncomfortable as he realizes that this is not his game or his life.

Karl, in the unfair game of life, sought to stack the cards in favor of Daniel and his best interests, but he also taught him that it's not okay to cheat. This is because cheating is a sign of weakness that generally leads to failure to secure a goal, such as completing dental school. Karl contemplates Daniel's eventual return with relish for he understands that Daniel trusts him and that trust is a prerequisite for a request for help. When Daniel returns to the ancestral home, his parents will have regained the right and the obligation to implement ground rules.

Karl himself is not a heavy drinker, but he does turn to alcohol under stress. Daniel may do the same, and in the eventuality that he becomes a returning son with an alcohol problem, he should not be allowed to range at will in the family liquor cabinet. A depressed Daniel should not be permitted to forego showers or proper personal hygiene or to hang around in a ratty bathrobe. *The offspring has to realize that his return is, to no small degree, an invasion of parental privacy.* Loving parents may be prepared to accept this invasion, but an adult son or daughter should understand that they cannot do whatever they want when not on their own turf. For example, a parent can, and indeed must, insist on good eating habits; the price of a free lunch is surely manners at the dinner table. The dinner table is often not a good venue for the prolonged ventilation of problems on the part of the aggrieved returnee.

Whether it is the dinner table or a neighborhood walk, the venue of the conversation is important. Meal times should be characterized by quiet conversation and simple food. For example, if a son comes home ranting and raving about being treated unfairly, a parent should encourage him to leave the dinner table to "walk it off" with an hour-long power walk. Exercise has many beneficial by-products including melting away anger. *It is difficult, if not impossible, to sustain anger or anxiety during sustained physical activity.* The problems themselves do not get solved by a power walk, but exercise causes the brain to produce endorphins that have a calming influence on the mind and ease bodily aches and pains.

The security of home and neighborhood may calm the adult child. However, sometimes this is not practical if the younger generation lives in a different location than the parents. In such a case, the choice of relocation depends upon a pragmatic evaluation of resources available. Where Daniel should relocate to when in crisis is a major issue. In helping adult children deal with medical problems, cities are generally better than small towns because the medical institutions in large urban areas are usually bigger and more sophisticated. There are generally more specialists, better special education services, more child-care options, more churches and synagogues, as well as a greater variety in job opportunities. All things being equal, the quality of life in small towns may be very high and provide a psychic comfort level, but in times of crisis, access to experts in cities may be more important than comfort.

REBUKING IN PLACE OF PUNISHMENT

The tendency of parents to juvenilize their adult children is inevitable and understandable. However, parents should strive to treat their adult children according to their chronological age. It is therefore the parents' obligation to rebuke or reprimand or chide their offspring whenever they make a bad judgment call in an effort to ground them in reality. Rebuking is harsh, yet at the same time respectful, because it deals with adult children according to their chronological age and prevents the emergence of blame. Of course, in order for the parental rebuke to be heeded, parents should first straighten out their relationship with their adult children and only then deal with the matter at hand. Otherwise, irrelevant anger might cloud the perception of the adult child, leading to a failure to internalize the parental rebuke. Further, the rebuke should be gentle in order to steer the adult child's return to the correct path.

Persistence, rather than wisdom, is the key to understanding and growth. In order for the child to understand that his parents are speaking for his own good and long-term benefit, the parents should speak with a soft tongue; it is self-defeating to speak to the child in a harsh or disrespectful way. They should persist when their advice is not heeded immediately. Parents, while talking, should pay attention to minute changes in the child's emotional state. They should be prepared to present their position time and time again until the child accepts the advice or else explicitly rejects the advice, saying, "I am not prepared to listen to you anymore." Even in the face of such rejection on the part of the child, the parents' continuous protest against the child's negative actions, combined with an acceptance of the individual as he is, will eventually reduce the adult child's level of anger and violence and allow him to listen to the message.

Parents should speak softly and gently and pay special attention to matters of respect and honor so as to avoid pouring salt on an open wound. *Being punitive can tap into the all-too-human tendency to enjoy the unfortunate plight of others.* If one has that bent – as many of us do, even if we are loathe to admit it – it is easy enough to find a good reason or rationale for inflicting punishment. Often the adult child will be unconsciously seeking severe psychic punishment, but parents should not be tempted to enhance their child's punishment. One should be wary of falling into that trap. *Even if returning adult children are, in fact, seeking punishment in order to relieve their sense of guilt, they should not be allowed to succeed.*

The rule of thumb here is to act according to the letter of the law, and not stretch it one way or the other. Parents should use the law to help define reality for their adult children and to help them internalize it in order to avoid excessive punishment, but they should not be tougher on their children than the law requires. For example, parents of a divorcing son with young children should inform him that the law generally gives custody to the mother. When the son insists that he will never give up custody of his children to "that evil witch," the parents should accept his words as a statement of pain, rather than as a legal plan of action.

There should be recognition of the fact that people in crisis are in a weakened state, and this loss of status should be met with compassion. In such instances parents should take particular care not to add to the pain of a person already being punished. Parents must be wary of engaging in excessive punishment of their wayward children or shaming their adult children in public by recounting over and over again embarrassing incidents from the past. *If an adult child is not in denial, the unbearable shame of his past actions has already been internalized.* Recapitulating the events would only be making the adult child experience a battering as painful as a physical lashing. Parents may be tempted to give their wayward adult child a tongue-lashing in order to maintain the inherent hierarchy between the family members. On the other hand, confrontational discussions between family members generate a false sense of equality. Assuming equality only lowers the level of discourse of the parent to that of the child in trouble.

Mature parents should be aware that a tongue can be a soft instrument or an excessively sharp one. They should not behave like a lawyer with excessive pride in their verbal ability, for this can border on verbal sadism. One lawyer, when asked why he had given up the practice of medicine, since his personality was well-suited for a surgeon, replied, "You're right about my personality. I still think of myself as a surgeon who likes to cut. But the tongue cuts sharper and deeper than any scalpel yet invented."

Even more painful than punishing, shaming and making cutting comments is the violation of trust, for it hurts in a spot peculiarly sensitive and internal. Parents should never tell their adult children "white lies" to make them feel better temporarily, because this often rebounds to damage the parents' credibility. Offspring must know that whatever happens, their parents will always be honest with them, especially when the adult child is in a delicate emotional situation. That honesty stands as a protective firewall against the various problems and tragedies in life that befall everyone. It is better to know the truth, no matter how painful, than to live with lies. The old adage that in certain circumstances it is kinder to lie rarely applies to any of the situations that bring wounded offspring home to the parental nest.

A parent should listen to whatever the child says, even though it may be unreasonable or untrue. Parents are being honest when listening to whatever the child says and indicating through gestures and expressions that they consider the statements unreasonable or untrue. However, even if they do not agree with what is said, they should be ready to comfort the child and give support with hugs, food and a place to rest. Parents should let their child ventilate and drive out the pain, for when a child is in extreme pain it often doesn't matter what the parents say as long as they are calm and honest throughout the narrative of woes. The awareness of the parents' honesty comforts the child and alleviates pain, for it evokes memories of acceptance.

But adult children in trouble must not only be accepted, they should also be rebuked as they were in their youth in order to enable them to deal with the errors of their ways. Parents should be ready for the long road to repentance following the initial rebuke. The first steps to repentance are generally false; the offense is often repeated despite promises that "I'll never do it again." Still, parents should continue to expect real repentance, even if they are frustrated time and time again by their child's actions. And parents should keep on doing whatever is appropriate in order to foster true repentance. Mature parents should be able to offer continuous love and an ongoing faith that things will ultimately work out for their children.

They should confront the continuous lies of a distressed adult child. If a returning son has a drinking problem, for example, there should be no liquor in the house. If an unhappy daughter overeats, parents should make sure that the fridge is full of limited quantities of a large variety of healthful foods. Repentance is a slow process, and persistence, not wisdom, is the key to progress. Patience and an internal sense of security in the truth of the message can sustain parents for a long time. Parents must wait. The period of rebuking stops only when the person is truly repentant. Then forgiveness can begin.

GOSSIP

Karl's excessive concern for his son has led him to take a supercilious position vis-à-vis his daughter-in-law, who may simply want to earn a professional degree, improve her position in life, and make a good marriage. Is Karl justified in his instinctive negativism towards his daughter-in-law, secretly wishing her failure in life and hoping for divorce so that his son will return to him? Karl is spending an excessive amount of time blackening her reputation, smearing her motives and impugning her intentions toward Daniel. Is his lashing out at the anticipated object of his unhappiness justified by the reality of the situation? Has Karl become a gossip dedicated to gathering information and impressions to malign Sondra? The unwritten underpinning of gossip is the delight of ruining another person's name or reputation; it is the verbal equivalent of the enjoyment of causing injury to another person's body. This behavior constitutes violence to the person's soul.

Gossip is responsible for serious damage to the souls of the three people involved: the object of the gossip, the one who tells the gossip, and the listener. Gossip destroys the reputation and good name of the object of the gossip. The object of gossip is in the unenviable position of denying the presupposition underlying the lie: for example, Sondra must prove that she is going for a professional degree for the future financial security of the couple and not only herself. The pain of damage to one's identity in the community is the equivalent of losing one's world, for what remains in this world is his name and reputation.

Gossips get a bad reputation, as they become known as people "who can't keep their mouths shut." "You'd have to be nuts to tell them anything personal! It would be all over town in a day." A gossip is shunned and avoided by people who succeed in overcoming the natural appeal of this sin. A gossip relishes being first with any bad breaking news, but earns a bad reputation as being indiscreet and untrustworthy. No one discloses a secret to a gossip because he or she cannot be trusted to promote normal communication. An adult offspring who may have been conditioned by bad experiences with a gossip can fear turning to a parent or a professional for help. Normal people confronting problems often do not confide their woes to a parent, a friend or a professional for fear that a gossip will use their vulnerabilities against them. While communication is an absolute good for the soul, gossip is at the other end of the moral spectrum and is an absolute evil.

Honesty opens up the lines of communication that gossip closes, for gossip is the opposite of honest speech among adults. The negative story told about a person is generally not the same as the actual story, as indicated by the gossip's insistence that "my" story is the "real" one because he or she has access to an unnamed source; all other versions are, by this definition, full of lies.

Those who listen to gossip appear to be harmless and doing nothing wrong. After all, hearing bad stories about others can make one feel better and virtuous about one's self. The readers of the tabloids seem to enjoy some harmless hearsay, learning about the evil behavior and sexual activities of celebrities. Still, people relish listening if the piece of gossip is a really good juicy item that exposes the sexual foibles of people they know. This voyeurism does little to uplift the human race and spreads misinformation. The factual inaccuracy indicates a mean streak in normal people who are denied access to the truth and realities of people's psychic lives. Yet those interested in gossip are the ultimate gladiatorial audience of this blood sport. Although they may be more innocent than those who actually dish out the dirt, the listeners are certainly dusty.

Adult children in pain may engage the parent in gossip as actor, object or as a listener. They may mark the parent as being responsible for their plight – and if so will not hesitate to dredge up irrelevant items from the past. This is not surprising, for adult children returning home come with the baggage of bad relations with people close to them in their daily lives. They sometimes bear a grudge against their parents for their ill fortune in life. They may complain that they were not brought up properly and that the parents did not prepare them to handle bad situations in life. They may feel that they did not receive a proper education. They are likely to highlight some failure of moral or financial support at a vital time, or to bring up some critical incident over and over again out of bitterness. They may approach their parents not with the expectation of having their problems solved but with the desire to settle old scores. These endless tales of inadequacies of the parents are purveyed to friends with absolute certainty. No disagreement or argument is permitted. More often than not such an adult child cites an unimpeachable authority to prove a point about the parents. Distorting reality about the parents makes them indistinguishable from an ordinary gossip.

Parents should listen to the lengthy recitations of sins of the past. The appropriate response is acceptance and understanding of the child's pain. This alone makes dialogue and social relations possible. The parent should not respond in kind by saying, "You're an adult now. All of that is history and doesn't matter now. And what about all the grief you've given us over the years?" The crisis that the child has brought home presents mature parents with the chance to grow into the kind of parents that they had always wanted to be, perhaps by becoming closer to their own parents; at the same time they can correct previous errors in parenting.

Knowing your own parents at any age can be rewarding to your own family. For example, one parent had a father who was a compulsive gambler and a mother who was saintly. He had suffered because of these circumstances his entire life and had worked through his issues. When his own daughter married a psychopath – a man who drank, stole money from his employers, and was emotionally cruel – he was instinctively able to connect to his daughter because of his own success in resolving his past conflicts. He became like his own mother, but far more pragmatic. From this position he was able to help his daughter evaluate her own situation more accurately and help her separate from her abusive husband. The daughter remained an innocent. Her second husband was drawn to her innocence. This parent had no magic words to help his daughter, but his magic feelings about his own parents sufficed for his daughter's happy ending.

Daniel, Karl and Rita each anticipate a "happy ending" to Daniel's marriage to Sondra. For Daniel, the happy ending would be love, professional fulfillment and success – Sondra's getting her defining degree as a dentist without bankrupting him or his family, having a child to keep Rita happy, and preferably a male child to keep Karl happy. For Karl a happy ending would be a quick divorce without too much financial loss. Karl doesn't believe that Sondra loves Daniel, so he prefers to talk about money instead of love. He expects Daniel's money for his honey to melt away in time. Rita is neither bitter nor saccharine about her children's marriages. She is prepared to deal with adversity in an emotional state of equanimity.

Karl was not totally in the wrong in finding it difficult to deal with requests to fund the future, even if it was selfish. Karl never worked through his initial dislike of Sondra and, instead, focused on the financial request as the real problem. He didn't look within himself to discover a more personal reason for such antagonism. Finding that personal reason might have allowed him to bring his anger under control and might have led to steps that would allow for a resolution with each member of the young couple. Instead, his anger, his "witty" remarks and his fear of losing Daniel leads him to criticism, condemnation, arguments with Rita and an uncertain future relationship with his son. Karl's anger continues to spin endlessly because it has no outlet. This failure to deal directly with the problem has turned him into an arrogant gossip. His unambiguous dislike of Sondra is so out of proportion that neither his wife in the present, nor his son in the future, may be able to deal with him. But what if he's right about Sondra? Alternatively, what if Daniel's view of Sondra prevails in the end and Karl is left an arrogant maligner of a nice family? Whatever the circumstances, the mature parent will find the resources to cope.

Chapter Five

THE LIMITS OF
HIGHER EDUCATION

INTRODUCTION

Karl may have been weakened emotionally because of his Holocaust subculture. He may have become overly close to his son and unable to say "no" to him concerning financing his daughter-in-law's education. He may feel powerless to prevent his son's going on a wrong path and ill at ease with family disagreements, and may not be able to walk away from his emotional paralysis.

The following story is about Ben, also a teacher like Karl, but more internally secure because of firm family roots. Karl can't set limits by just saying "no" to a financial request that he disagrees with emotionally, while Ben finds the internal strength to set limits. Karl and Ben are equally committed to higher education, but when Ben reaches an emotional limit on a vital topic he can draw a line in the sand, while Karl cannot. Ben can be selfish and selfless. He knows when to give and when to withhold. These are essential characteristics of a mature parent.

Synopsis

Ben is committed to providing higher education for his sons, but even he has his limits. He wants to enjoy his twilight years with his wife, doing the things they always dreamed about. Simon, their scholarly head-in-the-clouds son, has profound respect and honor for him as a father, as a person and as a teacher. Ben has a final lesson to teach his son Simon: the meaning of the word "no."

THE DILEMMA

Ben and Jane, in their early sixties, have worked in the public school system of Baltimore for almost thirty years – he as a high-school teacher of chemistry and she as a college guidance counselor. They are currently earning at the top of their salary range and, although they enjoy a comfortable standard of living, both are savers who choose not to live extravagantly.

They own one major asset, the house they have lived in for twenty-six years. They were able to buy the property only because they secured a twenty-five-year mortgage on good terms and, as Ben dryly comments, "Our home was the mother of all handyman specials." "Which," Jane adds, "would have been great if either of us had been handy. As it is, whenever I want to hang a picture, Ben wants to call a carpenter."

Over the years they have managed to refurbish their place little by little, but they could not afford to do the extensive renovations they would have liked. They had other priorities, namely twin sons to put through college. Since Simon and Mo were bright, they both gained acceptance to different but equally prestigious Ivy League schools in New England. "Which," Jane puts in, "would have been great if the kids had qualified for financial-need scholarships. But our salaries are too high." "And," Ben grimaces, "our zip code area is too good." The boys received partial funding for their costly tuition as a result of good grades, but their parents had to come up with the remainder of their tuition and cover all their dormitory and living expenses. The boys worked full-time every summer to pay for books and pocket money. They also held down part-time jobs on campus whenever they could.

Ben and Jane were justifiably proud when they attended the twins' graduation ceremonies. It was a foregone conclusion that their BAs would not be their final degrees, since Simon had majored in earth sciences and Mo in economics. And, although teaching assistantships and nominal tuition fees for graduate study helped ease Ben and Jane's financial burden, they were still obliged to supplement their sons' living expenses. These rose considerably because the twins, by then in their twenties, had chosen to move out of their dormitories and into apartments. Both had girlfriends and had purchased secondhand cars with their graduation gift money. Ben and Jane agreed to cover the insurance premiums for their sons' cars while they completed their master's degrees.

Because their cash savings were minimal and the boys' needs still high, the parents decided to take out a second mortgage on their home. The new kitchen, patio and guest bathroom they were yearning for would have to wait. For them it was not a question of money or material possessions, but of values. Education was a primary value in and of itself. Moreover, the future professional success of their progeny was dependent upon their obtaining first-rate educations and top-drawer professional credentials. The sacrifice was made willingly, though not without regret. "We had just finished with one mortgage," Jane explained wistfully. "If we hadn't had to subsidize the boys we could have put the second mortgage into the house. Maybe we would have taken a cruise as well. Some of our neighbors went on a cruise to Alaska. They came back ten pounds heavier but with great snapshots and, of course, wonderful memories." Ben stated flatly "It was not a matter for debate. We had no alternative."

It took two years for the twins to receive their MA degrees. During this time a friend and colleague of Ben and Jane died suddenly of pancreatic cancer. In addition to their shock and grief, the friend's death forced the couple to confront their own mortality. They spent long hours discussing their friend's life, death and dreams, many of which mirrored their own. "She was a wonderful, hard-working teacher," Ben observed sadly, "and she never got to do the things she really wanted to do, things she could only do in retirement."

As for the twins, Mo earned his master's in business administration and was done with formal education. He sold his jalopy, and with his parents' blessing set out for Wall Street in search of a job. Simon, intent upon saving the Brazilian rain forest, required a PhD. As he had done for as long as he could remember, Simon turned to his parents for financial help. His tuition was covered by a grant, his living expenses would be much the same, his car was headed to the graveyard, but he had his eye on a two-year-old sports utility vehicle that fitted his image as a savior of the woods. Much to Simon's surprise, Ben baulked.

"Enough is enough," Ben told Jane. "We've given both boys a good start in life, better than anything our parents gave us. When is it going to be our turn? I'm not saying the kid can't get his doctorate. I'm all for it. But let him do it under his own steam. I want to sip martinis on a new patio. I want to see the northern lights from a cruise ship. I want to go to my favorite restaurant once a month instead of once every six months. I want you to have help in the house. Everybody else on the block has a maid. Why not us? I want the good things while we're still young enough to enjoy them. I want us to enjoy our lives while we still have lives to enjoy. Is that too much to ask?" Jane, torn between her wish to help her son and her agreement in her heart with her husband, shook her head and said nothing.

THE REASONING

In view of the emotional needs of the parents, as well as Simon's ongoing monetary needs, Ben and Jane should adopt a united front. Together they should tell him that they cannot continue to assist him financially. *Nurturing sometimes has to assume the form of not giving.* Jane will probably have some difficulty with this strategy, but she should do the best she can with her ambiguous feelings and support Ben. Concurring with Ben does not mean that Jane is acting against her son's best interests. Jane is a wife as well as a mother. She has to recognize that, in siding with her husband at this point in their lives, she is strengthening her marriage and, at the same time, motivating her son to attain financial independence.

Ben and Jane, once they have agreed on their common stance, should have a talk with Simon. They may discuss the emotional impact of the death of their friend and the implications of that tragedy for them. They should point out that they have needs of their own, and that they want to enjoy life while they can. Finally, they should point out that the time has come for Simon to achieve his final educational goal on his own. He has lived the life of a student since early childhood. His college years have been, in a sense, an extended adolescence. At the age of twenty-seven it is time for his adolescence to end. He may need a car, but he will have to get his own.

Ben and Jane should be prepared for surprise and resentment from their son. He has been brought up to feel that he is entitled to an education and that his parents are obliged to see that he gets as much of it as he wants. The fact that he already possesses two degrees may not seem relevant to him, particularly if he is angry. Ben and Jane should counter this resentment and anger firmly and gently, reminding him of what they have given him until now. And they should insist that they, too, have rights, including the right to enjoy the fruits of their own labor.

The underlying assumption is that parents always help their children, even when these children are themselves grown-ups. So here, as always, the question is not whether Ben and Jane will assist their son in getting his doctorate, but what form this assistance will assume. Their refusal to maintain their son financially is precisely that assistance. In the long run their refusal will give the young man more than they would achieve by digging into the parental wallet yet again.

Parents seek to foster autonomy in their offspring. It may take the son longer to receive his PhD. He may have to put himself on a strict budget, take out a student loan for the first time in his life and deal with debt. It will not be as convenient for him as it has been in the past. But based on his proven academic performance, it is reasonable to assume that he will successfully complete his formal education, even if it takes him longer.

The status of the degree from a name university can no longer be the sole criterion for decision-making. One should assess the advantages of a theoretical degree in the field of one's choice against job possibilities expected to be available at the end of the line. After all, the letters following one's name do not ensure one's ability to earn a living. A PhD in a jobless field should be weighed up against a steady job in the building trade or the establishment of a prosperous business. There are no longer absolutes in rewards received for degrees or areas of specialty in the rapidly changing fortunes of the economy. Prejudices about the nature of a good education should not prevent a pragmatic decision of the parent and the adult child.

EXERCISING A PARENT'S FINANCIAL PREROGATIVE

When Ben says "no" to his son in the same tone he uses in his business and professional dealings, he is teaching Simon a valuable lesson. The message is that his son is no longer a teenager. Adolescence is finally over, and the task of relating to one another as equals is upon us. Even when a son is fully mature, a parent will continue to view his or her adult child simultaneously as a child and as an adult. Some remnant of the original parent-child connection always remains because of the overwhelming experience of being a parent and the time spent together from infancy and childhood until the current adult state. Previously constructed *age-appropriate relationships continue to exist concurrently with age-inappropriate absurdities, which apparently, are structured into the parenting relationship.*

Ben is reminded of a childhood friend of his who had returned to their hometown. He and Ben had set out for the evening to have a couple of drinks for old times' sake. His friend's mother had called the police station at 3 A.M. to report her son's absence.

She was worried that something bad might have had happened to him. The policeman responded "Don't worry, we'll get right on it, ma'am. How old is your son?" She replied, "Well, let me see now. He's fifty-two!"

Ben wants a grown-up relationship with Simon. *Adult offspring who are accepted unconditionally by parents are weakened, not strengthened.* Ben understands that just giving his son "more" will not help him grow up. Moreover, when "more" is handed over to the adult offspring on a platter by indulgent or worried parents, it will not be valued. After all, true value consists of the parents' giving of themselves, not only of their material possessions. Children have a good sense of when they are being "bought." When Simon begins to see his parents as people with financial problems just like everyone else, he is beginning to grow up. Furthermore, if Simon can understand his parents' hardship and their psychological reluctance to help, the pain ensuing from his parents' refusal – inevitably interpreted as their refusal to help – will be eased. Only when the adult child can focus on his parents' real problems related to their own deprivation in childhood will he begin to view them as people in their own right and not merely as a loving checkbook. A fringe benefit of not receiving money from one's parents is that it forces the person to seek alternative channels of communication with them.

Where did Ben learn the growth value of "no"? He learned about being a parent from his own parents, who served as role models of people who gave of themselves. Indeed, giving material possessions or money was not an option, for they had few possessions and little money to dispense among their children. He recalled that his own parents had gone to extraordinary lengths to buy a bike for him, just as the parents of his friends had done. The ability to make such a major capital investment in their children clarified their parents' economic status for the children and taught them where they stood in the economic hierarchy. Seeing their parents wrestle with the desire to help their child acquire a bike while faced with limited financial resources made a lasting impression. Few adult males of previous generations have ever forgotten their own "bike story," which had been so critical in bringing them in touch with the economic reality and hierarchy of their family at that time.

Ben, too, had an MBA of sorts, although not quite the same as Mo's. His was the MBA of childhood that taught Ben the reality of economics. All the children in Ben's childhood neighborhood had wanted a new bike. Naturally, they were all refused because of the cost, but the parents entered into negotiations to learn what the children would settle for. One bought a used bike, fixed it up, and painted it. Its value consequently increased, making him content if not happy. He thus learned that by means of some effort he could improve his condition, and in later years he managed to get by economically. Another was able to borrow from his family on the grounds that a bike was an economic investment. He fitted the bike out with a basket and paid off his loan out of his earnings as a delivery boy. He later went into business, having learned that if you want something really badly, you can take out a loan and work hard to pay it off. A third neighbor was told flat out that there was no way the family could afford a bike and that he was on his own. He saved 35 cents a week from his paper-route money, a job he held down for two years, until he was able to pay cash for a premium bike that had by then inflated to over $30. He learned to live with both deprivation and inflation, and the lesson of self-reliance allowed him eventually to overcome the ego insult inherent in poverty. Another boy said he didn't really want a bike anyway. Everyone knew he was lying because he didn't have a father to ask for money, so they let him ride their bikes instead. He learned not to invest in material goods, and his subsequent life has taught him that the main payoff in life comes from family and friends.

Bikes provide a common ground of discourse between the generations. After all, the way a bike is acquired in childhood is of paramount importance as a precedent for choosing cars in adulthood. The lessons of the parents' childhood can serve as a guide for their adult children's perceived legitimate right to wheels. The parent as a child felt truly entitled to two wheels, but had to make compromises in the face of family reality. The adult offspring is not entitled to the desired form of transportation, just as the parents were not. Thus the parameters of a negotiating situation are established.

A pragmatic discussion about the objective problem of Simon's wheels should result in Ben's setting clear limits. He would rather spend his resources on his long-term goals of fix-ing up the house or taking a vacation. But he also wishes to help his son not only to get a car, but also to grow up economically. Even if Ben had the money to buy their son a new car, will getting him the car of his dreams teach Simon the same lessons of value that Ben had learned as a child? Under what circumstances should a person confront his own economic reality? A child in such a situation may feel disappointed or angry about not getting exactly what he wants, but Simon must become an adult in order to understand that his parents' value system – not just their bank account – comes into play.

Compromise is a concept all adults should be capable of grasping, and it is a concept that *can be taught at any age*. Young children cannot compromise, but adults can and should if they are asking for something they have not earned. A sports utility vehicle may make Simon happy as he labors to save the rain forest, but he may have to make do with his disastrous old lemon, or even with no car at all. Necessity, not style, is the critical component.

HONOR THY TEACHER

Life-long education for mature parents and their adult offspring is desirable for civilized society. Humans are learning animals who will lose their native intelligence if they do not go to school. Quality education over a lifetime teaches respect and honor for others, especially teachers. Naturally, important teachers influence young individuals more easily than older ones, and Simon is glad that he has had a father to respect and a teacher to honor until now.

Many students remember an occasional teacher or librarian as the person who changed his life, but few find an adequate role model without even setting foot outside the home. Not all students are as fortunate as Simon, but those few who do find great teachers or mentors are truly blessed and know it in their hearts.

Simon will ultimately accept his father's "no" because he is part of a learning community headed by his father. Only with the broad participation of all its members can a learning community exist and prosper. Scholars spring from such a learning community and teach subjects not available to other parents. Simon has chosen the route mapped out for him by his father's example. They both agree that everyone must study – women as well as men, the elderly as well as the very young. Simon's formal study began as soon as he could talk, and he envisions it continuing until his death. The prolongation of his education was taken for granted by his family, and even though he will now have to pay attention to its funding, he knows that his education will continue throughout his lifetime.

Studying for a PhD and teaching go hand in hand. Simon would like to spread knowledge to others, for a student eventually develops a teacher's wisdom and feels driven to teach what he has learned. Furthermore, the occasional disciple develops a teacher's wisdom and opens up his mind. Simon feels compelled to continue studying because he fears that otherwise he will forget what he has already learned. He would like to be involved in quality education with a reasonable number of pupils of any age in his class. In fact, he defends studying as a worthwhile activity prior to working and marrying, with the argument – and the hope – that present sacrifices will be recompensed by later lifetime earnings. Mo, in contrast, is more likely to end up financing a school than teaching in it.

Simon sometimes wonders if he is living in a brain-cloud, like his father who is under the misguided impression that his childhood bike experiences are relevant to Simon's current problem of wheels. But then the son recalls a critical childhood event.

Ben often used to sit in his yard reading books while his neighbors mowed their lawns on their upscale street. His neighbors were upset with Ben because his was the only house on the block whose lawn was not mown; it destroyed the military-like, austere appearance of the street and might even lower the property values. Ben didn't care. But his neighbors continued to pester not only him, but his boys as well. Simon remembered asking his father why he didn't make a small gesture of goodwill toward his neighbors and cut the lawn. Ben explained that the lawn was only a beginning and that soon enough they would be concerned with other aspects of the family's appearance. Simon mulled that over and didn't think anything wrong with that approach until his father added, "They start with the lawn because they like the world to be trim and neat, but eventually they'll want to trim that rain forest on your head that they mistakenly see as long, unruly, matted hair. Is that what you want?"

Simon felt deeply about his long hair, and his father's words penetrated deep, perhaps too deep for his own good. Mo had reacted to the problem differently, saying, "What great neighbors! They're lending me that new model motorized lawn mower to use on our lawn and they're paying me to do it. It's pure profit. They even let me take their mower to do other people's lawns. They talked some nonsense about keeping the neighborhood neat and clean, but that's their problem. Mine is to get some money in my pocket!"

Simon has deep respect for Ben as a father, but honors him even more as a teacher. His father has been his role model until now, but Simon will need even more specialized teachers for his future. He is grateful for the discipline he received from Ben, because perseverance, and not merely raw intelligence, is what is needed to enable him to complete his PhD. Respect and honor for others is the basis of a quality education over a lifetime. His relationship with Ben gives him the confidence to deal with matters as great as ecology and as small as trimming the lawn. He needs the relationship with Ben now, for Ben and his mother will inevitably fade as educators or bearers of culture with the passing of years. Simon has sought mentors at various periods in his life, and the memory of those teachers or mentors will stay with him to the end of his days. Maimonides sums this up in his well-known maxim: "Honor a teacher even more than a father. A father gives life in this world, a teacher in the next."

Many people from different walks of life respect their teachers because the chord of the heart that they touch does not reverberate only to intelligence but to honor as well. These teachers serve as an alternative role model in a society whose purpose is the accumulation of material goods, rather than of knowledge. Teaching involves a monetary sacrifice for capable individuals, but people in more lucrative occupations continue to hang on to their every word. Their evaluation of the child or adult is taken with utmost seriousness, as if their sage comments had divine content. Individuals continue to have faith in the words of respected and honored teachers even as their own souls wrestle with their unwillingness to pay teachers decently.

Simon is a student by nature and has no doubts about his ability to save the rain forest. Still, he now has the vexing problem of what to do about a car. One of the neat and trim neighbors has commented on both his car and Mo's as being "fixed up beyond all recognition," but Simon admits truth from any source, be it trim or unruly. He is surprised that Ben didn't go for the sports utility vehicle, and it might be a parting of the ways between them – or maybe a role reversal. Ben's ecological dream is apparently limited to seeing the Northern Lights, while Simon, like Ben until now, has to deal with economic reality. Simon can see a ray of light streaming in through his brain-cloud as he realizes that he hasn't the foggiest idea of what to do about getting a car. He'll just have to figure it out for himself. He patted his hair and felt good about his life and his relationship with his parents.

Chapter Six

LOSING A CHILD

INTRODUCTION

Ben and Karl are well-educated individuals with enough educational and financial resources to solve problems that may be
emotionally draining or academically taxing. They succeed because not liking your daughter-in-law or becoming fed up with
unlimited expectations of higher education are within the realm
of normal difficulties that yield to exertion. Their problems may
be difficult, but they are not overwhelming.

By contrast, a problem that is truly overwhelming emotionally and cognitively is rare. The story of Jesse is of an ordinary,
uneducated woman who lost two of her children to an act of terror in 1983. Education and financial resources cannot help here.
Profoundly human spiritual resources must be found within if
one is to continue in the face of such a crushing tragedy. Jesse is
a parent like others who wants to continue giving to her children
but she cannot because they are no longer living. They continue
to exist in her memory, by their names, and within words written
written about them in the present.

Beneficent words allow life to revive against the committed
evil and the malicious rationalizations pardoning or understanding the feelings and mind of the perpetrator. A parent singled out

to be deprived of parenting itself can only listen to the reasoning and rhythm of words in the hope of furthering the long process of spiritual and psychological healing. Jesse's sad story is told in the hope that perhaps it will help other parents of terror victims since then to survive their unendurable loss.

Synopsis

This story traces the psychological sequence of thoughts and feelings of a mother following the loss of two of her children in a bus bombing in 1983. The bombing was carried out by means of a parcel loaded with explosives, rather than by a "suicide bomber" (perhaps more aptly called a "homicide bomber"), but the story has been updated to keep abreast of the latter style of murder, currently in vogue. This case, which took place on the author's professional watch, has been followed by him for the last twenty years, and it is presented in the hope that it may be of benefit in the post-9/11 world.

The actual events are recorded by David Shipler, Jerusalem correspondent for The New York Times *in 1983, in his book* Arab and Jew: Wounded Spirits in a Promised Land *(Times Books, a division of Random House Inc., New York, 1986, pp. 94–96), as well as in articles in* The New York Times. *The mother's name in the story has been changed to Jesse, in memory of Jesse Jacobson, the daughter of family friends who died of Tay-Sachs disease long before she had the opportunity to fulfill herself as a neverending parent.*

SEARCHING FOR WORDS

Bus Number 18 exploded late Thursday afternoon. Years later one always remembers where one was, what one was doing at the moment tragedy struck. I was coming home from army reserve duty and upon hearing the news on the radio went straight to the hospital where I worked as a psychologist. The psychiatrist on duty was assigning cases to the staff and he pointed out a particular family. I knew the drill.

The young man was in a panic. His sisters Nurit and Etti had been on their way home from school and had not arrived on time. He had been to three emergency rooms in the city already and each time had waited impatiently while the helpful clerk ran his finger down the list, finally shaking his head in an impotent gesture of helplessness. With each negative, the young man – not much older than a boy really – experienced a mixture of relief and a growing sense of impending doom. I offered to accompany him to the only other emergency room in the city of Jerusalem. This time he didn't draw a blank. A nurse informed him that his sisters were in surgery.

The waiting room quickly filled as more and more family members arrived. After what seemed like an eternity a nurse told the gathering that the thirteen-year-old girl was dead and that the eleven-year-old was not expected to live, either. "We are continuing to do our best, but you should not develop false hopes." The mother looked around, confusion radiating from her eyes, and asked the nurse, a familiar face from the neighborhood, what she should do. I told the nurse to tell her to go home and sit *shiva*, the traditional week of mourning. The mother said loudly, in a toneless voice that rang out eerily, piercing the hollow chamber of the room, "There is nothing left for us here. Let's go home!" The whole family broke down, crying and wailing, and was accompanied home.

A few hours later: the sound of a key grating in the lock. Upon opening the door, a scrawny young Israeli soldier stood there with a rifle and asked, with a look of foreboding etched on his features, what I was doing in his house. Placing my hands on his shoulders I led him into the parlor where the family was sitting, cleared a place for the soldier next to his mother, and told her to tell him. She told him and he collapsed in her arms.

The initial response in such critical moments is always to deny the presence of death. It takes time for death to sink into one's soul. It is natural to think about what might have been, what could have been, what should have been. All the professionals involved in this case presented a united front to prevent the human arousal of hope, for false hope keeps people in limbo at the moment of tragedy and does not allow them to move on with the process of mourning.

David Shipler called for more information about the tragedy and asked whether there was any hope for the surviving sister and whether he could write in his *New York Times* story that she was in critical condition. I told him, "She is expected to die and there is no hope of saving her life. You don't want to know details of her condition. She is expected to die. That is all you need to know." She was officially pronounced dead a few days later. Despair, in a final show of strength, extinguished the almost imperceptible hope that had been steadily fading in the mother's heart over the endless hours of merged days and nights. The professional staff felt their words to be inadequate as they accompanied the family through the many words spoken in the mourning period.

Words, produced out of mere air, are surely impotent against any physical object, let alone a bomb. Bombs are always referred to as "powerful," because their impact on people is so swift, compelling and deadly. What could be more "powerful" than the willful infliction of death on an innocent human being? In contrast, words begin slowly and haltingly, and in their confusion and disorder do not seem to come from a "powerful" source in the person. They seem to be needed the most when people cannot imagine having anything to say. Nonetheless, words, whether adequate, inadequate or profound, seem to erode horror gradually and have a "powerful" and occasionally therapeutic effect on the soul at critical moments. The consoling words of family, friends and community helped configure Jesse's soul through visits, talks and prayer.

The written words of *New York Times* correspondent David Shipler were adequate. The spoken words of the government representatives were inadequate. Of all the words spoken in those early days of adjustment, it was those spoken by a rabbi from the family's own cultural background that mesmerized everyone. The rhythm of his words was like a hymn. He touched the family's soul at the height of the mourning process for one brief, profound moment. The words spoken had an impact on some different part of the spirit, and the family members were gently led down the path of belief in a way that was at one and the same time familiar and new.

Words could not cope with the images in Jesse's head of the most cruel injury and death inflicted upon her two precious girls. The images penetrated deeply into her brain and prevented her from speaking. Yet she had been stirred by words or fragments of words, or chants which touched something within her. They existed uncomfortably alongside the horrific images of her mangled and dead children. Jesse was numb and did not know if she had the resources to ever chant or sing soothing psalms again, but she was sure she would never speak again in any meaningful manner.

A month later, Jesse observed herself in a full-length mirror. She was still attractive for a mother of five, but she felt disfigured, somewhat as if two parts of her body had been ripped away, leaving gaping holes in her soul. The reflection of her tragedy was ever visible in other people's eyes, people who were inevitably drawn to the thought that, "There, but for the grace of God, go I." Her innocents had been slaughtered for no human reason imaginable, and she felt her life constricting as she lost two of her worlds. She did not feel like going out or getting on a bus or a plane; she did not feel like making love; and she did not think she would ever feel anything again for the rest of her life. She looked into the void created by evil. And as she gazed at her face in the mirror, she knew that she was looking at every mother's worst nightmare. She was a mother who had lost two of her children in a terrorist attack on a bus.

A year later, shortly after the birth of a child in the extended family, the same rabbi spoke words of jubilation. His declaration that the souls of the two dead girls would live on in this newborn child – a concept not accepted by mainstream Judaism – continued to mesmerize. The mood in the family continued to be abysmal, but his words and rhythms had evoked a moment of grace.

LOOKING BACK WITH WORDS

All involved in that terrible incident in 1983 have moved on. Natural changes have taken place within the family – generally for the better – but the sisters always continue to be a part of the extended family in some way. Jesse continued her mothering of her dead children by talking about them and reminiscing with all those who knew them and even with some who didn't. She felt that parenting never ends, and she believed that Nurit and Etti would always appreciate the gesture of her caresses.

The city built a little park in memory of the sisters. Sometimes Jesse sits on a bench in that park and muses upon their tragic deaths. She is amazed that she can get up and walk on her own two legs, but somehow she manages to move forward.

My regular annual visits to the family on the memorial day for fallen soldiers and victims of terror have had some kind of long-term healing effect. On one of these visits, twenty years after that fateful day, the conversation became lighter, more expressive, and Jesse looked radiant. She seemed to see me for the first time and asked me if I were American. She asked whether I liked American music, started singing, and asked me to join in with her.

> *You are my sunshine, my only sunshine,*
> *You make me happy when skies are gray,*
> *You'll never know, dear, how much I love you,*
> *Please don't take my sunshine away.*

FINDING WORDS

Even while dealing with the devastation of the loss of her two girls, Jesse felt a surge of rage at the way the act of terrorism was dealt with in the press. The foreign news networks gave reports on "a tornado in the Caribbean, an earthquake in Turkey and a bus bombing in Jerusalem." The implication was that this was just one other natural event, no more premeditated or malicious than a tornado, which, although potentially devastating, cannot be conceived of as anything but an act of God or of Nature. Some news networks went even further, injecting a subjective slant into their reporting. Jesse was particularly irritated with a CNN reporter who continuously referred to "the justified anger of the people who produced the suicide bomber," implying that the victims, by their very presence on the bus, were somehow at fault. The unfocused reporting defiled the good names of the victims and justified the words of incitement that generate pure violence. The condoning of such verbal violence wreaks devastation on a person's soul and reputation. Expressing an understanding of the bomber's position, suggesting that he was merely giving vent to his "justified anger," enhances the vulnerability of the victim by taking from him his good name and reputation, as well as his life.

Miscommunication or misrepresentation is responsible for the poisoning of both the reporter's reputation and the listener's mind. In the case in question, the journalist's reputation was eventually destroyed by the miscommunication she perpetrated, deliberate or otherwise. The victims' names and memories were the object of misrepresentation and were sullied by their eternal association with the perpetrator. The media, through its continuous search for "news," can unwittingly collude with the dark side of people's minds.

Terrorists cater to people's insatiable need to listen and watch: they want their acts of terror to be shown in all their gory details on the news. In some twisted trickery of "suicide," the bombers often make videos of themselves prior to the act, and these videos are later shown on the news. They feed on the inquisitive and somewhat sadistic eye of society. If it were not for people's insatiable desire to "hear the latest news," bombers might have less incentive to murder others.

Jesse was unable to speak and barely able to think a month after the event, feeling that she no longer understood words. She ruminated to herself: Why is the person who set out to kill her children called a "suicide bomber" by the press, when he deliberately murdered her children and other innocent civilians on their daily rounds of work and school? Aren't words of incitement, ideas of killing and revenge-taking akin to homicide, not suicide? If the bomber was on the bus on purpose and the victims were there by accident, why does the reported number of people killed sometimes include the suicide bomber, as if he were a victim himself? The victims were there by accident, but he was there on purpose. He was not "killed" like the innocent victims. He actively killed them, and his name does not deserve a position of equality with theirs. Her two girls were not passively "killed," as if by an earthquake or a tornado; they were deliberately murdered. They were not guilty of being on the bus. The bomber was guilty of being on the bus. Jesse's grief declines as her anger and rage ascend. She realizes that she is beginning to understand the meaning of words.

TERROR VERSUS FREEDOM

An act of terrorism is a sudden unanticipated violent attack that temporarily stuns the individuals involved into paralysis, puts them in an unbelieving "out of body" state, and freezes their feelings in pain. It is as though they are mesmerized by the presence of evil. These acts are akin to a short-range artillery shell designed to attack a random group of innocent people in a bus or a coffee shop. The natural military and human response to artillery shelling is to spread out and dig in to minimize losses. After living with individual fear – for a brief moment, terror is successful – the natural response is to come together, to regroup, and to prepare for action. Jesse's family regrouped, just as people regrouped after the tragedy of September 11, 2001, which mobilized believers and skeptics alike to increase attendance at churches, synagogues and mosques as they reached for something spiritual deep within themselves. This coming together in straightforward and undemanding settings, such as at church meetings or around the dinner table, leads to discussions and steadfastness that become more "powerful" than bombers in buses or planes or coffee shops. The resolve to punish people committed to random murder becomes even more "powerful."

Vengeance for the pain and suffering inflicted is then left to God and a few good men whose duty it is to arrange a meeting with Him.

Terror is a direct attack on freedom at the most elemental level. Getting on a plane or a bus, going shopping at the mall, stopping off for a pizza or relaxing with coffee are now activities that in Israel are carried out with extreme caution rooted in fear and a restriction of freedom. Under what other circumstances could a respected *New York Times* reporter be told not to ask about the condition of the second sister in the attack? Why was such control of critical information at that moment more important than the right of the public to know? And why did all concerned think this was acceptable? Can freedom be so easily curbed or lost because of terror? In Israel self-restrictions are imposed on daily activities that in other countries are normally taken for granted. Is this liable to happen in other democratic countries as well? The fear of the consequences of terror pervades all realms of human activity: work, travel, shopping and socializing. No one is immune to terror.

Freedom becomes temporarily limited, but the human spirit will not be denied and it fights back for its elemental rights of innocent travel. Following a wave of terror, it is the simple acts, such as getting on a bus or waiting at a bus stop, that require great individual courage. Occasionally, a security person comes on to check bags. If somebody puts down a shopping bag for a moment, comments are likely to come flying: "Whose bag is this?" "Who left it here?" When somebody sheepishly admits ownership, the friendly piece of advice never fails to come: "You know, you really shouldn't leave your bag unattended." The tension and alertness are palpable throughout the bus, and by the time one reaches one's destination one is often emotionally exhausted.

People often weigh up their odds when they decide where to sit on the bus. Strategically, what will improve one's chances of survival? Is it better to be sitting next to an exit when a bomb explodes? Or perhaps the back of the bus is safer? People look warily at their fellow travelers. Tense young girls sit alertly looking at the stomachs of every man on the bus. Suspicious glances are thrown toward attaché cases. Girls are concerned about their clothing, worrying that they might lose their dignity if a bomb goes off and they are tossed about. Regular bus riders are careful not to dress with bulky clothing, lest they be stared at endlessly. Nevertheless, people continue to travel on the bus. Life does not come to a standstill.

The attack on the bus in Jerusalem in 1983 was but a harbinger of the current wave of terror in the world which has swept throughout the globe, touching places as far-flung as Israel, Bali, Morocco, Egypt, New York City, Washington, D.C. and the Philippine Islands. Others have experienced the same processes that affected Jesse: horror, disbelief, denial, prayer, gatherings, the search for words, the urge to action. The attack on the Twin Towers in New York City was a shocking example of an unanticipated and inconceivable event. The lack of clarity of the situation confused those who saw it live on television. People were hypnotized by the snake eyes of evil and stunned into paralysis by the collapse of the skyscrapers. Terror, as in Jesse's case, temporarily reigned. People mourned, prayed and took stock of their situation, lives and values.

Like Jesse, people managed to move their legs in the face of tragedy. The firefighters rushed into the burning building and became role models of heroes with the courage to do their daily job, just as Jesse did hers in continuing to raise her other children. The professional healers, especially the ministers, revealed who we all are. The mayor stood up and said the right words, and people were moved. The president stood tall. The country was prepared to do its job and to move from darkness to sunshine.

PARENTING AFTER DEATH

Nothing has ever engaged Jesse's soul as deeply as being a parent. Caring for her five children, each according to his or her own nature, has been a transforming experience in her life, one that continues even after her children's deaths. She has a lifelong commitment to her children – and "lifelong" refers to her own life, not the lives of her children. She has always felt closer to the girls, whereas her husband has always felt closer to the boys. Her remaining daughter is now finishing high school, and Jesse is fearful for her future. She doesn't want her daughter to risk her life by going into the army, as girls in Israel often do to fulfill their duty to their country. Jesse feels that she needs one girl to carry on. Her oldest son is now a paratrooper, just like his father.

She has been a good parent to her children and she has learned and grown with her children, but she can no longer grow with her two youngest girls, for they are gone. She cannot tuck them in or fluff up their toys or tell them to switch off the TV and do their homework. She will always remember them and their birthdays and think of the schools they might have gone to and the boys they might have dated. Many a surviving parent, child or spouse would gladly have given his life in return for a natural life span for his loved one. But deals like that are never on the table. Life is filled with unexpected circumstances. No parent can anticipate his or her child's death.

Is Jesse's parenting over? Where will her life lead her now that she no longer has her daughters to help her grow? As she looks in the mirror, she feels deprived of the mothering she might have enjoyed with her children. She mourns for the women they might have become. While all their friends grow, marry, have children themselves, and eventually age, Nurit and Etti will remain eleven and thirteen years old for all eternity. Jesse is now aging herself in front of the mirror as she goes through the greatest hardship and stress that any parent can experience. She had always thought that her children would grow up, marry, settle down at a job, and come to visit with the grandchildren once a week. Jesse had always expected life to grow easier as time went on. That, after all, is what was written in the parenting contract. But nothing had prepared her for this abrupt violation of the contract.

Jesse feels an acute sense of the lack of justice when she sees other mothers, no different from herself in their devotion and ability. They will continue to parent their children, even if they face difficulties. Parents of children with physical and mental defects get to parent their children. Parents of children who lack intelligence, opportunity or psychological competence get to parent their children. Parents of divorced children get to re-parent their adult child and participate in the parenting of their grandchildren. Everybody makes mistakes in parenting, but they always have the chance to become better parents. Jesse has been denied that chance. Her daughters had the bad luck to be on the bus – in the wrong place at the wrong time. If God had granted her one moment of grace, she would have asked Him to grant them better luck.

Although Jesse goes on with her life, she has a constant feeling that she doesn't have the right number of children, a feeling shared by women who have lost their children to acts of God, such as miscarriage or genetic illness. Her pain shadows her mind, and people around her tell her that she needs help to move forward out of her misty state. They want to extend help, but not the kind of help she wants. She is unwilling to desert her children just because their absence has impaired her ability to continue parenting them. She feels guilty because she was unable to protect her children, as any good parent would. She wants her children back, and she wants to continue to parent them. She's mad at God for not letting her continue to parent her two children, more precious than her own two legs. Perhaps she should have gone to the mountain and asked God to bless her children with luck. Perhaps if she had been a brilliant lawyer she could have reversed His decision. Perhaps if she had been a gifted psychiatrist she could have emptied out the hatred in the bomber's mind. Perhaps if she had offered her life or her legs in return, God would have been "a perfect parent" and let them live.

As time passed she stopped looking in the mirror and looked down at her body. Her two legs were still there. They no longer ached. She flexed them. She gradually reached the realization that nobody, not even God, is a perfect parent, and perhaps even perfect parenting could not have saved them. And it was this realization that finally helped relieve Jesse's sense of guilt. Had her girls lived, Jesse would have parented them throughout their lives, and she feels – and will always feel – cheated. Jesse was meant to be a neverending parent to all her children.

LOSING A CHILD

The death of a member of the older generation or a peer is experienced as a sad, natural event. In contrast, the death of a child at any age and under any circumstances defies normal experience: it is not a natural life event. The death of a child even degrades the very identity of the parent, unlike other tragic occurrences. As pointed out to me by David Shipler, a mourning son remains a son, and a woman who has lost her husband is accorded a special status, conferred by the word "widow," but no special name exists for the parent of a dead child. Language must have abhorred the event to such a degree that it did not provide a name for it.

Does the hollowness recede as the person is consoled by family and children and society, or does a black nucleus always remain in one's soul? Is the parent prevented from going through the mourning process by continual reminders of the horrible particulars of the child's death? Does a parent ever become consoled about the loss of a child, or does he or she simply learn to live with the loss until the end of his or her days? Does a parent continue to be in constant emotional contact with the departed child to the extent that normal relationships with other children, the spouse and other significant people become seriously impaired? Does a parent's loss remain so central to his or her life that the ability to organize his or her own life for his or her own purposes in a satisfactory manner is never regained?

The place to seek answers to unanswerable questions remains the Bible. The patriarch Jacob's inconsolable grief upon seeing the evidence of the loss of his son Joseph is expressed as follows: "All his sons and daughters tried to comfort him; but he refused to be comforted, saying, 'No, I will go down mourning to my son in Sheol.' Thus his father bewailed him" (Genesis 37:35; JPS translation). If we are to follow the biblical example, mourning parents can expect to be reunited with the lost child only in an after-life and can expect that their relations with their other children will be impaired. They can expect to learn to live with their loss but not to be consoled by other relationships. No special name is conferred upon Jacob in his state of mourning, nor upon the thousands of parents who have lost children under violent circumstances to beast or man. But the biblical narrative does not end with Jacob's eternal mourning for his son Joseph. Jesse's life did not end with the death of her daughters. The story goes on.

Chapter Seven

ALMOST LOSING A CHILD

INTRODUCTION

The experience of losing a child is rare. As a result few parents have to endure the piercing tragedy of Jesse's life. However, the fear of losing a child is in the hearts of many parents every time a real or imagined medical emergency occurs. The increased use of emergency rooms for children of all ages is an indication of how compelling the death threat is to so many parents. The parents generally choose the wise course of dependence and passivity towards the doctors, "who know best." Deference to the authority of doctors may be the best available option to parents, but some parents are inherently incapable of such meekness

The following story focuses on Kimberley. Unlike Jesse, whose cognitive functioning almost evaporates, Kimberley's increases. She is an intelligent, independent and rebellious mother who responds differently from most parents facing a life-threatening illness to the authority of "doctors who, after all, went to medical school and therefore know what they are talking about." She is a model of a parent who seeks information and empowerment to allow parents to make an informed choice about proposed medical treatment for a seriously ill child. Kimberley's high-risk strategy extends beyond her relationships with the doctors and her child. She has to confront her husband, her mother and even God in her struggles against conformist authority.

Synopsis

Kimberley, a brilliant lawyer, takes on the medical establishment in an effort to save her daughter from a life-threatening illness. Her skepticism of all authority extends to include God, and she wrestles with issues of belief and faith. She has to remain focused on the present emergency, yet needs to delve deeply into her past in order to find the resources to do so. The stress inevitably affects her relationship with her husband, as each parent deals with the crisis differently. No medical or personal detail is too small to be overlooked by this grown-up parent in her struggle to save her daughter and her marriage.

THE DILEMMA

"It came," Charles said, "like lightning on a clear summer day – with no warning. Suddenly the storm broke over our heads." The managing director of his family's manufacturing concern, Charles and his wife Kimberley, a brilliant Philadelphia lawyer, had recently thrown a lavish wedding at a fancy country club for their daughter, Leslie. Life seemed to be going well for the parents and the young couple. Then, a couple of months later, they received a telephone call from Leslie's husband. He had come home for lunch to find Leslie lying in bed unable to move and had taken her to hospital. "They're going to run a few blood tests, but don't worry. Everything's fine," he blithely assured them. He hung up and her parents anxiously waited for further details. By early evening the results were available. In a subdued voice, although trying to make light of what she had learned, Leslie reported: "My hemoglobin count is seven. I'm so anemic my blood looks like pink lemonade. Nobody here can figure out why I'm still standing up."

Kimberley's adrenaline level soared as she tackled the problem much as she would a complex legal case. First she would embark upon a fact-finding mission; then, with all possible information at hand, she would decide on the optimal course of action. Using her contacts she quickly discovered the name of the hospital's top hematologist and engaged him as her daughter's private physician. "Tests were run today and I'm worried," she said. He calmly replied, "I'll look at the chart and get back to you."

He called back two hours later and advised Kimberley and Charles to get a good night's sleep and come to his office first thing in the morning. "We're keeping your daughter here, and I'm afraid the news is bad," he said. "Leslie has a virulent form of leukemia. Statistically, her chances for survival aren't good." Kimberley angrily retorted, "Don't talk to me about statistics. Talk to me about my daughter."

Each of the parents responded to the emergency in a manner appropriate to their personalities. For Charles, the news did not change the daily routine of life in any tangible way. Trusting the doctors to do their best for Leslie, he left them to their business and continued to go about his. He went to work every morning, calling his daughter several times a day at the hospital where she lay in a sterile room. "We had gotten through other medical emergencies with Les," he recalled, "and I figured we would get through this one, too. There was nothing for me to do but keep on running the show at the factory, and, since Kimberley wasn't there very much, at home, too. We had another daughter in high school at the time, and her life had to maintain a semblance of stability."

For Kimberley, business did not go on as usual. She took a leave of absence from her law firm, dividing her time between her daughter's sterile room, the hospital's medical library and her own kitchen, where she cooked special meals recommended by the hematologist. She sat for hours beside Leslie's bed, alternately talking with her daughter and filling the long silences with various game plans for Leslie's survival, her agile legal mind turning the fearful statistics over and over. When she could sit no longer, Kimberley scrubbed every surface in the sterile room. Leslie had begun a debilitating course of chemotherapy. When her lustrous blonde hair became dull and fell out, Kimberley brought her head coverings of every shape and color, from clown's curls to a black Cleopatra wig.

Visiting the library and surfing the Internet while Leslie slept, Kimberley read everything available on the subject of leukemia and its treatment, bent on correctly interpreting the statistics that haunted her. She called experts in Europe and America, running up huge telephone bills. The hematologist and various oncologists recommended chemotherapy and a bone marrow transplant as Leslie's only hope, but Kimberley had her doubts. By this time she had read dozens of articles on the subject with the eyes and mind of a lawyer and the heart of a frantic mother. She understood that transplant procedures, even if a suitable donor could be found, were problematic. Moreover, a transplant would require complete body radiation to prevent possible rejection of the new bone marrow. Such therapy could render Leslie, who wanted to have children one day, infertile.

"The statistics show that bone marrow transplants are likely to cure leukemia," Kimberley confided to a colleague. "But transplant patients still die from other complications of cancer linked to the transplant itself! In other words, the doctors cure the illness successfully, but kill the patient as a side effect. This course of treatment raises the specter of an iatrogenic illness – that is, one caused by medical treatment. I know that the doctors want to cure Leslie, but they are also willing to kill her in the process. We have similar but different interests. I'm not willing to entertain death for Leslie for any reason. But you can use statistics to make any point. I don't want my daughter to know any of the stats. I threw a doctor out of her room the other day when she started to discuss numbers with Leslie. Now the woman is very cool to me, but I really don't care. She was out of line. The nurses love Leslie. And so does her hematologist."

At the end of Leslie's second course of chemotherapy she contracted pneumonia and nearly died. Kimberley did not leave her side for three days. She shared her grim vigil with Charles, Leslie's husband, and her younger daughter in turn. However, in the darkest times, those hours defined by the clock as morning, Kimberley and Leslie were alone. Kimberley began to resent both her husband's absence and his adherence to a normal work schedule. On the second day of the pneumonia crisis, Kimberley snapped at Charles that she expected him to be with Leslie whenever she wasn't available, and that the least he could do was to put himself out more for his daughter. "I need to eat and sleep sometimes too, you know," she protested. Irritated, Charles curtly informed Kimberley that she had no right to reprimand or judge him. Leslie, he pointed out, was not his only daughter. But Kimberley did judge Charles. On the rare occasions that she found herself at home alone with him, their interaction was punctuated by fights and sulking.

After Leslie recovered from her pneumonia, Kimberley's feelings of resentment toward Charles abated somewhat. She had had time, as she watched her daughter's sleeping countenance, to consider Charles' response. Although she wasn't entirely happy about it, she came to understand that it was the only way he could respond. "He's like his mother. It's just how she would react. When anything went wrong in her life, she kept on doing what she always did, in the hope that a strict adherence to her daily routine would somehow make the problem go away. Charles inherited her dogged optimism and that's what keeps him functioning."

During Leslie's third course of chemotherapy Kimberley informed the hematologist that instead of undergoing a bone marrow transplant, her daughter would undertake an unprecedented fourth course of chemotherapy. She presented her findings, quoting the latest studies of leukemia, arguing her case before the hematologist much as she would have done before a judge. Such was her passion, the force of her logic, and the depth of her medical research that the hematologist accepted her opinion and agreed to proceed in accordance with her recommendations rather than those of the surgeons. "It's a gamble," Kimberley explained to

Leslie, "but the additional course of chemotherapy, and not the transplant, appears to be the lesser of two evils." Leslie, still bald, smiled wryly and said, "I'm with you, Mom."

Kimberley spent even more time in the sterile room. When Leslie awoke in the morning, the first face she saw was her mother's. At night, Kimberley's kiss on Leslie's forehead sent the younger woman to sleep. "I was not a robust child," Kimberley told the hematologist, when he asked her why she didn't take a night off. "At the age of ten I contracted scarlet fever and was hospitalized for six weeks. In that entire period my mother came to visit me only three times. And, come to think of it, she hasn't seen all that much of her granddaughter, either."

Leslie survived the fourth course of chemotherapy. After regaining her strength she was released from hospital and moved into her parents' spare room together with her husband. Having her daughter at home made life easier for Kimberley, but her anxiety for her daughter remained high. "Maybe I should pray," she confessed to a girlfriend, "but if there is a God, I don't see why He should listen to me since I'm barely on speaking terms with Him. Would He believe that I believe in Him even though I only talk to Him when I'm in serious trouble?" Her girlfriend answered: "Believing in God isn't the issue here, though I guess it doesn't hurt to pray. What's important is believing that your child will survive."

Leslie has now been in remission for three years. Every new day free from illness increases her chances for a cure. She and her husband returned to their own apartment six months after her release from the hospital. She is feeling well and has recently begun graduate studies in business administration. According to a sophisticated blood-testing procedure, she has no trace of leukemia. Life has returned to normal for Kimberley as well. She is working full-time at her law practice. Her marriage to Charles is still intact, and she continues to believe, with all her heart, that her oldest daughter will survive.

THE REASONING

Kimberley and Charles are both good parents, although for different reasons. Kimberley did what she does best: taking charge, studying, and throwing herself completely into the task at hand. Charles provided a framework of stability for both daughters by maintaining a semblance of normality. The combination of their responses to the problem also brought out the best in the medical staff. Consequently, the range and breadth of their separate parenting skills in meeting the needs of both their daughters ultimately resulted in the restoration of Leslie's health and in maintaining their good relationship with their younger daughter. In the process of aiding their offspring, Kimberley and Charles not only retained their own autonomy, but gained important insights into their marriage and their behavior under stress.

Kimberley, countering her fear of losing a daughter to leukemia, swiftly focused her formidable emotional and intellectual resources on saving Leslie's life. Whereas many parents in the throes of such a serious medical crisis tend to regard their doctors as gods, whose decisions should be accepted without question, Kimberley – an agnostic who was not in the habit of putting her faith in a higher being, supernatural or human – viewed herself as a major player in the game that would determine whether Leslie lived or died. And indeed, by the time she had completed her exhaustive research on the treatment of leukemia, Kimberley, who never forgot anything she read, had at her disposal a vast quantity and depth of knowledge within a narrow spectrum of medicine that allowed her to communicate with the doctors on an equal basis.

Kimberley felt that Charles was not a player in the game. She saw him as not totally giving of himself under the duress of a life-threatening disease. The totality of her commitment, in contrast to Charles' partial giving of himself, became impossible to ignore. She perceived him as having abandoned their daughter. Her own mother had spent little time with her when, as a youngster, she had been hospitalized. As a child she had felt abandoned by her mother, and now that feeling resurfaced and threatened to overwhelm her. The many solitary hours at Leslie's bedside merely served to increase her anger toward her husband.

It was only in retrospect, once the tide of her fear had ebbed, that Kimberley was able to scrutinize her own reactions and Charles' to their daughter's suffering. Kimberley, always analytical, understood that her husband was not in fact abandoning Leslie. Her husband had behaved, she finally realized, like his mother – and not like her own mother had behaved years ago. Kimberley, by contrast, had instinctively done precisely the opposite of what her mother had done. Fortunately for their offspring, both parental reactions were necessary in order to support Leslie in the hospital and her sibling at home.

"Acting out" is the psychological term for the behavior of an individual who unconsciously behaves in a way that is appropriate to a situation in the past but not necessarily appropriate to the present situation. Kimberley, in this case, was re-experiencing her feelings regarding her mother from the time she had been hospitalized with scarlet fever. When she finally realized that Charles was not, in fact, abandoning Leslie, she managed to relate to her husband in a more mature manner. Kimberley, determined to see that history did not repeat itself, made herself completely available to Leslie during her hospital stay. This total commitment was a spontaneous and unplanned reaction to her daughter's need. Only later, when Kimberley compared her reaction to her husband's, did she become aware of the roles her mother and mother-in-law had played in the family drama. She then came to understand why she had aided her daughter in one way and why Charles had done so in another. This understanding paved the way for tolerance and the desire for dialogue.

Kimberley and Charles analyzed the different approaches they had taken in support of their daughter's fight for life. Determined to re-stabilize their marriage in the aftermath of the crisis, they slowly worked through their misunderstandings and unintentional hurts. "It wasn't hard to forgive my husband for not being with Leslie in the hospital as much I had been," Kimberley admitted. "He was, after all, holding the fort at home. In terms of my own past, though, forgiving my mother is another story. She did come to see Leslie every once in a while, but her visits were invariably accompanied by critical comments. Still, it's comforting to know," Kimberley dead-panned, "that in this ever-changing world, some things stay the same."

IT TAKES AN AWESOME PARENT

The parent is not expected to have a god-like capability to resolve life-and-death issues. Kimberley possessed high intelligence, reasonable wisdom, and humility toward the unknown. Ever the skeptic, she respected the knowledge of doctors, but was well aware that a level of even more sophisticated thinking exists. Since that level of thinking and understanding was necessary to save her daughter's life, she tackled the problem head-on, confident in her ability to learn anything at the highest level.

Kimberley saved her daughter's life on a risky gambit based upon her close reading of the medical literature and her courage to make a difficult decision. Most parents under such circumstances would be seen as doctor wannabees by the medical staff and would be strenuously resisted. When discussing her daughter's condition with the doctors Kimberley was careful not to come across as being defiant of authority (even though she had a healthy disrespect for any authority not based on pure knowledge).

Kimberley, with her high level of self-awareness, knew that she needed the patience of God to maneuver among the doctors, and eventually to work out her relationship with Charles. She sought a higher force in the form of knowledge and expert medical advice to help save her child. She appealed to the better qualities of human beings by striving to maintain a balance between the different opinions on treatment until she reached her own conclusions. She persevered in wearing down various medical arguments until the optimal one, from her perspective, was reached.

Parents should make a conscious effort to take care of themselves while helping their children in distress. Kimberley was not only generally intelligent and extremely persevering, but was also attentive to details. She had worked through her issues of closeness and distance from her critical mother sufficiently to accept her without acrimony and with a wry sense of bitter humor. Observing her mother's behavior as Leslie's grandmother, standing by Leslie's bedside and emitting critical remarks in a seemingly unconscious way, Kimberley was reminded of her past relationship with her mother as a child in hospital. Kimberley was healthy enough to realize that she was overcompensating for her mother's neglect by doing everything possible to take care of Leslie.

Ironically she had developed a laser-like mind as a defense against her mother's constant criticism. This allowed her to focus on minor matters as well as on the big picture. The squabbles and irritation with her husband about Leslie were certainly minor issues in comparison with the life-and-death situation they were all facing. Gradually she became aware that Charles' psychological make-up was different from hers. She was thankful for that. *Survival of the marriage depends upon accepting differences and not losing sight of them in a crisis.*

An in-depth understanding of Leslie's condition and the intricacies of the possible courses of action were critical to her survival. But no less critical was Kimberley's gaining an understanding of the effects of her own mother's parenting on herself. She and Charles had different parenting modes; they had different mothers. The survival of their marriage depended upon this understanding. While the overall goal toward which everybody was striving was Leslie's physical survival, it was imperative for Kimberley and Charles' marriage to survive as well.

Kimberley strengthened her marriage by working through her anger toward her husband, as she gradually reached the realization that her model of over-reacting was based upon the pain that she had suffered from her mother. Still, if her behavior was explained psychologically by her relationship with her mother,

Charles was justified in having his own modes of behavior based perhaps upon his own relationship with his mother. Kimberley did not overlook their differences, coming to the realization that it is details like this that can save a marriage. Forgiveness was possible.

"It came, " Charles had said, "like lightning on a clear summer day – with no warning. Suddenly the storm broke over our heads." Kimberley mused over Charles' statement. "He speaks for both of us and assumes that his description is accurate." Kimberley, with wry bemusement, was reluctant to totally give up reminding him that she had a mind of her own. Continuing to mull over the matter, Kimberley added: "In fact, in some ways he is right. It was a shock of sorts, probably even more so for Charles who has always been easy-going and who expected the proper authorities, the doctors, to work things out and produce a good outcome. He has such an easy acceptance of authority, while I have been challenging authority all my life and was totally prepared emotionally to take the trip to the mountain by myself to ask God to save my child."

Kimberley didn't know whether she believed in God enough to ask Him anything, but she certainly believed in making the trip of Life to the top of the mountain to seek whatever truth was necessary. She had unwavering faith in her daughter's ultimate recovery and was prepared to wait patiently until the end of her days for the ultimate answer as to whether there really was a God on the mountaintop. In the meantime, she was glad to have a steady fellow like Charles along for the trip because he made life less lonely. Moreover, if she were to meet God at the end of her days, she wouldn't want to give Him or Her a hard time – as she so often does with authority figures. Charles is so accepting of authority that he would surely put in a good word for her. Besides, she would feel better if he held her hand at the last moment – like he had done in the hospital room.

Chapter Eight

WHEN YOUR CHILD GETS DIVORCED

INTRODUCTION

Losing or almost losing a child is a rare circumstance that requires the activation of the deepest human qualities: faith and lack of faith, the decrease or increase of cognitive capacity according the person's intelligence and circumstances, the acceptance of God's will and the refusal to submit to authority. The spiritual problems of a Jesse or the cognitive problems of a Kimberley undeniably drain a parent's inner resources. The pragmatic problems of managing the divorce of adult children can be just as enervating for the parents; it is an occurrence that is anything but rare.

The interminable complexity can be equivalent to profound spiritual and cognitive issues. Parents must take practical steps to perform necessary financial or vocational actions that may make them feel that they are dealing with ultimate issues of survival. The common goal in a divorce is not always its solution but the distribution of the inevitable psychic pain as equitably as possible throughout the family, including the allocation of resources for the education of grandchildren. In turn, while adult children may be entitled to support in a time of crisis, they must in turn be sensitive to the emotional and financial resources of the parents. Being supportive is also profoundly spiritual and human.

Adult children must be sensitive to be well-rounded human beings; they also must have thick skins in order to make their way in a world that is often cruel, brutish and unfair, especially in divorce situations. Parents have to realize that giving their adult child "good advice" seldom succeeds in changing that reality. By contrast, supporting an adult child through a divorce can often be a growth experience for the parent and child alike. A parent has to constantly provide a positive emotional role model. This can enable the child to return to an encouraging mode of thinking about the situation. The all-too-common divorce situation lends itself not to spiritual or intellectual answers but to pragmatic cookbook solutions.

The following "how to" chapter is presented step-by-step to simulate a divorce process. In the complex story of a beaten woman, the simplicity of diagnosis yields enlightenment to the victim. The phenomenon of beating must not only be forbidden, it must also be understood. Some of the beaten women of my professional acquaintance also have an idiosyncratic undiagnosed learning disability that serves as a trigger for violence by men who see themselves as "just trying to control her." The parents may be unprepared for parenting again in the unfamiliar modern world with its strange rules, new values and unfamiliar diagnostic terms. The parents may be able to benefit from an up-to-date Spock-like manual on how to raise a grown-up child to once again further their own growth.

Synopsis

Sy, recently retired and looking forward to a bit of leisure and travel, suddenly finds himself dealing with his daughter's divorce and taking care of his grandson. Now, all the decisions fall on his shoulders: he must take responsibility for the fallout from her inappropriate education and her lack of job skills for the marketplace and also decide whether

or not to put their grandson in a private school. As his fi-
nancial resources diminish, his expenses grow. He must deal
with his daughter's hurt, anger and disappointment without
being infected himself by his daughter's feelings. Sy rises to
the occasion and becomes a neverending parent.

THE DILEMMA

Sy and Ethel are in their mid-sixties. Sy, a self-educated man, was employed for thirty-five years in a middle-management position at a large meat-packing concern in Chicago. He recently retired on full pension. Ethel, a sprightly practical nurse at a neighborhood hospital, was also due to retire. Sy was happy to leave his daily grind. He was well paid, but bored with his administrative duties. He spent much of his time tending the garden around their home, hoping to win some recognition from the local horticultural society for his efforts.

Ethel, who loved her patients and the hustle and bustle of the hospital, was ambivalent about the prospect of leaving work. The only aspect of their upcoming retirement that genuinely appealed to her was the opportunity to do the traveling that she and Sy had postponed while they were raising four children and putting them through college. The couple had researched van rentals, collected maps, and were looking forward to touring national parks. They also wanted to fly to Disney World without their grandchildren, most of whom they saw several times a week. "The best is yet to be," Sy would remind his wife, quoting from his favorite poem. Ethel reflected wryly that retired husbands weren't required to clean a big silent house, go food shopping and cook three meals a day.

Their house wasn't silent for long. One night Ethel returned from the hospital to find her daughter Michelle unpacking suitcases in her old bedroom. Her face was tear-stained, her eyes frightened. Michelle's six-year-old son Jeffrey was asleep on the bed. Sy sat at their kitchen table, which was littered with the pamphlets and road maps that had been pushed to one side, sipping a drink. Ethel knew that something serious was going on. "What's wrong with Michelle? Is she staying with us for a while?" Sy took a long pull on his drink and told her the story.

There had been a fight. Michelle's husband Paul had struck her and threatened the boy. Although Paul had been against Michelle's working while their child was in nursery school, he had suddenly realized that Jeffrey would be a first grader next September. Why, he screamed at Michelle, wasn't she out job hunting? That is, if she could even get a job with a useless degree in sociology from a second-rate community college. Michelle did not reply, and Paul's rage had grown. In a voice oddly devoid of expression Sy told Ethel that their son-in-law had been beating their daughter ever since Jeffrey's birth. At the beginning Michelle had not quite believed what was happening. After the first quarrel and attendant beating, Paul had apologized and begged forgiveness, promising never to raise a hand to her again. But there had been more arguments – with never any warning – and more physical abuse. Michelle's arms were so bruised that she wore long-sleeved blouses to conceal the marks. Paul had refused to get professional help. He kept persuading Michelle that nothing was wrong. If there was any blame it was hers, he said, and given time their family life would come right again. Michelle had hoped for the best and prayed for a change in Paul. Ashamed and humiliated, she had kept her terrible secret to herself. The threat to her son that evening finally galvanized Michelle. Fear overcame shame and, in desperation, she sought shelter under her parents' roof. "Michelle's marriage," Sy told Ethel, "is over. She's not going back to Paul." A dazed Ethel nodded in agreement. She cast a mournful look at the scattered maps on the table before pushing them aside. "I called a lawyer," Sy said. "He wants us to take Michelle to the nearest emergency room and get a medical opinion about whether or not there's a history of beatings. He'll see us in a few days time."

THE REASONING

Sy and Ethel have to shelve their travel plans for a while. Their daughter requires the services of a doctor, a lawyer and, possibly, a psychologist. They will have to arrange all of this for her. In the meantime, Michelle should be encouraged to talk about the abuse she has suffered, and her parents should listen to her story without being judgmental. It is so easy to blame the victim. Demanding to know why she didn't walk out a long time ago will not help. *People who are being abused feel so trapped that the option of leaving does not exist for them.* Many, threatened with even more beatings if they try to escape, are too frightened to leave. Some feel they have no place to go. Still others remain bound to their abusers by feelings of guilt or an inappropriate sense of duty.

Sy and Ethel also have their grandson to consider. His mother was able to extract him from a potentially dangerous setting. The emotional effort required for her to take that courageous step will probably take its toll on her, and she may not be able to do anything further for herself for several months. For Jeffrey, however, life goes on. It will be up to his grandparents now to create a semblance of normality in his life, at least until his mother is strong enough to resume her responsibilities as primary caregiver. Jeffrey should be enrolled in the first grade of the elementary school near the grandparents' residence. His grandfather will have to be available to him after school, playing checkers or cards or, if Sy is up to it, baseball. Perhaps he should try to interest Jeffrey in gardening or some other hobby. Sy and Ethel will also have to spend time fielding painful questions from their grandson about his mommy and daddy. They should do so as honestly as they can, yet without demonizing Paul. The rest of the family can and should be involved. Since Sy and Ethel see their other grandchildren regularly, Jeffrey will have frequent access to playmates closer to him in age than Sy and Ethel.

Once the legal and medical formalities have been set in motion, and as soon as they feel she is ready, Sy and Ethel should sit quietly with their daughter and gently encourage her to talk about what she wants to do with the rest of her life. Some time back, when things still seemed to be going smoothly, Michelle had told her mother that she might be interested in further studies in sociology. This is now impractical, since Michelle can no longer count on financial support from her husband for herself or her son, even after a court decision. Thought should therefore be given to a new vocational direction.

Since Ethel is employed at the local hospital she thinks it might be worthwhile to check out the retraining programs offered there. When Michelle is ready, Ethel could take her to the hospital's personnel department. The hospital is always in need of licensed practical nurses, qualified laboratory technicians, EEG and EKG technologists and radiological technicians. The courses leading to employment in these fields generally last one or two years and, upon completion, grant certificates or associate degrees. If necessary, Sy and Ethel should subsidize Michelle's vocational retraining. It is part of their responsibility to make sure she has the skills necessary to be a contender in the job market.

It is tempting for the grandparents to consider taking Michelle and Jeffrey along for the trip that they had been planning for so long. It would be a good escape – even if only a temporary one – from their troubles, Ethel reflects, a good opportunity for all concerned to "recharge their batteries." But the timing is bad for Michelle, and such an option, however tempting, should be postponed. What Michelle needs is self-definition as a professional in the work force and validation of her own worth as a woman and not merely as an extension of her husband. Because Sy and Ethel are giving parents, their travel plans should be deferred in order to come to their daughter's aid, but should not be canceled. Ethel carefully folded the travel brochures and put them away.

The first order of business is for Sy and Ethel to make their daughter and grandson feel secure. Moving Michelle back into her old bedroom may seem to be an act of juvenilization, but it is natural in the circumstances. This room was, and should continue to be, a safe haven. If Ethel is like most mothers, her daughter's room still contains the beloved artifacts (stuffed animals, dolls, high-school yearbook) of safer, happier times. These objects offer silent support. They tell a frightened woman that she is now in a place where she can regroup and heal.

Jeffrey is in need of emotional support, too. He has lost a father, although the extent of the loss will only be determined in time. His grandfather, by playing with him after school, by listening to his questions and allaying his fears, is filling the void created by Paul's exit from his life. Sy is the stable nurturing father figure in Jeffrey's life. The assistance Michelle requires most from her parents now has to do with rebuilding her self-confidence and, later, her professional life. Paying legal fees, covering food and clothing expenses, even subsidizing vocational retraining may demand serious outlays of cash from Sy and Ethel, but the most serious demand will be for patience and encouragement. It will take Michelle some months, even in therapy, to feel that she is in control again.

Once the family has settled into a stabilizing daily routine, the next item on Sy and Ethel's agenda might be, perhaps in consultation with a therapist, the goal of helping Michelle regain her autonomy and become a working mother. If Michelle had a profession, even a semi-skilled one, this would be relatively simple to accomplish. But Michelle has no qualifications, and her parents cannot afford to send her to college a second time. Nevertheless, Michelle has to have something productive to do with her days, and eventually will need an income. She cannot ask her parents to meet her financial needs indefinitely, and even if she wanted to, parents should not consent to such a plan.

Because Michelle is in the process of getting divorced and looking for a job, she should retrain both emotionally and occupationally. She will have to contend with two issues: coming to terms with the fact that her marriage is indeed over, and accepting that her choice of field of study will not lead to gainful employment. Coming to terms with the end of her marriage is the first step toward recovery. Michelle will probably have difficulty in giving up her relationship with her former spouse even though her family and friends see clearly that the marriage is over. Coming to the realization that her relationship has ended is a necessary step without which she cannot recover her energy and make a decision about her new vocational training. And vocational training is crucial: whereas she may gain great comfort and compliments from rearranging her stuffed toys or oiling her son's baseball glove, these activities are not listed in the occupation index of available jobs and nobody will pay her for doing them. Consequently, she should retrain in a more practical field.

When Michelle is ready, and if she is sufficiently motivated, she might choose to attend night school in order to complete a full BA. Sy and Ethel should not expect their average-student daughter to attend a prestigious university because such an expectation would generate the illusion that Michelle could do better if only she really tried. But Michelle has always tried as hard as she could in school. Her results were mediocre, but she cheerfully plugged on without becoming discouraged. This pattern hints at the possibility of some problems in learning requiring professional consultation, perhaps an undiagnosed learning disability.

Michelle's problems with her husband must await the decision of the courts. Even in cases where divorce and custody are not contested, the handing down of decisions and rulings can take years. If she can prove that physical abuse took place, it will be easy for Michelle to obtain a divorce. This means that her ongoing contact with Paul will be fairly minimal. However, unless her former spouse is a totally disinterested father or is considered a danger to her son, Jeffrey's contact with Paul and the question of child support are issues that will also be determined by a judge.

Through it all, Sy and Ethel must be an unfailing source of strength for their daughter. Setting this kind of example for her is the best way to help Michelle reclaim her own strength. Michelle is right in her assumption that her parents will be there for her, just as they were there for her as a young child. They are, after all, the kind of parents who will always be there. But now the parameters of the developing relationship should be formally spelled

out or put down on paper, otherwise, a failure in the newly negotiated verbal agreement may result in regression to the parent-
child model in which full responsibility resides with the parents
and none with the child. Parents and adult child must come to
that unique psychic mid-point that highlights maturity, a modu-
lating of personal desires and the family's economic reality. They
will also be there for Jeffrey. A situation in which parents support
both the adult child and the grandchild may appear inappropriate from the elderly parents' perspective: after all, why should the
burden of the younger generations fall on their shoulders just
when they thought it was time to enjoy the remainder of their
lives? Ultimately, it is a responsibility that they must take upon
themselves. It is the way of the neverending parent.

MONEY FOR PRACTICAL EDUCATION

More care should be taken in the selection of an area of study than
before, for rules have to be established when the natural order of
things has been violated. Sy and Ethel should help Michelle take
stock of her current assets and deficits. Michelle has a high school
diploma, a driver's license, a community college degree, a certifi-
cate of completion of a course in modern dance, and a diploma
from a school of home economics in diet cooking. These are all
worthwhile achievements in their own rights. Michelle's degree
in the humanities and social sciences marks her as a classically
educated person who enjoys cultural events and intellectual conversation and discussion.

Michelle is likely to resist her parents' attempts to direct her
into another field. She may insist on trying to find work in an occupation that has no future merely because the field appeals to
her. She may point out that she is no good in math or science, a
claim supported by her academic history and high school grades.
It is Sy and Ethel's job to make her understand that an academic
evaluation of natural talents is no longer the focus of discussion.
Whether she will find a particular course of education or a vocational training program fulfilling is no longer the only relevant

factor. She has no choice but to undergo a retraining course. She now must yield to the unpleasant necessity of preparing for a job that pays in order to avoid being a burden on others. The mature parent with diminishing resources must insist that she choose a practical field such as computers or technology, rather than the previous fields of her choice.

Sy and Ethel can acknowledge the power of necessity more easily than their daughter. For Sy and Ethel's generation, school and childhood were over when one had to go out to work. In previous generations one left school at an early age, found a job, married and started a family. The age of maturity may have been younger then, but the process of socialization into the world of work is the same, regardless of whether the person is fourteen, twenty-four or thirty-four.

The harsher experience of previous generations in the work-world now becomes more relevant as the necessity of studying to get a job begins to take precedence over learning as a value unto itself. Michelle should get a job to support herself and her son. If Sy, Ethel and Michelle can agree, for example, that a retraining course is the path to pursue, a division of labor should be agreed upon among them to make it happen.

Studying requires an enormous expenditure of energy from an adult with a poor scholastic record – more so for those with a learning disability. The optimum choice for Michelle would be a practical on-the-job training course combined with a minimum of theoretical study. This type of studying is often effective for adult children with learning disabilities. They benefit more from focused education than from theoretical formal education, for the former type increases their sense of self worth in an area that makes sense to them. The self confidence gained by succeeding in a practical course is a defining positive educational experience that can compensate for the many years of negative feedback of previous schooling. Michelle has to contend both with the emotional stress that accompanies fear of failure in a school-like setting and with the deep sense of lack of self worth of a person beaten and in the process of recovering from a traumatic divorce.

Why, one may ask, should Michelle study a subject that holds no intrinsic interest for her? Adult children often choose to study and work in fields viewed as positive by the parents, even if they were not initially intrigued by the field itself. Fulfilling one's parents' wishes and responding positively to one's parents' underlying value system makes an adult child like Michelle feel good. Michelle is still not completely mature and will readily agree to seek guidance from her parents. By beginning to accept her parents' suggestions for studying, she will have secured her base with her parents before striving for security within herself and for Jeffrey.

Parents should be firm and gentle in maintaining the unwritten "contract" with their children. They should accept the responsibility of paying for Michelle's retraining if she is serious about taking the course, but money should not be given casually. The parents' authority is reinforced when they assume responsibility by paying; in addition, they are providing a good role model for Michelle, demonstrating responsibility as a prelude to authority. Michelle's dignity has suffered in the past at the hands of her husband, who was a source of authority for her. If she does not succeed in finding a job, her dignity will have suffered once again at the hands of another source of authority: the job market. A sense of relief will come to Sy and Ethel when the focus moves away from the emotionally charged relationship with Michelle's husband, but Michelle's dignity will be restored only when she obtains a marketable skill.

Michelle's recently acquired inclination to take a course in vocational training would entail her parents taking out a second mortgage on their house to subsidize further education. Michelle needs to know that although Sy and Ethel are willing to help her, this would constitute a major sacrifice on their part. She is likely to go along with their request because she senses that their recommendation is for her benefit, even though she doesn't have a strong desire for vocational training. However, Michelle's parents' resources are limited. If parents become eternally self-sacrificing for the good of their adult offspring, they are practicing a form of self-immolation that can do their needy adult child no good. Mature parents should distinguish between giving of themselves as neverending parents and giving of themselves as a neverending sacrifice. This point can be illustrated by a simple parable:

> A chicken and a pig are walking together in the neighborhood when they come across their needy adult children sitting together inside a family restaurant. The sight of their children being too poor to order bacon and a couple of eggs for breakfast stirs their little hearts. The chicken says, "How tragic! We must help. Let's go in and give them what they need. I'll provide the eggs." The pig answers, "Yes, it is tragic and we must help. For you to give them what they need is indeed a generous donation, but for me to give them what they need involves total commitment and self-immolation." The chicken saw his point and adapted to the middle way by offering only one egg in the morning. The pig offered a large salad and preached the virtues of vegetarianism to his adult child.

The moral of the story is that although few really prefer one egg and a salad to crisp bacon and eggs, mature parents should be giving to their children, but not to the point of neglecting their own needs. Conversely, adult children in trouble have to adapt to the reality of what they can realistically expect from their parents.

Sy and Ethel should create a new framework for re-educating Michelle about money. Michelle may view her financial predicament as composed of a number of immediate concrete issues, such as the need to pay off a pressing debt, paying nursery school tuition or fueling her car. Although Sy and Ethel can empathize with her, they must not join her in being stressed about immediate needs. Their job as mature parents is to join her in her long-term struggle to stabilize her financial situation, for it is this that can lead her out of her emotional pit. Their urging further education or job training may shift the focus of attention away from her disastrous past relationship with her husband to her future.

Discussions about schooling can provide a mutual frame of reference for the rules to be established by Michelle and her parents. They should, together, try to create a common platform of financial responsibility leading toward the future. Whereas Michelle may want to relapse into talking about her husband's failings, Sy and Ethel should focus on the "here and now" issues that concern them, such as, "Did Jeffrey wash his hands before coming to the dining table?" *Looking back is useful only if it leads to moving forward.*

Michelle's lack of fulfilment in education and work stems from not having received an appropriate education at an earlier period of her life. She is now suffering from that failing. "Catching up" in education may prove to be a stressful mission as she finds herself attending school with younger people in unfamiliar circumstances. Everyone has to pitch in to make the situation right. *A fair distribution of the least amount of pain among all family members can lead to emotional cohesion.* Michelle may not be ecstatically happy or fulfilled with a job in data processing, for example, but she will feel a lot better when she holds her first paycheck in her hands. So will Sy and Ethel.

Sy and Ethel should express their state of conflict openly and explain to Michelle that at their age they are concerned with divesting themselves of financial and emotional burdens. This does not mean that they are unwilling to help, but that it is financially difficult for them. *Shedding burdens is an age-appropriate goal in the lives of the elderly.* However, financing an adult child's education empowers mature parents, reinforces their authority, and means that they will not have to give excuses for not having done the right thing in the past. Parents' support for education for returning adults, especially after one round of education has already taken place, should be conditional rather than absolute. Parents owe it to their children and grandchildren to support them at least to the level of education that they themselves attained. Beyond that, objective calculation should come into play. Science and technology training may not make an adult child feel good, but it usually results in jobs. Solid training in a field that will probably lead to gainful employment is likely to make the parents feel good. In short, returning adult children now have to consider seriously what they previously dismissed. Reality has arrived.

THE EDUCATIONAL RESPONSIBILITIES OF GRANDPARENTS

The grandparents' connection with grandchildren is no longer the traditional one of serving peanut-butter-and-jelly sandwiches to young visitors. Many grandparents long to be old-fashioned and emulate their own grandparents, but the modern world has propelled them into changes. The fact that most grandparents no longer live with their extended families, for example, has affected their role. The connection with grandchildren is now maintained through phone calls, e-mail and only occasional visits. Moreover, the involvement of grandparents with their grandchildren today often revolves around the disposition of money.

Michelle complains, "I don't have a job, but I still have to pay the mortgage and the child's schooling. I'm desperate. Help me." But Michelle is capable enough so the grandparents do not have to take full responsibility for Jeffrey, and this means sharing the authority in a non-demeaning manner. The relationship with Jeffrey should be handled delicately by the grandparents, with care not to undermine the authority of their already weakened daughter. It is not uncommon for a grandparent to raise grandchildren with responsibility and authority if the parents are incapable of raising and establishing a meaningful connection with their children. And some parents cannot finance the necessary education for their own children. Though Michelle's permission is not explicitly needed because of her dependent state, it is imperative to seek it in order to bolster her dignity.

Grandparents who recall the Depression may suffer from emotional sensibilities related to the financial insecurity of that period. When the adult child says, "I lost my job, but I still have to pay the mortgage and schooling," the grandparents might be hearing a regressive throwback to the more gut-wrenching question of the time of the Depression: "I lost my job, so how am I going to feed my kids?" These insecurities may be so powerful as to influence the grandparents to deal with their dependent off-spring in a negative way, exacerbating existing problems in the family. "I made my way when I was your age in harder times, and you should be able to make your way on your own."

Sy and Ethel are capable of responding realistically to the new financial expectations thrust upon them by the situation. Sy has a role model in his uncle, who became a guide or coach in good times and was prepared to be there for his family when a crisis occurred. When a parent uses money properly for constructive purposes, this practice teaches the adult offspring the wisdom of good money management. Parents who manage their money well are able to provide their offspring with a lesson that will serve them well for the rest of their lives. Sy is faced with a decision as to what extent he should emulate his uncle and what he should do differently.

Parents who observe their offspring floundering in a shaky marriage or a problematic job situation where a positive outcome is unlikely should evaluate the situation in a business-like manner. They should plan for the worst outcome, while being empathic with their offspring.

Parents often have a fantasy that with the end of their role as caregivers, parenthood will have ended and the children will be on their own and will never return. Only through an awareness that parenthood is a long-term commitment and that they are in for the long haul can reality replace this fantasy. Essentially, parents should be ready for the next shock to their ordered lives by evaluating the possible outcomes for their children.

Failure to rehearse one's emotional reactions is as inadvisable as failure to prepare for war or for an important business deal.

Constant examination of one's own strengths and weaknesses is beneficial in interpersonal family relations. Consulting with others can enable changes to take place; one can tone down the negative traits of instant anger or excessive generosity or stinginess. By consulting, mature parents can prepare to deal with the emotional outbursts and the financial onslaught of the returning child.

Being "downwardly mobile" is not the reverse of being upwardly mobile. Both processes should be approached with moderation, especially since the down trip is painful. On the way up, an adult often begins with a suit for the interview and then buys even better clothes. Later, "big toys" reflect a new social standing. But when downsizing occurs, it makes little economic sense to shed these possessions because they're now worth little.

Thinking ahead in these areas can make any potential decline more palatable. For example, the classic approach to clothes consisted of buying good-quality clothes rather than following the latest fashion. An example is the eighty-nine-year-old woman who used to receive compliments on her "new dress," although she hadn't purchased one in fifteen years, simply by recycling her clothes sensibly. When times become difficult, people do not buy new cars to show off, but maintain the old one. Poor people have always known this; the middle-class adult child, in contrast, may know it in theory, but has never had to put it into practice. A crisis provides this opportunity. Middle-class adult children assume they will never become poor. They were born with TVs, pianos and all the other fixtures of middle-classhood. Unlike their parents and grandparents, who probably had to suffer the indignity of deprivation, the "promise of plenty" appears as if in their birth contract. When that promise is violated – when poverty strikes in the form of divorce or downsizing at the workplace, for example – someone must pay for that. Often, that someone is the parent.

Grandparents often have difficulty acknowledging the high costs of putting a child or a grandchild through school today. When grandparents agree to help with educational expenses for their adult offspring and grandchildren, they are, in effect, acting as an updated version of the post-war American "G.I. bill." Even if the grandparents themselves acquired formal education with the help of the G.I. bill, tuition fees were markedly lower than today. That generation was seen as the educational elite since most adults did not go to college. Today, one needs a degree to succeed. The financial difficulties these grandparents encountered in getting a college degree are miniscule in comparison to current educational costs. Although Michelle's educational goals are modest, Sy and Ethel are liable to become impoverished themselves by Michelle's situation. After all, they have a fixed income and are now faced with budgeting for Michelle's educational, health and psychological expenses. Michelle may have chosen a life of poverty by marrying the wrong guy and neglecting her education, but she can't foist the same choices upon her parents.

Parents like Sy and Ethel are more pragmatic than Michelle, not out of choice but as a reflection of their life experiences. The Depression and World War II were crucial experiences for many parents who couldn't afford to fulfill their educational ambitions, which might have given them a lasting sense of worth. Their exposure to higher education came later during their lifetime and, naturally, they wanted their children to study. The more fortunate succeeded in acquiring an advanced degree, which created an educational gap with previous generations.

By contrast, parents who for financial reasons did not have the opportunity to study often praise the value of work and experience, because they learned in the real world, a world defined as being other than in school. They did not live in an abstract world of theorizing and studying for its own sake. They did not have the endless choices of which courses to take, which professions to enter or where to locate. They came from a world of limited jobs and choices laid down for them by their families. Their experience was practical and their choices self-evident. Their chores or jobs were taken seriously and taught them how to compete. Whoever could shovel more coal was the strongest. Whoever could climb trees the fastest was the most skillful. Whoever could ride the bike up a hill to deliver wet wash had the best legs. Whoever could work longer hours selling newspapers had more stamina. These chores and work experiences built character and life-long work habits for survival in a hard world. Character development features in many adventure sagas, such as J.R.R. Tolkien's *Lord of the Rings* Trilogy or Robert Pirsig's *Zen and the Art of Motorcycle Maintenance*.

In my opinion, acquiring financially rewarding skills for adult children who have not succeeded in establishing themselves financially should supercede higher education in relatively abstract fields such as sociology or art history. Michelle's weakness in translating her knowledge into money-making skills emphasizes the necessity for acquiring precisely those kinds of skills offered by practical experience.

Sy realizes that Michelle is contemplating a relatively low-level but practical course of study, and suddenly the insight that she is limited in her abilities comes to him. The awareness that this program suits Michelle is heart-wrenching because Sy now has to give up the fantasies about his daughter's abilities which sustained him through his own years of hard work. *The fantasy that "my children will lead easier lives than I did" seems to be universal, a way of projecting one's own unfulfilled desires onto one's offspring.* Sensitive children pick up on their parents' fantasies and often try to fulfill them because they feel their parents' pain and want to "make everything all right" for them. If the parents are fulfilled in their line of work, the children often follow in the same line of work.

The children may thus fulfill their own dreams, as well as the dreams of their parents, through their choices. However, Sy is beginning to learn that the nature of dreams is more conflict than harmony. Michelle does not want to go into a helping profession like her mother or into a standard business job like her father. Maybe it wasn't her dream to do so. Maybe she thought that she would just get married and live happily ever after. Maybe Sy and Ethel should evaluate their aspirations by looking at other people with high-end, middle-level and low-level parental aspirations for their children. At the high end of the educational goal spectrum is a family of physicists and engineers who did not consider their children educated until they had a doctorate from the Massachusetts Institute of Technology. The family members would only accept their children going into medicine, psychiatry or psychology when they were reassured that these fields had a sound scientific and research foundation and would provide a good living.

At the middle level of parental aspiration is that broad category of parents who particularly value a degree from a name university, symbolizing the mythology of fame, such as Harvard in Boston or Columbia in New York. This phenomenon of child-like mythical thinking by parents may be more obvious in name universities, but extends to numerous lower-level state universities. The child-like mind of the parent may believe in the omniscience of academic knowledge; it presents university education as a "perfect infant," dried and powdered in the cloak of excellence. One high-achieving mother placed the catalogue of her alma mater, Wellesley, in the family bathroom when her daughter was two years of age, presumably as an expression of her aspirations for both her present and future level of performance and learning!

Let mature parents put aside this modest mockery of educational goals. Most parental aspirations for their children are less in areas of status and more in the realms of learning that lead to spiritual and economic independence. Parents are interested in universities that teach practical subjects so that their children can afford their own bread and butter. According to the author, this level of practical education must be reached by adult children somewhere in their thirties and forties if they have not achieved their higher aspirations in their twenties.

Knowledge of the Bible and Shakespeare used to determine the pecking order of human society at one time. This is no longer the case. Degrees in the social sciences and humanities often do not allow adult children to eat, or even graze, in jobs and family relationships, while one course in data processing or computer programming guarantees a full dinner.

THE PITFALLS OF DISPENSING GOOD ADVICE

If parents keep trying, they will likely become the kind of parents their children need. They should not concern themselves with "what if" questions, such as: "If I had been a better parent the first time around, would my adult child be in such trouble now?" A child always in crisis seems to be willing to be re-parented at any age under most circumstances. Indeed, this is the ultimate opportunity to parent in a mature manner. The reunion between parent and adult child in trouble can expedite a healthy respect for the individuality of each, instead of an infantile merging. The purpose of the encounter is to assist the adult child in growing and developing independence and to enable the parent to become a wise giver and supporter, thus enhancing the parent's self respect. When one develops respect for one's self, respect for the adult child generally follows.

Hierarchical relationships carry the inherent possibility of a punitive relationship. To avoid a punitive response to an adult child's outburst, mature parents should put aside their tendency to rebuke or criticize and focus on caring. Argument and civilized discourse should come in place of direct orders, which generally only lead to sullen silences. Sy should be careful not to be arrogant toward his daughter or endlessly confrontational, lest Michelle respond with passive-aggressive behavior, withdrawal from the situation or sullen rebellion. When one person asks another for help, *the hierarchical issues between the helper and the helped should be dealt with gingerly and sensitively to prevent them from interfering with the healing process of the adult child.* Unfortunately, it is often the tendency of parents of adult children to initiate the relationship of helping by giving the child "good advice."

Sy and Ethel were spared the embarrassment of giving Michelle the "good advice" to leave her husband – advice she would not have been able to heed anyway until matters had reached a head – because they didn't know that he had been beating her for the last six years. Michelle finally left her husband not because she was threatened, but because Jeffrey was threatened.

Naturally, a host of questions arise. "Why didn't she leave him before this?" "Why did she put up with so much punishment and diminishment of her self?" "Why didn't she listen to the advice of her friends, who had told her Paul was no good for her?" When one ponders this question one realizes that Sy had put up with a grueling middle-management job until he was able to get out with a pension, and that Ethel had spent her entire professional life putting up with the decrees of doctors whose discourse with her was limited to giving orders. Could they have unwittingly served as role models of people who are supposed to absorb punishment? Whatever the reason, it is to Michelle's credit that she finally took a stand against passing on to her son any patterns of self-diminishment she may have inherited from her parents.

Sy and Ethel, however, have thicker skins than Michelle, perhaps because in their generation one was expected to suffer and they were prepared to absorb pain. If Sy and Ethel argue that their darling daughter is too sensitive for the harsh realities of this world, they will be giving Michelle a license to withdraw from a painful situation instead of toughening her up in preparation for the struggles ahead. While it is true that *adults need to be sensitive in order to be well-rounded human beings, they also need to have thick skins in order to make their way in a world that is often cruel, brutish and unfair.* A failed marriage, being passed over for promotion, sexual harassment and disrespect are all terrible occurrences, but, unfortunately, they are common events in daily life. Most adults will have to deal with at least one of them in the course of a lifetime. Sy remembers his uncle's boy-scout motto, "Be prepared," as he contemplates Michelle's and his next steps.

As mentioned above, the natural tendency of the concerned parent when called upon to help is to dispense "good advice." The mature parent should resist this pitfall. On the one hand, *someone in trouble may be willing to clutch at straws and listen to any advice, no matter how preposterous or far-fetched.* On the other hand, *someone who does not feel in crisis may be unwilling to listen to any advice, however sensible.* In my opinion, even if you do not feel the need, you should have the patience to listen to counsel, and even if you are in crisis, you should nevertheless be discerning in the advice you heed.

When in crisis, one recommendation is to tackle each problem separately so as to avoid being overwhelmed. However, failures in critical areas of functioning seldom involve one isolated portion of a person's life. *Serious problems come in clusters and unusual sequences.* To illustrate: failure to communicate in a relationship can lead to separation, which in turns puts financial pressure on an already stretched income. One of the partners in the relationship feels unloved and eats too much, thereby eliciting criticism from others and from one's self. Overeating leads to illnesses. People are willing to alter their bodies by elective or emergency surgery. On the one hand they are willing to do just about anything medically, but on the other hand they will not invest in communication by developing a relationship and talking about the issues.

One rule of thumb that Sy should use to determine whether his actions and advice in helping Michelle are appropriate is to ask himself the following question: "If I were her friend, would this be the right thing to do?" *Healthy parent-child relationships are characterized by bonds of friendship.* Hence, if the answer is in the affirmative, Sy is probably doing the right thing. Of course, if he knows his daughter's friends well, he can try out his "good advice" on them. If the friends respond positively, this is a sign that he is moving in the right direction. On the other hand, if the friends relate to Sy's advice as being good, but not relevant, Sy should think twice before passing on his advice to Michelle. Perhaps we should bear in mind the words of Oscar Wilde: "The only thing to do with good advice is pass it on. It is never any use to oneself."

DEALING WITH THE EVIL OF DIVORCE

Michelle presents herself as the good party in the conflict, who has finally and painfully become enlightened. Michelle's problems with her husband initially present as an unpleasant drama of a moral character. Clarity and obscurity vie with one another for the attention of the listener. Finding the truth in a morality play is notoriously difficult. Each detail of Michelle's story should be examined for verification from at least two independent sources to determine whether her perspective can be confirmed by evidence. Michelle's position, when she discusses matters with her parents, is black-and-white: she is good and in the right and her spouse is evil. Her tale of woe stretches the fabric of reality until it twists the woof of good and the warp of evil. She claims that she was previously in the dark about the personality of her spouse, but now the situation is crystal clear. He is just plain evil. Sy's job is to search for the truth in order to prevent his sweet young daughter from ending up as another bitter middle-aged divorcee. Michelle's familiar sweetness transforms itself into bitterness before the parents' eyes.

In a serious dispute between husband and wife, both their positions possess some degree of validity and neither can be dismissed out of hand. Sy looks around at his peer group, pondering over those who have separated, and notes that divorce is less likely to take place when both parties can admit their failings and seek forgiveness. Michelle's husband has a surfeit of failings, the most outstanding of which – and one not to be minimized – is his inclination to strike his wife. Because Michelle is no longer prepared to tolerate the disrespect of men, she has become truly free-thinking The only thing of which Sy is certain is that the relationship that began so sweetly has come to a bitter end.

Sy has little experience of divorce, but he has seen harsh separations take place in his place of work, and he has witnessed how much pain is involved in the experience of being fired, downsized or sent on early retirement, pain that is to a certain degree comparable to what Michelle is undergoing. Would he assume that an employee has been fired for no objective reason but due to the evil nature of the employer? Probably not. Sy is able to use the experience of his work-life to gain perspective on Michelle's problems, but he would do well to keep to himself for the time being the thought that perhaps a fair share of the blame lies with Michelle.

The emotional pain that accompanies separation from a loved one should be dealt with reasonably by bringing it to the surface through a process of re-experience and re-examination. This process should constitute one step on the way to emotional and spiritual maturity – that is, unless a disproportionate emotion of anger crowds out all attempts to soothe and salve the hurt or insult. Michelle's *immediate task is to regain a sense of self-respect and dignity from work, rather than from a relationship with a man.* If she can make appropriate decisions about money, she is less likely to collapse emotionally within or outside any serious relationship.

Why should a mature parent like Sy demonstrate forbearance when his daughter returns home with a problem that is obscured by the child's own anger? To compound the problem, Sy's anger is liable to be ignited when he is forced to deal with his daughter's crisis and its ramifications in his own life. Parents like Sy should use their formal education, their work experiences and their stable social relationships to serve as a role model for their adult children. Sy should adopt a policy of avoiding responding to an insult with anger. This process may take months to perfect. Sy should carefully consider the context of his conflict with Michelle. He might consult two other objective or emotionally uninvolved people before coming to an independent conclusion of his own.

If Sy's own judgment is not clouded by anger, his chances of helping to resolve any problem of Michelle's are greater. Analysis and consultation are skills that few are born with; they are acquired through learning and/or necessity. Like all skills, the more one uses them, the more proficient one becomes in using them. When Michelle sees Sy acting with restraint, she will have a role model for resolving her own conflicts without anger and will have learned that Sy thinks problems through without letting himself become totally submerged by his anger. She will have learned that Sy tries to solve problems himself. Michelle will have learned that it's acceptable to consult with people outside the immediate conflict. Michelle will have learned that her father tries to deal with pragmatic problems rationally and with a clear head despite the fact that he is angry. She will have become re-introduced to supportive, lasting parental love, which can kindle hope and thus help to lift her out of her depressed state. Michelle will hopefully learn that her dependency on her father is temporary. She will have learned that Sy is a different kind of man than her husband. Michelle will have developed a healthy dependency on a stable man – and perhaps eventually she will be able to do the same with another man. She will have learned that behaving like a human firecracker is not the mature way to behave. Sy will feel good about himself for making this effort. Sy would not do this for himself, but he will put himself through such a difficult emotional exercise for the sake of his daughter. *Parents do things for their children that they would never do for themselves.*

Anger shadows the mind and prevents clarity of thought. This may be true both for Sy and for Michelle's husband, but the most serious negative consequences fall mostly on Michelle, who, like most battered women, believes herself to be partially responsible for getting beaten and is likely to continue to punish herself in many ways long after the beatings have stopped. If Sy, in contrast to Paul, refrains from exploding in anger at her inappropriate behavior, he will maintain his wisdom and his ability to guide his hurting child. By demonstrating control of anger he will be facilitating change in Michelle's thinking and behavior, thus encouraging Michelle to begin to gain control over her anger and to realize that she is not solely responsible for provoking her husband's anger. Being in control of her own anger helps bring Michelle closer to her father. Sy should refrain from reproaching Michelle, lest she feel insulted, ashamed or defensive, and therefore unreceptive to her parents' suggestions. Her mind must slowly become unshaded from her depressed feelings, and, by being able to listen to her parents' words, her thoughts should gradually become clear.

Sy should focus his energy on the question of whether Jeffrey will get a better education at a public or private institution and should refrain from expressing anger at the fact that he will have to pick up the tab for Jeffrey's education. Sy's irritation at the added expense would only fuel the flames of Michelle's anger and deepen her despair and depression. Having to spend unanticipated money for someone else's problem naturally may fuel discord – which school to attend, which parent should leave the house, which re-training or education program is most likely to cover the shortfall of money stemming from the separation. Getting to the bottom line too quickly is likely to increase the frustration and anger of all concerned and prevent that clarity of thought so necessary in a crisis.

Michelle should begin to deal with the issue of whether her husband is truly repentant for abusing her. Repentance means as-suming responsibility for past misdeeds and being prepared to go through all the necessary steps to guarantee that the offensive acts come to an end. It is not enough for the offense to cease, because it may occur again after a semi-serious promise never to do it again. Most abusive husbands go through a sequence of beating, begging forgiveness and promising never to do it again, sending flowers and candy and professing their true love. Michelle has to decide whether to believe him or not this time, for failure to believe him inevitably entails divorce. If Michelle has been hurt physically or psychologically, it is not enough for Michelle alone to forgive him. Her parents should insist that amends be made to Michelle and Jeffrey, as well as to themselves, for the grief all have suffered.

Repentance begins with a personal discussion with the of-fended party, Michelle, but the truly repentant person should "go public" with his repentance and make amends to family, friends and son, so that all can see that justice will be done. Even if his apologies are at first rejected, the repentant offending husband should continue to offer them repeatedly until they are accepted. The husband should make every effort to gain acceptance, even if he has to enlist other people to reinforce his request for absolution.

The longer one has sinned, the longer the process of seeking repentance.

If the offended person, Michelle, refuses to be compensated in any way when the repentant husband has done everything possible, then the husband can take the final step and forgive himself. Repentance should be sincere and serious and seen so that both Michelle and her husband can move on to the next episode of their life. Sy will know that he has been effective when Michelle stops blaming her husband and recognizes her own role in the nearly permanent chronic crisis of her marriage. At this point, the burden to move forward shifts to Michelle. She should forgive herself for having been in a relationship with an abusive husband.

Michelle is in the process of becoming a single mother, and *single mothers tend to over-compensate because of guilt over not providing a father.* The single mother cannot pursue a policy of trying to be both mother and father to her children. Because one salary cannot cover what two salaries do, the custodial parent must learn to say "no" without projecting personal disappointments onto the child's feelings. The up-front "no" may inflict short-term disappointment on Jeffrey, but it is a courageous step that the parent must take with any-age child because it is less harmful than the chronic pain ensuing from disappointing a child. When money runs out and promises are not kept, the child – no matter what his age – learns not to trust adults. An undermining of Jeffrey's trust in his parent's word and in all authority figures who could help might weaken his subsequent ability to cope with life. *Saying "no" grounds the child in reality.*

Younger custodial parents living on a limited income may not be able to take their children out for good times on weekdays, buy them expensive gifts or take them on vacations. They can waste their limited psychic energy on jealousy as they watch their children and former spouses go out for a good time while Cinderella stays home to do the dishes, make the sandwiches, do the laundry and sweep the floor. Further damage to the single parents' image of themselves can occur if they must turn to their own parents to help them keep promises made to their offspring. These unnecessary promises not only increase dependence on aging parents, but also undermine the child's confidence when he or she realizes that his or her parents cannot keep their word. Like any individual in any bureaucracy, young children may learn to bypass their own parents and go directly to the grandparents. Promises toward a child are not meant to be broken, so that keeping one's mouth shut or saying "no" under conditions of uncertainty is a good strategy.

Sy and Ethel should view Michelle's failure as hers alone and not wallow in guilt at alleged deficiencies in their parenting skills. They should focus on the gift of love they have given her. The parental impulse to sacrifice one's self out of love for the adult child should be curbed by time and circumstances. The initial love that one feels towards a child as he grows older does not wax or wane with time, and that element of stable love and attachment is virtually permanent and neverending. However, parents should trust their instincts and resist regressing to the satisfaction of being eternally giving to their children, as when they were growing up – getting up in the middle of the night to nurse a sick baby, and the like. It is impossible for parents to love the same child the same way for twenty years running, because after twenty years, it is no longer the same child. Michelle at thirty-four years of age is not Michelle at fourteen. *Although the parent's love has not changed, the child has.* Simply reaffirming that love and acting as if the child were still a fourteen-year-old may reaffirm that warm feeling in Sy, but will not be helpful to Michelle, the adult child in crisis.

WOMEN WITH UNDIAGNOSED LEARNING DISABILITIES

The beating of a woman is such a dramatic event that it can obscure details that otherwise might have come to the surface. Some women in shelters for battered women have learning disabilities that affect communication, including with their husbands or boyfriends. *Many women, and indeed men, would rather be considered disturbed than dumb.* They prefer behaving outrageously to get attention, and only after questioning may they reluctantly admit their inability to focus in reading.

Consistent failures in an adult's private life and work experience, coupled with the avoidance of revealing high school and/or college grades in various subjects, a dismissive attitude of being insulted by the questions, and the blaming of teachers and schools for learning failures, all these may be symptoms of an undiagnosed learning disability cleverly concealed throughout a lifetime. Adult women like Michelle, with an average college history, but who never did much with their education, may show talent in specific scientific endeavors or possess good verbal facility as salespeople. They get by with their abilities but often seem unfulfilled. Disappointment plagues them and they run around in circles. Their sense of not being fulfilled in some deep way is consistent with an instability of attention disorder. Hyperactive learning-disabled adults are doers, not talkers; they get things done, but don't like to talk too much. Their laconic speech can either be a deficit or an asset, depending upon the work environment. They are reliable and pleasant but not as happy as they might be. Michelle might be one of them. This might explain what Sy sensed as Michelle's own "responsibility" in the failed marriage with Paul.

Sy's job is to facilitate the professional help that Michelle might need. My clinical estimate of the number of learning-disabled adult women in the population at large is about eight percent, making it by far the single largest undiagnosed group. Many more men are diagnosed while still at school because they present as behavior problems, but those women who sit quietly at the back of the room and don't bother anyone merely get a reputation for being a bit slow and limited. As long as they get married and have children, that's "all that can be expected of them."

This diagnostic group is most often overlooked by psychologists in modern society, probably because previous theories did not emphasize a search for a learning disability. Many psychologists treat the presenting symptoms of this disorder well, but until the complete configuration of being unable to attend is recognized, any progress made is unstable and sporadic. Many women with attention instability disorder have spent years in long-term intensive psychotherapy, to no avail. This failure is not due to the type of therapy or therapist, but to the unwillingness of so many diagnosticians to look at a woman as a potentially flawed electronic circuit and their tendency to regard a learning disability, probably based on a neurological weakness rather than a serious emotional disturbance, as not within their province of specialization. No wonder these woman often go undiagnosed. They have a great deal of social intelligence, are masters of concealment and are frequently proud of having passed their test with the psychologist because he could not determine what was the matter with them. They are experts at focusing the problem on the school or their spouse or even on the therapist, but do not see their part in any conflict.

Perhaps if the best and the brightest of these learning-disabled adults became therapists, they could make better progress. After all, clients would then have someone to work with who instantly understood them. The great sin of not diagnosing them denies them their destiny of a near-normal life. In my opinion, their problems are easily resolved or mitigated by physical exercise, the occasional use of prescribed neurological medication such as Ritalin and short-term counseling. But *a woman's subterfuges to avoid involvement in the diagnosis are amazing in their subtlety.*

After a highly intelligent wife was diagnosed with Attention Deficit Hyperactivity Disorder with special difficulties in the production of verbal material, she watched her husband discuss the couple's communication problems with their psychologist. She finally said, "I'm glad that you figured out the problem and are talking about it between you, but I'm getting a little bored listening to the both of you going over what I just said. I understand the issue and you just keep repeating yourselves. I can see that both of you like talking about it and seem to get on well together. So, may I be excused? I've had enough of listening to you, but I don't mind if you want to talk some more."

When it was pointed out that they were communicating in order to help her communicate with her husband later on, she was astonished to hear that he had problems communicating with her. "Even so," she said, " if my husband needs someone to communicate with, I am happy that he now has someone to talk to. I'd like to know later on how you two got along." She changed the subject and left with a lame excuse for her next appointment, as if nothing significant had taken place. The husband volunteered, "Sometimes, I get so frustrated trying to talk with her that I feel that I'm going to lose control of myself and do something rash. It just makes me feel terrible about myself and our relationship."

Michelle was referred to a psychologist for vocational evaluation and was indeed diagnosed as having a learning disability. The purpose of a professional diagnosis is not the attainment of enlightenment, but getting a practical prescription for education. The psychologist explained to her that adults with learning disabilities often value focused education more highly than theoretical formal education because it increases their sense of self-worth in an area that made sense to them. The pragmatic education used in simple business transactions or the clearly defined jobs in the army have put many a learning disabled adult on the right track. Self-confidence attained by succeeding in a practical course can be a definitive positive educational experience that diminishes – and perhaps even erases – the pain of many years of negative feedback in school, wrestling with an academic education that "made no sense."

Michelle listened to the psychologist's diagnosis and thought, "How can he be so verbose? Why is he talking so much about this problem that I've had all my life and managed well enough? Is he disrespecting me? The hell with him and the hell with Paul! Why should I care about having a learning disability? I've got a vocational training course to complete and a child to take care of." She walks out smiling to herself and feeling that she has outwitted the psychologist. Her mood picks up. She is ready to move on.

Chapter Nine

CHOICES YOU'D RATHER NOT MAKE

INTRODUCTION

In contrast to laid-back Sy, Herb, the protagonist of the following story, is not dealing with unanticipated events such as a divorce. This pragmatic businessman does not require a trail of discovery; he knows all too well his financial and emotional problems. He is a rational man who worked through his emotional problems logically to lead a full life and overcame obstacles, but his good emotional control and high level of competency does not shelter him from stress of his own making. This natural leader is confident of his anticipated decisions about his children. He proves capable of withstanding the emotional demands of his son, who is named after his deceased brother.

He must face the predictable problem of the disposition of his money as he contemplates the end of his life. He has to find the courage to also deal with an unhealed emotional and moral wound from his youth as a prelude to helping his adult children become fiscally responsible. His emotional journey is not tortuous. Herbert must come to grips with his hidden and deep secret regarding money and trust in family relationships. He can have an emotionally corrective experience and do for his adult children what he was unable to do in the past for his brother. He must take the courageous step for his own peace of mind and for the sake of heaven.

Synopsis

As Herbert grows old, he is haunted by a guilty secret from his past. He needs to make a decision that will affect his adult children's financial future, but must first deal with his unresolved guilt over a previous decision made years ago when he betrayed the trust placed in him by his brother Robert. Herbert, like many other members of the "Scrooge Syndrome" generation, finds it difficult to relinquish control over his money and to trust his children financially. He and his wife face a difficult decision: do they dare reveal to their children the truth hitherto known only to God and themselves and risk losing their respect, or should they take their secret with them to the grave?

THE DILEMMA

Herbert and Doris head a large family and, over a working life spanning some fifty-five years, have created a successful business. Now in their mid-eighties, they have reared three children who have given them ten grandchildren. Having lived together for so long and in such harmony, they look more like brother and sister than husband and wife. Both are slight, gray-haired, and still boast ramrod-straight backs.

Herbert always possessed, according to his wife, "a good head for business," which he exploited to the full. In his twenties he acquired enough money to open a clothing store in a poor neighborhood. In due course, and with Doris working at his side after their youngest child reached school age, the small store became a large one. Eventually, it spawned five more stores, most in a working-class sector of the big city where they lived.

As Doris and Herbert's business thrived, so did their children. Anne, the eldest, earned a law degree and went on to become an assistant district attorney. Herbert was immensely proud when she passed her bar exams, although he would have preferred to see her in a corporate practice rather than criminal law. She continued to work full-time after giving birth, juggling her work schedule with her home life. One of their sons became a doctor and young Bob became an English teacher. Herbert didn't care for Bob's wife and considered her somewhat manipulative, but his son seemed more settled than in the past.

All three children seem to have stable marriages and enjoy good relationships with their own children. Doris and Herbert's grandchildren are now either in college or are college-bound in the near future. Doris and Herbert were both delighted that their sons elected not to follow them into the family business. "We worked long hours and were constantly on our feet," Doris recalls. "Waiting on the public is no pleasure, and sometimes it was downright dangerous because our stores were in such bad neighborhoods."

Herbert and Doris are considering putting their children's inheritance into a trust fund for them, not trusting their ability to deal with financial matters. "They're smart," Herbert sighs, "but they're book smart, not street smart. I would even say that when it comes to money, they're virtually idiots!" Doris nods in agreement and adds, "We won't be around forever, and if the kids don't know how to take care of the money we leave them, they're not going to have it for long." "Can you believe it," Herbert asks rhetorically, "they rarely have contact with any cash other than their salaries and what we give them periodically? They don't know the difference between stocks and bonds. My son, the English teacher, doesn't even have an accountant. When it's time to do his taxes, he puts all his receipts in a paper bag and goes to a bottom-of-the-line accounting firm! Plus, he's having difficulty paying his municipal taxes, and he and his wife recently came to us for help."

Herbert is wary of professional trustees for personal reasons. "If the trustee is honest," he notes, "everything will be fine and we'll only be out the administration fees. If he's not honest, our kids could get swindled big-time. What I think is, if you're going to get clipped, you're better off going to a barber."

Herbert recalls his own past history. He is painfully aware of the dangers of placing one's trust in a stranger – or even, for that matter, in a family member. He himself had once been in a position of financial trust and had betrayed that trust. Looking back on that period, Herbert's features cloud over. "I don't want my children to know how I made my money in the beginning. There were things I had to do, corners I had to cut. Nothing illegal, mind you. But I did things I'm not proud of. It's better the kids don't know about those things. They respect me and I'd like to keep it that way. I don't want any of them, especially my daughter the lawyer, sitting in judgment of me."

But despite all his efforts to repress the events of his past, they keep coming back to haunt him. He acknowledges reluctantly, "I betrayed the trust that my kid brother placed in me." Robert had recently married, shortly before enlisting in the Navy. His government life insurance policy ensured that if he didn't survive the war, his bride, then in the early stages of pregnancy, would not be left penniless. "Your wife is only nineteen," Herbert had argued. "Make me the beneficiary of the policy. If, God forbid, you're killed, you don't want her blowing all her benefits. I'll take care of her and the baby." Robert, who trusted his older brother and knew that his wife was inexperienced in financial matters, had had no hesitation in signing the papers that made Herbert the policy's sole beneficiary. Four months later Robert had been killed in action.

Herbert, desperate for capital to purchase his first clothing store, had decided to use all the insurance money for "the family benefit." A bitter showdown had followed between Herbert and Doris and their widowed sister-in-law, who had angrily demanded that her late husband's wishes be honored. Herbert had hedged, offering to give her the money, plus interest, as soon as he could. The sister-in-law had cursed Herbert, taken her infant daughter and left town. Three years later after he had established himself in the clothing trade, Herbert had tried to locate his sister-in-law and niece to make restitution. But they had both vanished and no contact had ever been established between the two families again. Herbert and Doris had never told their children what had happened, choosing instead to stand guard over their only family skeleton.

Herbert and Doris now face a "choice point." A choice point is a juncture at which one has to make a decision, and the decision made will have a profound effect on your life course. Choice points are usually associated with crisis and are often spurred on by dark clouds. The decision of many Jews to emigrate from Europe before the rise of Hitler, like the decision of many Chinese and Mexican families to flee the poverty of their homelands for a better future in America, have altered these families' futures. The decision maker is generally faced with an "either/or" situation, just like the one in which Herbert and Doris now find themselves.

This is a choice point for Herbert and Doris because they must either put their money in trust for their offspring or encourage their daughter and sons to learn how to administer the money for their own benefit. Even if their heirs do comprehend the downside of having their assets controlled by someone else, they may still be reluctant to take time out from their busy professional lives to manage their own assets. After all, these are adults who have never known financial need and who were not encouraged to assume responsibility for the sums of money that would one day be theirs. If Herbert and Doris opt for the former and put the money in a trust fund, their children will not have direct control over their own inheritances. If they choose the latter, Herbert and Doris will have to give their children a personal illustration of the meaning of trust. Revealing the dark secret of their past might cost them their children's respect. They do not want to be judged harshly by them for sins of the past.

The courageous and educational choice is to opt for the second alternative and risk the possibility of harsh judgment. Herbert and

Doris should reveal the whole truth. After all, it is only by doing so that their offspring can be taught that positions of trust are not always inviolate. Herbert and Doris should have one-on-one dialogues with their children in an effort to encourage them to maintain fiscal independence by learning how to manage their inheritance.

Dialogue can only occur between equals. The parents should speak calmly and honestly with each of their offspring and should be matter-of-fact about the past and not wallow in guilt. They can explain that times were hard, that they had young mouths to feed, that their opportunities were limited. They can relate to the guilt they have carried through the years and their unsuccessful attempts to make amends. But this preamble should not obscure the primary message: if a family member is capable of betraying one of his own, surely strangers are capable of doing the same. The parents' shameful secret is a warning bell that should be rung during their dialogues with their children, no matter how shocked or angry the latter may be, and no matter how painful such revelations are for Herbert and Doris.

Their children will, in all likelihood, be willing to listen to their aging parents when they raise this difficult topic because of their joint history. At every stage of their children's development Herb and Doris encouraged them toward independence – independence, of course, meaning different things at different ages – but at the same time taught their offspring to respect boundaries and know their limitations. While the children knew that being independent meant doing certain things themselves, they always assumed that their parents would be there for them. As a six-year-old girl their daughter had decided to express her independence by getting up early in the morning in order to spend time with her father. Nevertheless, she had still expected her mother to lay out her clothes for her. She would not accept responsibility for her clothes, considering her early rising enough of a sign of responsibility and independence. Her mother's services were not sought; they were taken for granted.

The classical model of independence and dependence or assumed support was similarly exhibited by young Bob as an adolescent, and later as a college student whose view of responsible sharing was, "All you have to do is to pay for my education, buy me a car and set me up in an apartment. I'll get the girlfriend myself!" He assumed that Herbert and Doris would pick up the tab for tuition fees and living expenses. Although these economic patterns were fine when they were children, it is no longer cute or amusing now that they have passed the threshold into adulthood. Herbert and Doris are getting closer to the end, and their children's assumptions about money will have to change.

Herbert and Doris are responsible for encouraging their children's autonomy. This autonomy may assume many forms: earning a college degree, acquiring a trade, learning social skills through interaction with family, friends and people in the workplace, etc. However, parents should provide not only a formal education for their offspring but also an informal education or "street smarts" as well as "book smarts."

THE REASONING

Few children at any age are blessed with being able to learn the lessons of life merely by listening to family stories or seeing a perfect personal example. Herbert and Doris should teach their children through their own negative example, in the hope that their children will not repeat their mistakes. No parent can offer children great wisdom in all areas of endeavor. No one knows everything there is to know. However, every parent has a distinct history and a unique spin on the lessons to be learned from life. *Parents have an obligation to pass on to their children the practical wisdom of their life experiences.* Herbert and Doris learned some of their most valuable lessons in life because they made errors in judgment or because they were inexperienced, naive, greedy or afraid. They should find the courage to reveal their family skeleton and expose their failure to live up to their own moral standards. In short, they should reveal their weaknesses and show their children that they are only human.

Herbert and Doris know that they will become absent role models in God's good time. If it is possible to teach their children to maintain their financial independence, it is a lesson best taught while the teachers are still alive. True, even after the death of one's parents, critical lessons of life can still be learned. But these lessons are more difficult to internalize without the availability of mentors.

Parents and adult children continuously seek a common path through the perplexities of modern life as they strive to maintain the closeness of family life. Herbert and Doris are indeed fortunate that they are still available to their grown-up children to serve as role models. This model is one of hard work, steadfastness and dedication to the job and to one's family, a model that is respected and recognized as valuable by the younger generation. Whereas in previous generations role models were continuously at hand, today – with the increased mobility and dispersion of the new generation – such role models are not automatically available. Many extended families no longer dwell under one roof, in the same neighborhood or even in the same city. Nonetheless, parents continue to communicate with their children all the time. Parents are in touch with their offspring through cellular phones and e-mail. The very presence of the emotionally available elderly parent may strengthen the entire family complex; conversely, the absence of role models generates an illusion of independence, of "being on your own," which can leave the children vulnerable to life's stresses and anxieties.

WORK AND MONEY – THE GENERATIONS

Two major events, the Depression and World War II, shaped Doris and Herbert's lives economically. Their generation had to assume responsibility early in life, sometimes by selling newspapers, apples, magazines and the like. As they grew older, they gradually assumed more responsibilities in the world of work. Life was so tough that they comforted themselves with the fantasy that life could and would be easier for their kids. The shame of the loss of human dignity and the penetrating arrow of poverty impacted strongly on their lives. Herbert and Doris swore that their children would not have to suffer these, as they had in their day. They shared their feelings about poverty with their children but they did not connect emotionally to them, since the children passed off their stories of this era as unrelated to them. The parents' focus on their own financial deprivations didn't teach the children about potential poverty of their own. They figured it was Herbert's problem, not theirs.

Different generations face different issues. Herbert's main concern in his youth was having a nickel to rub in his hand. He was afraid of becoming so tight-fisted as to squeeze the nickel so hard that he would "make the Indian on the head side ride on the back of the buffalo on the tail side." In contrast, today's youth may be obsessed with whether they can afford a "nickel" bag of cocaine. The older generation faced the consequences of unwanted pregnancy and whether they should "do the right thing" by getting married; the current generation is concerned with the fearful disease of AIDS.

Herbert and Doris, for example, assumed responsibility gradually as they developed and became stronger with the successful completion of each task. By contrast, their adult children had fewer opportunities for personal growth because of their improved economic circumstances. The entry-level jobs – those menial tasks, such as paper boy, that were available to kids of Doris and Herbert's generation as a means to supplement family income – no longer exist for today's middle-class kids. Instead, these privileged children are urged to do well in school before getting a job. They enter the job market better prepared academically but without the "calloused skin" that is gradually formed by coming up against the minor irritations of life. They haven't had to develop the ego strength necessary to deal with real problems of relationships and work. *Parental affluence often encourages grown-up children to remain adolescent and immature.* Doris and Herbert's adult children have been protected from making their own financial decisions by their ever-caring parents. However, knowing that they will not be there forever, these parents should take steps to ensure their children's future economic well-being.

THE SCROOGE SYNDROME

Herbert is reluctant to discuss his financial matters with his family – and the reasons for this reluctance go beyond his personal issues. He feels that he is the guardian of his generation's attitude toward money and that he shares its underlying code of beliefs and behavior engendered by the Depression and World War II. Will his underlying financial beliefs impede progress in resolving intergenerational issues in his family? Will he be betraying the values of his generation if he opens his wallet? Many of his peers believe that money determines everything, including family relationships.

The fear of not having money is a paralyzing feeling for many men and women. Sex and money are often interconnected. It has not escaped Herbert's attention that increasingly people seem to have more financial secrets than sexual secrets and that the former are more deeply rooted and harder to reveal. Apparently men with mistresses don't talk about their happy feelings, Herbert muses, but instead grumble about being deprived of cash in hand. Further, he has observed that many of the widows he knows complain about having to pick up major expenses of a new boyfriend instead of being grateful for the companionship. How did the belief that interpersonal relations must be subsumed to the financial necessities of life come to be so universally accepted?

Early years of financial deprivation, fueled by the unique stories absorbed by the generation of the Great Depression, have generated the "Scrooge Syndrome," an abnormal and inappropriate tightness with money that persists into the third and even the fourth generation after the events that engendered it. The penny-pinching Scrooge in *A Christmas Carol* lost his empathy for children – withholding his bounty from them on Christmas – because of his fear of going without. Like him, Herbert was afraid of ending up with nothing unless he could amass enough capital to go into the clothing business, but he was also worried that people might see him as a modern version of Ebenezer Scrooge. "Oh! But he was a tight-fisted hand at the grindstone Scrooge! A squeezing, wrenching, grasping, scraping, clutching, covetous old sinner! Hard and sharp as flint, from which no steel had ever struck out generous fire; secret, and self-contained, and solitary as an oyster." Herbert has spent his entire life struggling with his Scrooge Syndrome, working hard to feel that he will never have to do without. Paradoxically, no amount of money will enable him to feel secure.

Psychological victims of early money problems are expected to be able to take their noses out of their preoccupation with counting their cholesterol or looking at the stock market quotations on their wireless phones. They should take the time to respond appropriately to the immediate genuine needs of their troubled children. This is by no means easy to accomplish. Any time that a modern-day Scrooge is petitioned for money, the person in need may be subjected to withering criticism of his personal traits. Those who experience the Scrooge Syndrome often justify their instinct for keeping a tight grip on their money by defining the petitioner as a member of the "undeserving poor," to use George Bernard Shaw's felicitous phrase. By way of contrast, mature parents look at the merits of the case in their families impartially and calmly.

No support group exists to share the experiences of financial shame. People go to great lengths to try to escape poverty and prefer not to dwell on it except as a bad memory. No feverish imagination could invent the stories of the Depression. The harshness of these stories and their life-long defining characteristics stand in stark contrast to the normality of life today in the Western world. For this reason the children and grandchildren of those who endured the Depression regard their stories as extra-galactic and irrelevant to daily life. But such is the force of past experiences of poverty that those who suffered them may continue to feel an immediate threat in daily personal habits. Even if they are now wealthy, they always look and behave as if they are poor. Every life has been touched either directly by the actual experiences of the Depression, or indirectly by the stories of these experiences. The stories and experiences of poverty may no longer chill the body, but they may be frozen and imprinted on the soul, thus impeding problem solving.

The experience of poverty may have a long-term ripple effect on each member of that generation, as demonstrated by the following stories.

One young lad became the "man of the house" at age six when his father had a serious heart attack. When he was eight his chore was to take the streetcar into town and stand in line with strange men and women to collect his family's welfare check of six dollars a week. He became his mother's confidant and a man to his friends. He faithfully carried out the job he was given in life and continues to do so to this day. Many people describe him as being "as tight as wallpaper" with money.

Habits of poverty die hard and last longer than poverty itself. Even though the economic distinctions between children growing up in poor conditions may have been minimal, sometimes these differences assumed gigantic proportions in the eye of the beholder. For example, three boys who had to share a room would envy a boy who was lucky enough to have his own room with his own bed. Today these aged "boys" continuously discuss square footage in their business. The boys who wore hand-me-down clothes cannot forgot the humiliation of never getting any item of clothing new; at their advanced age they go shopping for suits in their spare time in order to reassure themselves of their ability to pay for any suit with ease. One child who grew up never sure whether he would have shoes to go to school routinely checks his forty pairs before selecting which pair to wear to work. Another child, having witnessed families rationing milk to their children to avoid the embarrassment of asking for credit at the local store, is always reminded of this as he savors his occasional milk shake. A boy who used to walk a long way to high school to save a nickel feels good being able to walk into a travel agency and order an airline ticket to wherever he wants. A young man unemployed for seven years of the Depression now sells financial security to others and regards it as a privilege to keep on working into his advanced years.

A woman born well after the Depression grew up listening to her father's stories of sleeping in subways and selling apples and chestnuts. Her father coerced her into taking a commercial course in high school instead of gaining an academic background; his fear of her being unemployed outweighed his concern about her being fulfilled. She later managed to do well for herself academically, but was humiliated by the fact that her father did not view her as a person in her own right. Ultimately, she became a parent dedicated to providing her children with proper schooling – in line with their individual abilities. *Poverty continues to exert its influence long after it recedes into the past.*

THE CRAFTING OF PECUNIARY COMPROMISE

Most stories about financial conflict highlight different sets of expectations and often do not end amicably. Young Bob and his wife recently came to Herbert with the request for help in paying this year's municipal taxes on their house – after he had helped them out with last year's taxes. True, the daughter-in-law did not feel comfortable begging for money from her in-laws because of the potential emotional price tag. Herbert, although a man of means, refused, knowing that once a particular expense becomes a line item in a budget, it is never deleted.

Young Bob and his wife then turned to the weaker link. Doris, whose guilt overrode her need for unity with her husband, gave in to them. Doris rationalized her acquiescence to her husband: "I know that I should have said no, but I just couldn't. Not to our son who is named after your brother. I just couldn't go through that again. I can't forget that look in Robert's wife's eyes and I don't want to see a look like that in the eyes of young Bob's wife. Never again." Thus, the young couple learned that instead of finding ways to meet their own expenses by facing the issues realistically they could manipulate the mother into giving them a handout.

Herbert said nothing because he had nothing to say. With time, Herbert's initial rage and feeling of exploitation diminished and he began to analyze the situation more rationally. Upon re-flection he acknowledged that the responsibility for raising their grown children lies with both Doris and himself, and that consid-erations other than purely financial ones might play a role. Herbert was not one to slam the door in his son's face. Fully prepared to negotiate with the young couple, he was miffed at the fact that they had opted for the easy and irresponsible way out. Had they explained their financial plight to Herbert, stating their awareness of the potential pattern they were slipping into but demonstrating their goodwill and resolution to avoid long-term financial depen-dence, they would have been taking some critical steps to devel-oping a healthy family dialogue. Negotiating with young Bob and his wife to craft a pecuniary compromise would not have left him feeling exploited and angry. Finally, Herbert came to the conclu-sion that he felt responsibility for his family, especially young Bob, but that he no longer had the authority to lay down the rules. He was aware of the fact that he, too, would eventually have given in to the young couple's financial demands – not because of its in-herent worthiness, but because of the guilt he carried to this day. He didn't know if he could explain his financial decisions to any of his children. How could they possibly relate to his overwhelm-ing burden of guilt?

Awareness can make a difference between the generations. In the past, when young Bob had asked for a small amount of money so he could show his girl a good time, Herbert had jok-ingly hedged. "Young Bob," he had said, "I had nothing when I was your age and I survived. Why should I give you more than I had? It wouldn't be good for you. Besides, you would only spend it foolishly." Bob, aware of his father's Scrooge Syndrome, had retaliated in jest, "Of course I'll spend your money foolishly. What's more, I'll enjoy every minute of it. You wouldn't want me to spend my own money foolishly, would you? I wouldn't want to be an embarrassment to you!"

Conversely, lack of awareness may be psychologically destructive. Giving funds may be as devastating as withholding funds, if there is no awareness of the underlying motives and strings.

CHOICE POINTS

At certain points in life one "gets stuck" – in a marriage that just isn't working, for instance, or not quite managing to finish one's degree. When adult children reach such a choice point, when they have to make a momentous decision yet seem unable to take that last step, one function of mature parents is to try to help their children get past it and move ahead. Parents are not destined to gaze passively from the sidelines, but should be involved in their adult children's choices. Getting through choice points breaks the cycle of despair for both the adult child and the parent. Paradoxically, the older parent's experience of limited choices – after all, with each generation, the range of choices increases exponentially – is a source of strength. These parents are in a good position to help their adult children separate crucial choices in life from non-essential ones.

Herbert had stumbled onto a choice point in his own life when he had asked his brother Robert to make him the beneficiary of his life insurance policy, but he only became aware of the true meaning of this crucial concept years later while trying to counsel a friend. Elliot's father had died in the 1950s while Elliot had been trying to finish his undergraduate courses, forcing him to drop out and become financially responsible for the family. Elliot had received an offer to work for a small company in Hartford, Connecticut, that had offered to pay well for his creative mathematical and logical abilities. Herbert urged him to take the job.

The offer sounded too good to be true, and even though Hartford was miles away, Herbert reasoned, Elliot could buy a small car and commute from his family home. True, the logistics were complicated, but the problems could be overcome, or so Herbert had thought. Unfortunately Elliot thought otherwise. He turned down the offer from that small company in Hartford in 1953, a company called IBM.

Elliot told Herbert years later that he had been the only one to recognize the realities of his family situation and to attempt to provide a practical solution by trying to help him through his choice point. Herbert's awareness of his friend's critical point in life and his own role in resolving it suddenly made him aware of his own choice point – that critical moment in life when he had become his brother's insurance policy beneficiary. *It is easier to see other people's choice points than one's own.*

Herbert, like Elliot, did not realize the potential of the job with this small Hartford company. Nevertheless, his instincts told him that a move should be made when this choice point presented itself. The only way he could articulate his feelings was to say, "It's important to be at the right place at the right time to make a difference." Often one gets stuck in a grind for a long time before being able to reach a fantasized choice point. People harbor the hope that, given enough time and patience, they will eventually succeed in reversing a negative decision they have made and reach a choice point that will change their lives. The graduate student thinks, while grinding out his thesis, "One day I will be famous for the work I'm doing now and will not have to tolerate the arrogance of my professors." The woman beaten by her husband thinks, "One day this will no longer happen and I will leave or he will realize that I'm a good person and stop it." There is the financial fantasy that, "I prefer to do this menial job instead of getting a job that requires more work. That way I can wait until my ship comes in." Or the classic fantasy response to a difficult reality: "One day I'll fire the boss and then he'll know how bad it feels."

FROM SELF-CENTEREDNESS TO "DOING THE RIGHT THING"

Even though Herbert is not too fond of his daughter-in-law, he is worried that young Bob may be too self-centered to meet his wife's needs, and he is concerned that the marriage might end up on the rocks. Marriage requires each partner to meet the other's needs. It is the responsibility of parents to point out any lack of reciprocity in the offspring's basic relationships. This point should be stressed time and time again. Parents may sometimes have to wait months or even years for the dime to drop because the principle of reciprocity is generally not understood at the beginning of a critical relationship. Parents must wait patiently as the falling apart of the relationship, the consequence of lack of reciprocity, becomes apparent to the adult child. The drop of the dime – when the light first goes on for the adult child – is the starting point for understanding the role of narcissism in the troubled relationship.

Herbert does not like the way young Bob describes his marital relationship. He was horrified when Bob once said, "True, she had money, education, connections and a good family. What did I bring to the relationship? How can you ask me that? Isn't it obvious? I brought *me*." Narcissistic adult children have no trouble telling their spouse that if they don't like the way things are, well, there's the door. They aren't unduly concerned because they have a deep-seated belief that even if their current partner/spouse leaves, there will always be someone to take up the slack – and that "someone" is likely to be the parent. The natural mode for parents is to keep on giving. The role of parents is to help their children become aware of their narcissistic behavior and its potential outcome, and to help them work on their marriages.

Herbert knows that if his son leaves his wife, sooner or later he will end up on Herbert's own doorstep. He dreads the thought of young Bob coming home for a breather – knowing full well that this "breather" may turn into an arrangement too permanent for comfort. But he should be prepared for this eventuality by preparing a teaching strategy.

Parents should realize that their child has returned in order to learn from them. The returning adult offspring may not even be conscious of this need to learn, but may want to be taken care of by the parent, financially or emotionally. Even if these children do not want to learn about themselves, their narcissistic selves must be explored with another person who will neither reflect upon nor reinforce this narcissism. Parents should not say, "You were too good for her. You were better looking than your wife anyway. If I were you, I would just rise above the whole matter and walk away, punishing her by leaving her with the children." Parents should remain calm and serve as a role model of appropriate involvement, saying, for instance, "Each one of you has contributed to the crisis. Let's look at it from an objective standpoint, as if you were not personally involved in the situation and were advising a friend... It's not a matter of how she looks; it's a matter of how she feels... You can't walk away from the situation... Too many people are involved, especially the children... Whether or not you were too good for her is irrelevant. You have to find some way out of this without wasting your energy on blaming her."

Mature parents are frequently equipped to bail their adult children out of trouble because of their age and experience with critical relationships. They've been there. Parents should give their adult children a crash course in the development of "street smarts." The parents should feel secure in their ability to handle difficult situations because of their own experience. They should teach their children all that their children need to know. Adult children are often receptive to listening to their parents' "street smarts," the ability to handle a real-life situation that has been triggered by an external crisis. Their willingness to receive on-the-job training in life is a result of the need for relevant knowledge. The churlish claim of young people to superior knowledge may well be warranted with regard to book learning and computer skills, but not in dealing with interpersonal relationships. The odds of winning in life, as in professional sports, are generally stacked in favor of the more experienced party, as in the "street smart" NBA acknowledgement of the importance of having a winning history instead of just talent. As a more experienced team plays a younger, more talented team struggling to win a championship, the basketball aficionados say, "You can't get there if you haven't been there."

Nevertheless, age and longevity do not always guarantee wisdom. Parents also have the uncomfortable task of warning the returning offspring not to repeat the mistakes of their parents. Unfortunately, the price of wisdom is learning more from mistakes than from triumphs. While on the one hand, by revealing past errors parents run the risk of damaging their emotional credibility in the eyes of their children, on the other hand they can argue that regardless of the mistakes they have made in the past, it is immoral for the next generation – and generations to come – to be trapped in a blemished family history.

Herbert wants to pass on to his children his earthly gains, not his moral lapse or his personal loss when he lost his brother in combat. A person who has experienced one crucial loss in his life may become overwhelmed with fear of further loss. This emotional paralysis may render him incapable of behavioral change. He may, indeed, suffer further loss by continuously bemoaning his fate rather than taking steps to change his current unhappy reality. He will eventually alienate his family and friends, who grow tired of listening repeatedly to the same tales of woe. They will become irritated with him for having their advice rejected. A parent should acknowledge the child's fear of loss and empathize with the distressed offspring. A parent should, at the same time, make the child understand that not being prepared to risk loss means giving up the chance of ever gaining anything. Parents should convey to their children at any age that growing and developing is dependent on being prepared to take a risk.

Parents must attach a positive value to risk-taking by using examples from their own lives. The willingness of parents to serve as models of risk-taking may help them arm their adult children with a potent weapon in the arsenal of human coping. Growth, development and independence march forward by taking risks as in any conflict. Success is contingent upon courage, which means doing the right thing at the right time because it presents itself as something that must be done. After all, nobody goes ahead deliberately taking needless risks; courage is not defined as recklessness.

Parents who were affected emotionally by the Depression or World War II were forced to take risks by financial circumstances or military necessity. Now, Herbert is again being forced to be courageous: he will have to reveal his skeletons, explaining to his children what happened and risking his own self-esteem in the process. He is unwilling to face God as a coward.

The legal tradition with which Herbert is familiar recommends releasing trust funds by age, for this, after all, was the generally accepted indicator of maturity in a society with limited options for growth and development. Today, parents should recommend the release of funds using firm indicators of maturity: achievement of a defining degree, possessing certain character traits, job satisfaction, and money earned. In Herbert's day any paying job was worthwhile and satisfying. Satisfaction came from having money to feed the family; no one gave much thought as to whether the job suited one's personal inclinations. Each generation is called upon to support a family. A generation forced to deal with pragmatics knows the score better at a choice point than a generation that had the "luxury" of freedom of choice. The parents' lives focused on necessity that offered limited educational and vocational opportunities. Later generations might often become overwhelmed or immobilized by too many options.

Herbert made his mistake because he was facing limited options. He doesn't want his children ever to be in such a situation. He feels that he represents his generation as well as himself and is determined not to be remembered as Scrooge. He is determined to be courageous and take the risk of educating them about money and teaching them the merits of giving. It may be his last chance to prove himself as a mature parent.

Herbert intends to continue to maintain control of his life until the end, when he will find himself alone on the mountain. He has always been looked up to by his family and his community. A long time ago he was looked up to by his brother Robert. The trip up the mountain of life has been long and arduous, and he has often felt himself to be a man alone without his brother. He doesn't really want to leave his family, but it would be good to see Robert again. His warm spot for his little brother has always remained with him, and he has missed him every day of his life. Surely Robert will forgive him when he explains that all he ever wanted to be to every member of his family was a neverending parent.

Chapter Ten

A SECOND CHANCE AT PARENTING

INTRODUCTION

Sy and Herbert are parents with the necessary financial and emotional resources to cope with a divorcing or potentially divorcing adult child. The next chapter deals with Thomas, an intelligent lawyer and judge whose personality flaw hinders his ability to cope with a diagnosed learning disability in his son. The denial of a learning disability in a young or even adult child is often offered with clever psychological alternative explanations; they possess face validity but little relevance to dealing with the problem. Learning-disabled adults often present as emotionally disturbed adults and pointing out their flaws is a common but ineffective path of inquiry taken by an intelligent and prudent man such as Thomas. He is representative of the intelligence of lawyers and school board members whose own personality diamond may be blemished because their specific expertise is irrelevant to psychological and educational issues.

Thomas' incapacity to properly use money at a critical point in his relationship with his son is redeemed as he gains the necessary insight into his imperfection and has a second chance at parenting. Thomas discovers the importance of his ancestors as positive and negative role models for parenting and is able to choose wisely among them. He learns to walk and talk his adult child through his troubles and reach a pragmatic solution that allows each generation to grow. The choice between "tough love" and staying close to the adult child in trouble is dealt with. New learning is necessary, since the world has changed so much that often the parents' life experience is no longer valid for this generation. It's never too late to learn for parents who want to help their children.

Synopsis

Thomas, a retired judge, has a son, Bill, who heads West to get his act together after his divorce. Thomas "forgets" to uphold his promise to make Bill's alimony payments, thereby casting his learning-disabled son in a "dead-beat" dad role, commensurate with Thomas' perception of his own father who had abandoned him as a boy.

But Bill, far from being a "dead-beat" dad, returns a year later with recharged batteries and a fresh outlook on life to assume his paternal responsibilities, gain custody of his child, and pick up where he left off. How can the damage be repaired? What can Thomas do to make amends for his transgression?

This chapter looks at the problems that arise when one's own issues are not fully worked through. Thomas' inability to accept Bill for who he is, learning disability and all, stems from his failure to resolve his own issues. Acting out these issues with one's offspring clouds the picture, making it harder to deal adequately with objective problems, such as learning disabilities. But everyone gets a second chance at parenting; it is never too late. However, in order to get that second chance, the parent should first examine himself before tackling his wayward offspring's issues.

THE DILEMMA

Thomas and Mary are in their early eighties. Thomas had been an outstanding student and had attended university and law school on scholarships. He had been raised by his mother after his father had abandoned them. He is now a retired attorney-turned-judge who earned a name for himself as a fighter for the underdog when he practiced law, and later when he sat on the bench. Politically he is a liberal. His wife is a conservative, an honors graduate who kept house for Thomas and their two children and gave dinner parties on a grand scale whenever his career might benefit from it. The couple has done well and they live in a spacious condominium in Florida.

Thomas and Mary, both high achievers, never fully understood or accepted the implications of their son's learning difficulties. Bill is a computer programmer, divorced from a mentally unstable woman, and the father of a teenage daughter. Bill's learning disability was detected and diagnosed when he enlisted in the air force immediately after receiving his high school diploma. Thomas was skeptical of all military information, including this diagnosis of his son. Bill's decision to become a technician in the air force rather than attend university, coupled with his failed marriage, are topics that emotionally baffle Thomas. When the public schools in Trenton, New Jersey, where Bill was raised and still lives, picked up on his daughter's dyslexia in fifth grade, it dawned on Thomas that it might be true that they both had a mild form of a learning disability, but certainly not from his side of the family.

Bill's wife, from a different cultural background, suffered from post-partum depression; Bill realized that something was "not quite right" with her. He encouraged his wife to go into therapy, but she rejected the idea. For his daughter's sake, Bill remained in the marriage for six years. By the time he had obtained a divorce, he was in serious physical, emotional and economic trouble himself. At almost 300 pounds he was seriously overweight. His parents were not supportive of the divorce, feeling that their son should have "persevered" in order to save the marriage, despite his wife's "little problem." They saw Bill as a man who had abandoned his wife and daughter. For Thomas, abandoned by his own father in childhood, his son had committed a mortal sin.

Bill had not, in fact, abandoned his wife and daughter. On the contrary, recognizing that he was not able to be a good father to his young daughter at that point in his life, Bill headed West to work for a year on the farm of a former air force buddy. He did this on the clear understanding that his father would take over the monthly support and alimony payments that he owed his ex-wife and pay them out of his own pocket. He also asked his parents to visit their granddaughter periodically and to make sure that his ex-wife was functioning, however minimally, as a mother. Bill returned to Trenton at the end of the year 100 lbs. lighter and ready to resume his responsibilities as a father. To his dismay he discovered that not only was he unable to make a bid for joint or full custody of his beloved daughter, but that he was wanted by the Trenton police for failure to financially maintain his family.

Thomas had "forgotten" to make any alimony or support payments on his son's behalf, and the authorities threatened to put Bill in jail on a "dead-beat" dad charge. Thomas was blithely unconcerned with this situation and was convinced that when he, known throughout New Jersey as a fine judge, got into the court-room to present Bill's case, order and justice would be restored to Bill and his daughter. In court Thomas and Bill faced an unsympathetic judge who declined to hear a motion for custody. Bill was given two choices – he could immediately hand over $4,800 to his ex-wife, or he could go to jail. Faced with these alternatives, Thomas, in a state of shock, mechanically wrote out a personal check and gave it to the county clerk. He had an overwhelming feeling of having been in this place before, powerless to control his emotional environment. He was not used to being out of control. In some strange way he even felt almost grateful to the judge for giving them a clear framework and instructions on what to do.

He comforted himself by being glad that he possessed sufficient means and power to do something for his child.

It was not the money he was worried about. What bothered him was that he was no longer in control – and he had told himself he would never allow himself to be in that situation again after that one time, so many years ago, when his father had left. But in fact, he was no longer in the control seat. The custody battle had been severely compromised by his "emotional oversight." A date for the custody hearing was set, but Bill's case had been weakened considerably. The mother's lawyer convincingly contended that the reason his client's former husband sought custody was not because the mother was unfit. The real motivation, he alleged, was to avoid future child-support payments. In view of Thomas' "oversight," the court readily accepted this argument. The case dragged on, and six months later the mother was awarded full custody. To top things off, the mother had accused Bill of sexually abusing their little girl. Bill was permitted to visit his daughter only one afternoon a week, and in the presence of a court-appointed social worker. Counter-charges were promptly leveled at the mother, and these allegations resulted in periodic visits to the mother's home by the social worker.

The tide turned in Bill's favor once the social worker was granted access to the mother's home. The findings indicated that Bill's ex-wife did, indeed, suffer from a host of emotional problems that at times rendered her dysfunctional as a mother, if not actually abusive. During these periods the daughter would tell her mother that she wished to live with her father. "But I love you," her mother would respond with hurt and surprise. "How could you want to leave me?" The daughter, always a pragmatist, would answer, "I love you too, Mom, but you can't take care of me."

Bill, meanwhile, had found a steady job and managed to create a stable home environment. Some of the credit for this went to Thomas and Mary. Overwhelmed with shock and guilt at the role they had played in their son's disastrous court case, they purchased a modest house for Bill near his daughter's school. Despite these redeeming factors, it took the court seven years to remove Bill's daughter from her mother's care and even then, it was to place her in a foster home and not with her father. Eventually, and with the ongoing supervision of the social worker, Bill was granted full custody of his by-now sixteen-year-old daughter, custody he will retain until she reaches the age of majority.

THE REASONING

Thomas could not get over his state of shock at what had happened in court. After all, he, too, was a judge, and the courtroom was like home to him. He had seen and presided over numerous custody battles and none of this was new to him. He had seen people engaged in all sorts of incomprehensible behaviors in court, but now he was astounded at his own behavior. His failure to make the promised payments was an oversight intrinsically inexplicable for someone of his intelligence and sophistication. The sense of shock that he experienced at the judge's decision not even to listen to him made him feel that the courtroom was no longer his home. Mary pointed out to him that the courtroom is not really a home and that the only two homes he ever had were with herself and with his mother. And if the problem wasn't in the home with Mary, then it must be in his childhood home. Thomas didn't think that she was right because it didn't feel right, but finally he concluded that if it walks like a duck, quacks like a duck and looks like a duck, it must be a duck.

Thomas began to realize that he was acting out his own childhood drama. He had been reacting to his gut feelings of abandonment instead of looking objectively at Bill's plight. Unsupportive of Bill's decision to go out West, he had viewed his son as an abandoning father and instinctively identified him with his own father. In Thomas' script Bill was the villain of the piece. This might explain why Thomas did not honor his commitment to pay child support during the year of his son's absence. By this omission Thomas, in effect, transformed Bill into the role of his own "dead-beat" dad.

The pain of his own childhood abandonment was something Thomas had never acknowledged or come to terms with. Had he been able to do so he might have been able to work through the hurt and anger he felt toward his father instead of displacing and channeling those negative emotions onto Bill, casting him in the role of villain. The non-payment of child support, which doomed Bill's bid for custody, was, in fact, an act of hostility on Thomas' part, designed unconsciously to punish his son for having left his wife and child.

This behavior also demonstrates that Thomas, despite his age and intellect, had not yet "grown up." Although the circumstances of Thomas' unhappy childhood may shed light upon his behavior as a parent and a grandparent, they in no way excuse it, because in a very real sense it resulted in his not being there for his son and granddaughter. Thomas and Mary redeemed themselves when they belatedly provided child-support payments to keep their son from jail and subsequently purchased the house that Bill and his daughter now call home. Although these acts of generosity were carried out partly for the wrong reasons (guilt being a strong motivating factor), their impact had a positive and healing influence.

Thomas was not sure why he was making amends, but it felt satisfying to be able to look after his son the way he would have wanted his own father to have looked after him. True, it was painful to re-experience his own abandonment as a child, but being there for Bill felt right. He was not only making amends for his failure to come through for Bill, and his motives were not purely altruistic: in redeeming himself by his subsequent actions he was also coming through for himself. Thomas met Bill's need for security, but more importantly, he met his own need for security.

Bill was luckier than Thomas – he had a better father. His decision to leave his child temporarily was devoid of any intention of abandonment. He was totally committed to doing his best for his daughter against enormous odds. He was obstructed by his former wife and betrayed by his parents. Nevertheless, he took responsibility for his mistakes, rehabilitated himself, and, in the final analysis gave his daughter a stable and secure home life. Bill and his child now share the joys and contentment of a caring relationship. Bill finally received justice from both his father, the judge and from the state when he finally obtained custody of his daughter.

A SECOND CHANCE AT PARENTING

Thomas' second chance to re-parent Bill was an opportunity for him to make amends for parenting errors made in the past. Further, it may be Thomas' last opportunity to complete any unfinished business with his own parents. He will know that he has succeeded if he doesn't act out the next time Bill needs his help. If he has succeeded in working through his own problems, he will be able to demonstrate empathy for Bill while retaining the objectivity to analyze Bill's problems and help find appropriate solutions. This second chance is an opportunity for Thomas to develop into a mature parent who must be "selfless" for the sake of his child, but also "selfish" in solving his own problems. *Crisis provides an opportunity to correct the original outline of child-raising, to get a second chance at parenting. The parent and the adult child have both changed and have the capacity to be different people.*

Parents who want or need to re-parent their adult offspring must be constantly on guard against age-inappropriate perspectives, for most parents continue to view their offspring as children, regardless of their age or status. Viewing them as children is one thing, but treating them as children is another. Bill showed an awareness of his own maturity when he wryly noted that he now related to his father less like an eight-year-old and more like a twelve-year-old. *Progress, however small, is still progress.*

Thomas, in addition to his problem of acting out his personal family drama, faces the normal temptation of any parent to slip into age-inappropriate behaviors. For example, he cherishes tender memories from Bill's childhood rather than his adulthood. A grandparent should take care not to be drawn into infantile modes of response when inappropriate. The grandchild's behavior may be reminiscent of his own child. Inevitably, tender moments with adult children are revived by baby pictures, and the emotional pull to regard adult offspring as children once again is bound to subconsciously cross the parent's mind. One must constantly bear in mind that one's children are now adults, with problems requiring adult solutions.

GENERATIONAL DIFFERENCES: SOCIAL AND SEXUAL

Thomas can be forgiven for the lack of awareness of acting out the family drama with his son. After all, his generation was not one that sought help from professionals to overcome such a personal problem, easily dealt with in short-term therapy. He and Mary must be applauded for seizing a second chance to correct their parenting pattern of Bill. But if Thomas and Mary are so intelligent, why didn't they recognize the seriousness of their daughter-in-law's problems early in Bill's marriage?

Thomas and Mary, like many of their generation, chose their mates out of a rather narrow pool of possibilities. For their generation one's mate was in all likelihood of a similar family background, introduced by relatives or friends, and often attending the same or a similar school or college. Fidelity, even when breached, was highly valued and was a vital common bond. The conventional courting rituals of that generation are characterized in the following laconic sentences: "He seemed like a nice person. We got along. I thought he was smart. His family seemed nice. His friends didn't bother me. All of my friends were getting married, so it seemed like the right thing to do."

Because these relationships started out with fewer expectations and less knowledge than those of Bill's generation, there were fewer disappointments. Those that did occur surfaced relatively late in the marriage, as seen for example in couples who divorce after twenty or thirty years of marriage. By contrast, children of the current generation are more likely to date and perhaps marry someone from a different background. They are likely to shy away from formal introductions, preferring to meet potential partners in neutral venues, such as a bar, a social or sports event or a class. They are likely to have higher expectations of relationships than their parents' generation. They are not as concerned with whether nice girls should or shouldn't kiss on the first date, and they have more varied sexual experiences. Despite this, they tend to know their partner less well than in earlier generations. They may lack a common life-path and similar goals within a supportive environment; and they do not have a like-minded community to sustain them through the bumps on the road. *Today's adult children have many more sexual relations than their parents did, but seem to be less satisfied with what they have.* They are awed by their parents' commitment to one another and are constantly searching for a committed relationship for themselves. This desire to imitate a successful model of commitment fuels their courage to break away from their pattern of instability and to risk making the leap from many short-term relationships to one long-term commitment.

Many parents of the older generation profess to envy the sexual freedom of their children, but when asked whether they would actually rather have belonged to a different generation and lived like their children, they tend to back off from this suggestion. Most parents will tell you that they enjoy the idea of an affair to spice up their lives, while in fact they are content with their relationship just the way it is, because they prefer the safety of the familiar over risky encounters. Their adult children are more susceptible and less mindful of risks because, like most young people, they believe themselves to be invulnerable and too distant from their own mortality to think about it. The parents, who have less time ahead on this earth than behind them, are more prudent in their risk-taking behavior and its consequences.

The social and sexual stability of the older generation is reinforced by stability of occupation and work. Many parents can also serve as role models of job commitment for their adult offspring. In many cases, they stayed in the same or a similar job for many years at a time and were dependent upon this job. Even though they could ill afford to lose the job, they did not feel vulnerable. The necessities of life were simply different back then. Although members of the younger generation have a wider range of job possibilities, they also have more gripes about them. Whereas remuneration for work today may be higher, the instability of the job market and the fear of being laid off make members of the younger generation feel even more vulnerable than their parents.

Parents, when faced with the job of counseling adult offspring, should try to focus on the similarities rather than the differences between the generations, and should not allow themselves to be sidetracked by issues of age, employment or other generational issues. Parents like Thomas and Mary might have been in a better position to educate Bill about his wife had he married a woman from the same or a similar cultural background. But Bill's choice to marry a woman from a different culture made it impossible for his parents to determine whether her eccentricities were due to a cultural pattern or to psychopathology. Unfortunately, *the total picture of important relationships does not usually present itself in full immediately, but as a partial and unclear jigsaw puzzle* to be pieced together until everything suddenly falls into place.

ACUTE VS. CHRONIC CONDITIONS

Thomas misinterpreted Bill's acute situation (necessitating a temporary cash flow for alimony payments) as a chronic condition – a misinterpretation that stemmed from his own acting out of the problem of abandonment, Thomas' own chronic condition.

The solution to a given problem depends on the severity of the problem and its duration, as well as on a judgment call as to whether the problem is acute or chronic. Both should be taken into account in making a judgment about the appropriate course of action. For example, a temporary dependency might be deemed proper when the married children move in with their parents for four months while their apartment is being renovated. The period of dependency of an adult child requiring parental care after a car accident may be long and unpleasant, but there is an end to the period of rehabilitation. The parents' payment of a one-time credit debt may generate immediate relief and lead to improved budgeting skills and warmer feelings. Often, however, what is considered by the parties to be a temporary solution to an acute problem may develop into a permanent state of dependency, assuming different forms at different times.

Most requests of adult children to their parents do not stem from acute problems. A legitimate reason for referral to professionals is to clarify the difference between an acute and a chronic condition. Chronic requests for help stem from long-term problems, such as the inability to hold down a job, a neurological dysfunction, a learning disability, a physical ailment or a mental illness. Divorce might at first appear to generate a short-term dependency on parents, but because of feelings that smolder between the two divorcing parties, manipulation of the children as a vehicle for ongoing hostilities, and withholding of alimony and child support payments, it may become a chronic financial burden on all concerned.

An acute problem requires a simple decision as to how to help, whereas a chronic problem requires a long-term strategy. Parents who assume that the problems of their adult children are acute tend to see them as being in a state of youthful growth. Conversely, parents who assume that the problem is chronic tend to see their children as being in a state of decline or stagnation. But whether a problem is acute or chronic is an objective question, not in the eye of the beholder (the parent), but in the elementary measure of frequency. How many missed payments does it take for the issue to qualify as a chronic credit card problem? How many missed child-support payments create a "dead-beat" dad? How many years of poor grades constitute a learning disability? How long must it take for a separation to turn into a full-scale divorce? How many years of not working constitute a disability? The awareness that a problem is chronic and not acute may also take time to become apparent, but eventually a point in time for a re-evaluation of the problem becomes inevitable.

An investment in a positive gesture for an acute problem is likely to pay off in the short run, whereas investing in a "quick fix" for a chronic problem is likely to prove ineffective. Picking up the tab for an adult child's chance poor decision may be rewarding for everyone, as it relieves stress and anxiety. Making an investment in the adult child's future is an even more positive gesture, although it is also a financial burden; nevertheless, the payoff is clear. However, when the parents find themselves investing money in their adult children to keep matters from deteriorating, the problem is clearly chronic. The goal for some parents of chronically dependent adult offspring may be to adhere to fiscal policies that prevent matters from getting worse, rather than investing in a quick cure.

Each person contains within himself an "intra-psychic point of balance" that allows one to navigate the shoals of one's psychic life. Finding the intra-psychic point of balance between appropriate and inappropriate dependency in chronic conditions is unique for each individual. It should ultimately result in growth for the child and relief from stress for the parent.

THERAPY AND LEARNING

As previously noted, therapy would have eventually brought Thomas to the realization that his own abandonment by his father was coloring his perception of family relationships, including those between Bill and his wife and daughter. Was he just born too soon to benefit from therapy? Perhaps. Would he have been better off had he had the choice between therapy and a form of learning which would have emphasized an internal dialogue about the problem of abandonment, as well as pointing out his acting out behavior? Probably. Before the 1950s and 1960s problems were resolved either by oneself, or, if one was lucky, in consultation with the parents. In subsequent decades, therapy with a competent professional became the "in" way to resolve problems. Over the years styles of therapy have changed and become broader – more varied but not necessarily more effective.

There has always been a place for an external source to help resolve one's problems. *People have always sought guidance – from the village elder, the witch doctor or the modern-day psychologist.* Adult offspring who are young, attractive, vital, intelligent and socially integrated are likely to overcome their problems no matter what advice they follow, no matter what type of therapy they pursue. Therapy for them can therefore be characterized as helpful but not essential. Therapy has historically been the most effective way of treating offspring up to the age of approximately thirty. However, it becomes increasingly age-inappropriate and age-ineffective as the adult child becomes nominally independent. Although therapy is a good option for gaining insights into dilemmas hampering adult offspring, research on psychotherapy seems to indicate that the general success rate is only about one-third, regardless of the type of therapy. Parents may initiate sending their children to therapy, and indeed may go to therapy themselves, for they are competent people who have done a relatively decent job of child raising. Furthermore, therapy is considered the "right thing to do." Unfortunately, *adult children after thirty turn to their parents because they have not overcome problems that should have been dealt with in their twenties, such as choice of occupation and choice of partner.* Thus therapy by itself is often insufficient to cement the connection between parent and child in order to engender extensive change; it remains a positive but not necessarily an essential part of parenting.

In contrast to therapy, the dual roles of the parent as teacher and pupil are critical to the mature parents who want to improve their parenting skills. Mature parents need to be good teachers to their adult children, but *it is even more important to be good pupils, for that is a more powerful and defining emotional experience than being a "professor."* Hopefully, the parent – and in fact, each and every one of us – carries within the memories of one outstanding teacher; it is these memories that can be tapped for guidelines. Once parents succeed in recreating that positive memory and experience, the actual "teaching" of their adult child should progress more easily and effectively. They should try to create a semblance of equality in a relationship of structural inequality, as in the classroom and in delicate family relationships.

Had Thomas been able to connect emotionally with a teacher or father figure from his youth, he may not have acted out against Bill. Thomas might have scoffed at therapy, but he certainly could not mock the teachers he emotionally valued. In the dual alternating role of teacher and student, mature parents should be prepared to modify their own characteristic responses to the offspring's plea for help, while simultaneously identifying those characteristics in adult children that should be adapted or altered. It may be fitting to return to a reliance upon parental wisdom and to go back to more traditional ways of solving human problems, instead of relying solely on therapy, for *learning patterns are as neverending as parenting in their constant availability.*

INTER-GENERATIONAL DIALOGUE:
TALKING AND WALKING

Optimally, the two generations should combine their joint resources in an effort to resolve a given problem. To reach that state of successful inter-generational dialogue, the parent should first work through his issues prior to such a discussion. The purpose is not to achieve a victory for one position or another – life is too complex for simplistic answers – but to resolve an issue and reach a practical compromise between the two generational positions through the give-and-take of the negotiating process. The negotiating process supercedes therapy and education because it can become a self-reinforcing "intra-psychic compromise," or a middle way between the generational positions.

The "intra-psychic point of balance" is a middle point between two positions with which both generations can live. That point is intra-psychic and not objective, because just how far a person can compromise is a subjective matter. One person may say about another: "It may not seem like much to me, but for him it's a big step forward." Each person, because of his own history, can bend only so far. Achieving *compromise in negotiations requires tolerance, understanding and respect for* the *differences* between people. These differences may be major ones. For example, a man with a good education but little money may view education as a top priority and be willing to spend money on his children's education, but will not feel obliged to buy his adult offspring a fancy car. He himself doesn't have one and doesn't suffer from its absence. By contrast, a man who has had little education but who has made a lot of money may feel compelled to buy his adult offspring the newest, most ostentatious vehicle, but only grudgingly give money for education, which he does not perceive as having a financial payoff. Such a person does not know the true value of education because he has not had the powerful experience of being a student or the thrill of curling up with a good book. For him, the American dream of pursuing happiness has been translated into the pursuit of money and possessions.

The intra-psychic point of balance between the generations is often achieved through an adult form of negotiation that involves money and material goods changing hands. Mature parents should make decisions that encourage their offspring to reduce or even completely overcome their unreasonable fiscal dependence on their aging parents. By treating their offspring as capable adults instead of dependent children, parents are teaching them to adapt.

Thomas and his son eventually resolved their problems in a relatively satisfactory manner. Thomas finally became a supportive father, even though he never completely resolved his own problems with his absent father, an issue that clouded his usually impeccable judgment. Overcoming the anger and hurt that had accrued on both sides was the crucial factor. Thomas, with his superior intellect, should have sensed that something was wrong and should have made the effort to communicate with his son when both were in a bad emotional state.

A good way to achieve this kind of dialogue is by going on a long walk together, especially if the adult child is in a state of heightened agitation, as when Bill hit the roof when faced with jail because Thomas had "forgotten" to make child support payments. A change of place or physical activity will frequently allow the parent to calm the agitated adult child. Often such *a change of venue helps in dealing with verbal vehemence.* When a break in the angry flow occurs and the parent can be heard, he should calmly suggest going out for a walk in a public place. If an adult child is stomping and fuming around the living room, going outside the house will generally induce the distraught person to exert control for fear of public exposure and may make the adult child realize that his behavior is socially unacceptable. The adult child, even at the height of a tantrum, is capable of being aware that some explaining will be necessary when coming out of a state of agitation. If still upset, some excess energy can be worked off by shouting at the wind. The parent should listen patiently to the violent shouting and wait for that point of poignant golden silence that becomes such a valuable vehicle to ferry an adult child to true dialogue – one that is not verbally violent, but calmly reasonable.

Parents who were brought up to speak only when spoken to have built-in controls to contain irritation, in contrast to children of a later generation, who insist that they are entitled to say what they like to whomever they like whenever they like. While it is generally true that parents have an obligation to listen to their children, this need not apply when the offspring is out of control with anger.

In sum, parents should first listen then respond when the child is willing to listen. If in doubt about the willingness of the child to listen, they should remain silent, for no parent can meet the needs of an angry child until the anger is first dispersed. Only silence and gentleness of speech can allow a parent to gain control of the painful situation of the agitated child. This approach represents a pragmatic pattern of presenting the limits for which the adult child craves.

Nobody likes a critic, especially when the truth is spoken. Parents should be diplomatic if they are to get through to their adult children. The parents should be careful not to "edit" their children's emotionally laden stories, by saying things such as: "You shouldn't speak that way," or "You should use a more appropriate word." An adult child in a shouting frenzy does not need an editor. Criticism should be muted unless imperative (such as in the event of a car accident due to driving under the influence of alcohol). Reminding adult children that they had been warned not to do something ("I told you so") is demeaning and is never a good strategy. The adult child's shortcomings are generally obvious; helplessness in coping with a problem is evident when help is sought.

A power walk will rid the adult child of excess and disturbing energy. The adult child may at first walk stiffly, as if ready to burst with anger, but the parent should not tread tentatively as if afraid. The ability to keep pace with the child speaks volumes more than actual conversation. The way to encourage communication with an adult child in crisis is to walk side by side, so that the parent is seen to be accompanying, not leading. This announces to the world that the parent is there for the child and by his side in every sense of the word. This companionship in walking is a precursor to communication. As the walk progresses, the pain in the child's soul diminishes. If a companion has a sympathetic ear, the child will be encouraged to open up and can venture to look at troubles.

Once parents succeed in opening a dialogue, they should be prepared to go wherever the dialogue takes them. The parents should not be overly concerned about the actual problem or its consequences. If the parents have "walked the walk" properly, they will be able to "talk the talk" successfully. They should be prepared to respond fully to their child's problem at this critical moment, even though they know that only a small portion of their words will be absorbed or accepted. Nonetheless, the portion that is absorbed can serve as the basis for the ensuing dialogue. The direction of the walk is unimportant; what really matters is the direction of the talk. For those individuals totally immersed in dialogue that results in genuine communication, wherever they're going is the right way.

THE FALLACY OF "TOUGH LOVE"

When an adult son or daughter comes home to solicit financial or emotional assistance, parents should take pause and say little in order to avoid saying something they might regret in response to the assaults on their pocketbooks and their emotions. Parents might also be tempted to respond with what now passes as "tough love." This argument assumes the following form: "Life is hard. Everyone must suffer in this life. This is your turn. I survived tough times. You will, too." However, this response is devoid of emotional empathy and the "tough" response is merely a way of justifying the parents' own problems in life. Had the parents worked out their own issues of coping with difficult situations, the response would not have been in terms of survival at the lowest level. Parents who have worked out their prior difficulties should not be put off by the adult child's dilemma, and should confidently be prepared to enter into a bargaining situation with their wayward offspring in the routine manner of any negotiation.

Adult children in crisis are often so depressed that they are unable to do anything, let alone take control of their lives. The goal of the parent should be to help them regain control. One effective way of achieving this goal is by "resocializing" the children into the world of responsibilities. This can be achieved by asking them to carry out minor tasks: to fuel the car, shop, take the parent to the doctor or wash the dishes. In short, they should do chores and run errands for the welfare of the family as an integral part of their lifestyle; the goal should be their return to work and their ability to develop relationships, like the parent in the family of origin.

Instead of an empty, patronizing "poor baby" approach, or a rejection disguised as "tough love," the parent should dig deep within and empathize with the adult child's state of not being quite grown up enough, a state parents should recall from when they themselves were children. Parents should take it from there by asking them to do chores or provide services for the good of the family, so that when the parents actually help them, the children will not feel that they are entering the world of helplessness and welfare.

Bill has, perhaps, made some critically detrimental choices regarding his own life. The source of his financial and emotional defeat in divorce may have been his "silver spoon" upbringing in trendy Trenton. His "time out" working on the farm out West for a year provided a sense of competence that had not been available in the marriage and allowed Bill to reach a strong point of internal balance. "Doing chores" – carrying out odd jobs about the house, for example – has an ongoing, repetitive nature. It is one child's responsibility to take out the garbage and another is in charge of the dishes. These responsibilities provide a first step in socialization, educating the child in those fundamental values of work and relationships. Mature parents should use their own past adaptation successes to help re-socialize their adult children to cope with the dilemma. Parents should clarify in their own minds the precise message to be conveyed.

Youth cannot be denied with its optimism and sense of omnipotence; nonetheless, being older and more mature has its compensations, for the years have brought understanding and tools for problem solving. The mature parent's knowledge and love is sufficient to deal with the dependent adult offspring. Parents who withdraw from their adult children's difficult situation with lame excuses and complaints that they are feeling too old to cope are essentially saying: "I'm not going to meet this trouble because trouble didn't make an appointment with me." But *trouble drops in unexpectedly, without politeness or propriety*, and often without consideration of the parents' feelings. No one thinks of making reservations in advance for difficulties with family, and no one invites trouble at any age – whether early or late. Obviously, it is better not to have troubles at any age. Unfortunately, trouble comes when it comes.

DEPRESSION DETERMINISM

A parent like Thomas must stay focused on Bill's immediate problems and not regress into "depression determinism," the state of mind that deals with the very hard times of the mature parent's own generation. Those vivid experiences of poverty that undermine a personal sense of security are generally no longer helpful, for these bitter roots prevent the surfacing of reasonable and sweet understanding. Parents influenced by the Depression may reach into their pockets, sincerely wanting to help their adult offspring, but are ultimately unable to release the dime because they are afraid it might be their last one.

Thomas is a rags-to-riches parent. He constantly reminds Bill that he "worked fourteen hours a day when starting out," as if this were relevant to his son's situation. He is currently a professional parent on a limited income. "I paid my way through school and paid off my debt of $140,000 when I bought my practice," he reiterates. That number is as clear in Thomas's mind as if it were yesterday, but the amount of money that he made after setting up a practice is referred to with vagueness. "I make a living. I get by. But do you think I'm made of money?" "Times are tough," this particularly deprived parent from the period of the Depression said. "I've had to take out home equity loans to repair my home, so this is no time to expect me to repay your so-called debt of honor." The reason Thomas cannot recall the value of his properties is that he is still "psychologically" as poor as he was when he got through school on a scholarship. Instead of responding with assistance, Thomas responded to Bill with his own hard-luck story: "Oh, I've got the money all right, but it's tied up. Sorry. You caught me at a bad time." There never seems to be a good time for people who dread their own poverty.

Of course, the assumption that mature parents should use whatever resources they can to help a wayward adult child does not apply when financial options are simply not available. If the parents do not possess the means to help their needy adult children financially, there is no decision to make. An adult child must either find a way to resolve the problem or else live with the unpleasant consequences of not being able to resolve it. For example, an adult child who can't make alimony payments faces jail. The parent may look on full of worry and concern, or privately feel relieved because the burden is too much to handle emotionally or financially. Either way, no decision-making option exists for the parent.

But when parents possess the financial, physical and emotional means to resolve the problem presented by their adult offspring, they have to make a decision as to how to help in such a way that will avoid them becoming destitute themselves. Should they do all in their power to resolve the child's problem, no matter what the personal cost to themselves? Parents who have the money to resolve the financial problems of adult offspring often refuse for fear of becoming poor in their old age. If they decide to help, the parents should decide to what extent they will do so, because they may be afraid of giving their offspring resources that will be wasted and depleted so quickly that it will merely create a repetition of the current situation.

It is natural for people to fear growing old and becoming destitute. Parents who lived through the Depression often had to support their own old and needy parents financially or emotionally. They have experienced this first hand. For example, Thomas' young abandoned mother married a rather unpleasant older man so she and her son would have some financial security and so she could stop working at a terrible job. The son was aware that his mother was better off with her second husband although she was miserable, and he vowed that one day he would take care of her and his other family members.

Although this now over-eighty-year-old son established himself financially fifty years ago, he's still a scrimper and a saver. He turns off lights when he leaves a room, doesn't talk excessively on the phone and clips coupons from newspapers for the sales. His fear of poverty generated loyalty to friends and businessmen who could guarantee him a job. He praises the federal government for its disaster relief. Social security, although a minimal part of his income, provides him with a personal sense of financial security. His family and friends have waited many years in vain for him to pick up a check gracefully. He would love to be able to give money to the needy, and he willingly puts his hand in his pocket, but he can't pull it out. He is worth several million dollars and refers to himself as a "poor millionaire." No one will ever humiliate his mother again.

IT'S NEVER TOO LATE TO LEARN

A successful solution requires that both parties benefit from the outcome. Thomas has gained empathy with Bill, who has become the father figure in the family, and Thomas basks in a warmth that he never knew as a child. Thomas now lives in an emotional framework provided for him because of his love for Bill and his granddaughter. The judge in the courtroom forced emotional limits on him for the first time in his life. He had grown up without intellectual or emotional limits, for he had had no father to correct and channel and criticize him. As compensation for not having had a father, he had gained and reveled in the endless praise of his mother, and later of his wife. He was much admired by all, except, of course, by the father he never knew.

Thomas had developed an arrogance born out of success; because he was "right" in so many human conflicts, he never developed a modest self-image. That is why he was so shocked that the rules applied to him as well when an unsympathetic judge read his son the riot act – pay up or go to jail – without considering who Bill's father was. Thomas had finally run into an authority figure he couldn't handle. To add insult to injury, it was precisely in his bailiwick where he, as a judge himself, should have known the obvious ruling. His haughtiness and arrogance made him thoughtless at a delicate moment in his son's development, because he assumed that it was his day in court.

Such haughtiness is common in businessmen, lawyers or family leaders who expect their assumptions about any issue to be accepted because of their history of saving the situation at the last moment. Thomas, in effect, went into the courtroom with arguments prepared, confident of success and ready to win, as always. He forgot that it was Bill in the dock. Was Thomas so vain that he thought the case was about him and not Bill? How was Thomas, at the age of slightly over eighty, to grow and develop into a mature parent?

When he had a chance to collect himself and think about the judgment, he realized that it was a fair ruling and that he might have made the same decision had he been sitting in the chair. His arrogance and haughtiness introduced an error into his thinking because of his self-centeredness. He realized now that he was irrelevant to the case, just as he had been irrelevant, so he thought, to his own abandoning father. Maybe he was wrong about that, too. Maybe he was wrong about Bill. Thomas was entering a new zone. He realized that he could be mistaken about something. He had seen this in court cases and personal arguments where people "act out" conservative or liberal principles largely irrelevant to the issue at hand. He had a superior mother who gave excellent advice in the unshakable belief in its relevance. Was he following in her footsteps and becoming respected but not listened to? Was Thomas afraid of being a liberal father giving in to Bill's neediness and becoming a nice, but ineffective parent and a wimp?

Thomas learned his lesson in court and became supportive of the only father figure available to him. He bought a house for Bill to prove to himself that he was not an abandoning father. Thomas became a mature parent by beginning to doubt his own version of his personal history and by questioning his mother's outlook on the world. He had, at long last, found for himself a middle way between his parents. He finally felt that he was in the right place. For him, the intrapsychic mid-point was like the bear's bed in the fairy tale – just right.

LEARNING DISABILITIES: THE STRENGTHS
OF THE LEARNING DISABLED

Children with learning disabilities can suffer psychic pain so deep that, if left untreated, it can affect their self-image permanently. Yet despite the fact that learning-disabled children are at a disadvantage in a classroom setting, they cannot be exempt from going to school and taking examinations that from their point of view are impossible. School may be harder for a learning-disabled child than for "normal" children, but the greatest painful injustice of all is the long-term negative self-image developed. For example, an intelligent learning-disabled child like Bill knows that if his true understanding could somehow be evaluated, he would have received an 89 in a crucial examination, but because of time constraints and errors of inattention, he received a 74. Even if some teachers might, on occasion, consider taking the easy way out and just upgrading the mark, the learning-disabled child would not tolerate being disrespected as a dummy for whom the school has to make special allowances. He would prefer the power to protest being labeled a 74-grade type of person and would struggle to become an 89-grade student. A learning-disabled child, like any other, views the grade as a personal label evaluating him as a person, and not merely a measure of learning in a particular field. The learning-disabled child literally transforms himself into a grade-point average.

One would have expected learning-disabled adults to have overcome this insult to the ego, especially since they would probably have experienced many successes in life in the years after school, where their learning disability is less likely to be a handicap. Nonetheless, this blow to the ego comes up repeatedly in psychological sessions. These learning-disabled adults are among the most courageous people, both mentally and physically. Dealing head-on with the ongoing and profound insult to the ego, they are often able to put the pain aside and get on with their lives (although the pain and insult of that grade of 74 remains with them).

Learning-disabled children can take heart from knowing that the pain is of relatively short duration and need not affect their lives for a long time.

When Bill brought home a mediocre grade, his mother's response was "What's wrong with the teacher?" whereas Thomas' was, "I guess the kid is not as bright as we are." Ironically, his mother's practice of finding fault with the teacher worked to Bill's disadvantage; after all, a diagnosis is more likely if the focus is maintained on Bill while searching for the circumstances and the true cause of the mediocre grade.

Thomas' response was essentially an alienating one, because he adhered to the outmoded assumptions of his time that good students like himself fare well, but are not always blessed with children as bright as themselves. Thomas had over-learned the lessons of his generation and had no room for new, and what he assumed to be erroneous, views. Besides, he had always known the answers better than others. Because he had learned his lessons at school too well, he objected intellectually to the concept of a learning disability, passing it off with a wisecrack. In his day the children who failed had been classified as "limited," "lazy," or simply "not too bright," in contrast to himself, and he liked being at the top of the heap. The diagnosis of a learning disability did not fit into his world outlook. He preferred the terminology he had grown up with rather than this new-fangled diagnosis of learning disability. "It's just a cover story to excuse Bill's not doing well in school," said Thomas. "Bill is just a slow learner in the classroom." Thomas's unwillingness to accept the now conventional wisdom regarding a learning disability means that he uses misguided euphemisms to describe the same phenomenon. The word "lazy" is the most common descriptive word used by teachers and parents, and even the child. The phrase "slow learner in the classroom" is the title of a well-known classic book by Newell C. Kephart, a pioneer in learning disabilities. A good-natured parent can assume the "late-blooming" theory that says, "He just needs more time to find himself."

In summary, euphemisms lead to procrastination. Thomas' continuing to regard Bill as not having a disability in effect kept Bill from getting the support from his father that he needed to function as an adult. Any child, learning disabled or not, eventually must grow into an adult with enough education and sufficient ego strength to cope as an adult. Thomas' continuing stance of regarding the diagnosis of a learning disability as inaccurate for his child, now an adult, overlooks Bill's uniqueness. Any weakness of character on Bill's part can impede his ability to study, adapt at work and improve critical relationships. Thomas' refusing the diagnosis wasted precious time in Bill's youth and now, in his adulthood, it was jeopardizing his chances of surviving in the grown-up world.

Thomas' high intellectual ability had often put him on a collision course with commonly accepted verities, including the legitimate diagnosis of a learning disability. Thomas relied on his own cleverness, not authority, to solve problems. But now Thomas, at the age of eighty-three, was finally ready to deal with the sin of procrastination before time ran out for him. He began to realize that not only had he denied the existence of a learning disability, but he had also denied the reason for his refusal to accept authority in general, whether in personal relationships or in professional ones. Thomas was now ready to take advantage of his second chance at parenting.

Chapter Eleven

AN UNDIAGNOSED
LEARNING DISABILITY

INTRODUCTION

In the story of the divorce of Sy's daughter the learning disability is a minor matter among more somber problems. In the story of Thomas a personality flaw keeps him from dealing effectively with his son's learning disability. In the following story about Tony, the learning disability is missed because of socio-economic and cultural reasons. Learning disabilities are often found among respectable working people who may be unaware of the problem. When learning disabilities are erroneously conceived of as a middle-class diagnosis designed to serve as an excuse for children who can't study well, all people are done a disservice.

The failure of awareness can result in damage to the person's image of him or herself. Psychotherapy is helpful but is only partially beneficial. Parents, by becoming role models of the traditional values of work, diligence, loyalty and patience can teach the acceptance of necessity instead of individual desire. Techniques for building a person's self image include buying small gifts, verbal expressions of self worth and validating culturally appropriate expressions of emotions. Not only the parents, but also the family ancestors can be invoked as role models. Parents can be friends with their adult children, but not at the price of surrendering their parental authority.

Synopsis

Anthony's oldest son, Tony, who has been working toward his degree at a snail's pace, falls in love and drops out of college. Eventually, he comes home with his tail between his legs – no girlfriend, no college degree, no job. The host of woes that besets him is almost overwhelming. How is one to deal with an overweight thirty-year-old son back on one's doorstep, recently diagnosed as having a learning disability and apparently unprepared to "get back up and fight"? Anthony and his wife face a dilemma common to many parents. How are they to reassure their adult child without creating too comfortable a home for him?

THE DILEMMA

Theresa has known her husband Anthony for fifty-two of her fifty-seven years. They grew up together in the sprawling Italian neighborhood of a big city on the East Coast, their homes facing one another across a tidy, narrow street. They were married a year after Theresa graduated from Catholic high school. Anthony, three years her senior, did not graduate because he found school "boring." The nuns remember him well as "the boy who could fix anything." A good-looking youth, who frequently complained of headaches, he was smiling and belligerent in turn. Only Theresa never lost her patience with him and her unwavering acceptance of Anthony, moods and all, had a calming effect on him.

Anthony found employment through an uncle as a semi-skilled electrician with a construction company. But this child of working-class Italian parents had middle-class aspirations. He worked at the company until he was old enough to enlist in the army. Anthony managed to obtain a high-school equivalency diploma (GED), and by the time he had completed his service he was a fully qualified electrician.

After his wedding to Theresa – by then a secretary with a government agency – Anthony attended university on the GI bill. He studied mechanical engineering, working part-time as an electrician. Although he finished his sophomore year, it was hard for him to concentrate. He did not return to college. Instead, with the help of the electrical workers' union, he found a job as an electrician with his old construction firm. Anthony and Theresa's combined salaries did not make them rich, but the two were able to leave their modest apartment and buy a two-story row home, not unlike the row homes in which they themselves had been reared. They proceeded to have two children, Anthony Jr. and Frankie, in quick succession. Theresa remained in her job. The couple continued to raise their sons in a brand new house according to the old-world values characteristic of many Italian families.

At age twenty-seven, happy-go-lucky Frankie followed in Anthony Sr.'s footsteps and became an electrician, carefully avoiding the college route. He has a steady job, lives at home, dates frequently and on the weekends hangs out with his father and older brother. Theresa happily cooks "her three boys" their favorite foods. She attends to the house and continues to be what she has always been, the calm and steady linchpin of her family.

Tony Jr., a heavy-set young man of twenty-nine, landed a clerical position with the Department of Motor Vehicles after high school and went on to study at a community college. Pursuing a BA in marketing from a small liberal arts school with a decent reputation, he was an undergraduate for ten years, taking only two courses per semester. That was all he could manage because reading was so tedious for him and he found himself going over the same paragraph again and again, not being able to remain focused on the thread of the argument. Because of his light course load he was able to maintain a 3.8 cumulative average. He was proud of his grades and had hoped to graduate with honors, although still six credits short of his goal.

Last summer Anthony and Theresa sent Tony Jr. to Europe. It was his first time abroad and the first trip he had ever taken on his own. In the little town of St. Simon in the south of France he met a pretty college junior from Bridgeport, Connecticut and fell in love. After returning to the U.S., Tony dropped out of college and kept in touch with his new girlfriend, driving every other weekend to Bridgeport, five hours away, to see her. Anthony and Theresa viewed the situation with mixed feelings. On the one hand, they were happy their son had a girlfriend. On the other hand, he hadn't done anything academically since the summer. In addition, he was gaining weight. They assured him, as they had often assured Frankie, that if he chose to go into business they would give him financial backing up to a sum of $40,000. Tony received these tidings with a grateful smile, but he did not take them up on their offer. Nor did he re-register for school.

Toward the end of the year he told Anthony and Theresa that he wanted to relocate to Bridgeport to work in an advertising firm there, owned by his girlfriend's uncle. Anthony wondered whether he would be expected to fork out a payment to make his son a junior partner in a field he didn't really understand. Neither parent objected to the move, although Theresa knew she would miss him. After all, Tony was a grown man, and there was nothing unusual about his desire to be closer to the woman he would probably eventually marry.

One Saturday morning Tony packed the trunk of his car and a small U-Haul and drove to Bridgeport. He rented an apartment his girlfriend had found for him and went to work on a trial basis at the uncle's ad agency. Things began to go wrong almost immediately. The parents of Tony's girlfriend convinced her to remain in her college dormitory rather than move in with her new boyfriend. A stunned Tony found himself spending much time in his studio apartment alone. He started eating more during the evenings he was not with his girlfriend, evenings that were becoming increasingly frequent. The work at the agency was interesting, but there was a great deal of copy to read, and Tony was having trouble keeping up with it. The words kept swimming in front of his eyes. His new boss had noticed that Tony was lagging behind and had jokingly labeled him "lazybones." Tony did not appreciate the joke.

The phone in Theresa's kitchen rang while Anthony Sr. was once again considering his options for buying his son into a partnership. Theresa answered the phone and smiled when she heard her son's voice. The smile quickly faded. She stood, listening intently, for several minutes. "I'll speak to your father and call you at the apartment," she said slowly. She hung up and turned to Anthony. "Tony broke up with his girlfriend yesterday. She wasn't ready to commit to him." Anthony was stunned. "And there's another thing," Theresa frowned. "It seems that Tony's not getting along with his boss. He just can't seem to get through all the books and magazines they make him read at the office. He takes the stuff home and reads in bed until all hours. But he ends up falling asleep over it. The thing that just drove him around the bend is that this morning he took a long look at himself in the mirror. He knows that he is obese. He wants to come home."

THE REASONING

Anthony and Theresa are faced with multiple problems, only one of which is Tony Jr.'s desire to seek shelter once more beneath the parental roof. The most pressing of these problems is Tony Jr.'s weight. Even young men carrying over 100 lbs. of extra weight can be candidates for a heart attack. Inappropriate weight gain is usually associated with depression and low self-esteem. This adversely affects many other aspects of life, particularly in the social sphere. Although Tony's ego may have taken a beating because of his girlfriend's rejection – no small matter when a first love occurs just before age thirty – his depression and low self-esteem may have a very different origin. There is a suspicion that Tony's inability to process reading material quickly and his lack of concentration is a form of dyslexia or a learning disability. This suspicion is further supported by two facts: Tony did not have a sufficiently high average in high school to qualify for a regular four-year college, had to go to community college instead, and is taking an inordinate amount of time to complete his university degree. Under the circumstances, it is not surprising that Tony is seeking consolation from the refrigerator and asking to return to the comfort of his warm Italian home. He is living on his own, in unfamiliar surroundings, for the first time. His first serious affair of the heart has ended badly. His first attempt to hold down a demanding, responsible job has failed. All his woes are raining down on him at the same time.

Anthony and Theresa should convince their son to enroll in a resident weight-loss program as soon as possible, preferably at a "health farm" that is not an easy commute from their home. The expense for this program, which will be considerable, could be deducted from the $40,000 they earmarked for his business venture. At the health farm Tony will learn about diet and exercise. Group and one-on-one therapy sessions are standard components of good weight-loss programs. An alert psychologist and a group of supportive peers could make an enormous positive impact on Tony Jr. In addition, he may be able to be assessed at the health farm to determine whether or not he has a learning disability.

Since dialogue is an essential tool of the mature parent, Anthony should take his son for a long walk and discuss the idea of the weight-loss program thoroughly. If his son is reluctant, Anthony should try to convince Tony to adopt this radical and all-encompassing approach to losing weight. In order to more effectively make his point, Anthony should have at his fingertips the answers to all of Tony's questions about the health farm. And it should be made clear to Tony that both his parents approve of this course of action for him.

If Tony resists the idea of going to the health farm, Anthony's next step should be to play hardball. He could promise to give financial backing for a business on three conditions: Tony's participation in a resident weight-loss program, his loss of a significant amount of weight and the completion of his college education. His weight is a life-and-death issue. Therefore, even if Anthony and Theresa had not been in a position to send their son to a health farm and were facing going into debt to make this happen, all three would have had to assume some responsibility for paying off this debt. That's a tough way to experience togetherness.

SEEKING HELP

When an adult like Tony is in psychological trouble, as evidenced by his excessive weight, an initial approach is often to assume that the person can and should handle the problem himself by not eating so much. This focus on the person's internal resources essentially denies the existence of a problem. The very act of seeking help or intervention is an implicit acknowledgement that the person cannot handle it himself. Expecting the person in trouble to handle the problem himself is but a veiled way of telling him to go away and not bother anybody.

For a family as close-knit as this Italian one, a more likely approach is a vigorous argument that the issues should be dealt with only in the context of the family so as to avoid airing dirty laundry in public. Such a family defense mechanism may have been appropriate when the family lived huddled together for warmth in a primordial cave. Only those in the cave could see clearly, and only they are capable of having valid helpful opinions. Outsiders need not apply to help the family. But family defense mechanisms of this genre exclude any social intervention or the introduction of modern knowledge.

In stark contrast to this unhelpful cave mentality is the approach of people in trouble who are willing to seek help as needed from relevant professionals, self-help books and sources outside the family. Modern man is not expected to handle all problems alone or with his close family in a cave. He seeks help from professionals who respect one's privacy. Anthony and Theresa are in touch with the modern world through their jobs and medical experiences. Tony will need outside help for his obesity and a professional diagnosis about his suspected learning disability. Tony's parents are eager to help their son, and their proposed solutions require outside intervention to promote their son's independence and to maintain their ongoing life-style.

Although Tony's difficulties apparently arise from a number of unresolved issues, his obesity is a life-threatening condition that should take priority. His parents cannot resolve this problem themselves, so their job is to make sure that experts are available to assist their son in resolving it. If Tony's life had not been in patent disarray, and if he had weighed less than he did, a program such as Weight Watchers might have sufficed. From a parent's perspective, however, embarking on a standard weight-loss approach would do little to enhance Tony Jr.'s personal autonomy, as it would require bringing this almost thirty-year-old man back to his own room and, by extension, to his old life. By contrast, the new and total environment of short-term residence at a health farm, far from home, will address his physical and psychological problems without juvenilizing him. Once the weight-loss program gives Tony access to a psychologist on a regular basis, he can be tested for a possible learning disability.

Furthermore, learning disabilities often run in families. An interesting question to consider is whether Anthony Sr. has an undiagnosed learning disability himself, which might explain why he dropped out of high school. Confirmation of this hypothesis would strengthen his son Tony, as it would mean that he is not to blame for his plight, but shares a genetic problem with his father, whom he admires.

Tony's stated ambition to graduate with honors, despite his chronic part-time student status, may be due neither to psychological characteristics such as perfectionism nor to an inflated image of himself. He reads slowly at school, a condition often described as dyslexia. Tony probably knows that he should husband his energy because the effort of reading is so tiring for him. By restricting the number of courses he takes, Tony may be adapting to a learning disability. He is compensating for his inability to read efficiently by reducing the amount of reading he is required to do.

Many learning-disabled adolescents and adults achieve significantly more once they are out of school. They are often successful entrepreneurs. They succeed when they determine the structure of the task in a field of their own choosing. By contrast, high school and often college impose goals that may seem sensible to most, but not to the learning disabled. They exhibit stubborn persistence in achieving goals that others deem wise to give up. They often become leaders of large organizations because they are adept at getting others to do the work at hand. Their behavior and learning is frequently at a higher or a lower level than the majority of people and therefore may be less predictable. They are often outstanding soldiers because of their over-attending to one specific task for a long time. They are characterized as either under-attending or over-attending, according to the specific task at hand. *In sum, the learning disabled suffer from instability of attention in relation to an expected norm.*

If testing confirms this diagnosis, Tony's learning disability is a core problem, along with his weight. In therapy he will undoubtedly spend many hours letting off steam about how hard it is to lose weight, about the girl who got away, about his feelings of inadequacy and depression. These are all painful subjects that demand attention. But if Tony has indeed been coping unaware of a learning disability for most of his life, only after the learning disability has been diagnosed and dealt with can his pain and suffering be alleviated. A parent like Anthony can emphasize a shared problem of learning, perhaps by referring to his own problems in high school. In doing so, he can help his son to a better destiny.

FAMILY VALUES

Although Tony has a warm relationship with his father, sons no longer automatically follow in their father's footsteps, as they once did in the past. Anthony had become an electrician like his father and his grandfather before him, and he had benefited from the availability of a role model for work. His younger son Frankie chose to follow in the family footsteps, becoming an electrician as well, but the role modeling became eroded by the time it reached Tony.

Families used to have a matriarch or a patriarch who provided the role model for practical skills, such as how to cut meat, wire a home or business, paint a house or tend a garden. Sometimes such role models fade with time as unanticipated challenges appear, but often the spirituality, love and discipline of the previous generation continue long after the actual skills have passed on. Frankie learned more from his father than merely how to do the electrical wiring, and Tony learned family values as well.

As a mature parent, Anthony should reach inside himself to connect emotionally to the family matriarch or patriarch, find the love within for the child, and then switch to being totally pragmatic about the solution to the child's problems. Analogously, discussion of how the family matriarch or patriarch operated in their area of expertise is not meant to teach another generation the actual skills but to convey values such as dedication and hard work. A good illustration of this principle is the continuous discussion about the mechanics of the motorcycle in Robert Pirsig's *Zen and the Art of Motorcycle Maintenance*. The purpose of the father was to polish his son's personality, not merely to teach him how to maintain a motorcycle.

The traditional values derived from the family matriarch or patriarch constitute part of the foundation of parenting. These must be supplemented by expert guidance and modern information – of which there is no shortage in this day and age. Parents who knew how to muster expertise in their first round of child rearing – with the help of experts such as Dr. Spock or parental guidance magazines – should now enter the phase of adult child raising with the assistance of expert guidelines. Rather than stick dogmatically to only one approach, mature parents should resort to whatever information and guidance they can muster to help resolve the problems of the adult child.

When contradictions arise between a solution provided by the experts and the solution with which the parent comes up, the parent should delve deep within, read the relevant literature carefully and then make a decision. Sometimes a logical professional approach to a problem makes sense academically and analytically but doesn't feel right to the family. In such a case, the proper course of action is the approach that feels right, for that is the one more likely to result in a practical substantive solution to a real problem.

This book about parenting is addressed toward those parents who wish to become better parents in the future than they were in the past. *Although perfect parenthood is a fantasy, better parenting is always possible.* No parent is perfect, but lack of perfection is not incompetence. One should be aware of one's lack of perfection and strive for physical and mental health and goodness within one's self. Moreover, if an adult child falls short of perfection, the parent should not settle into the comfortable pattern of blaming the adult child for being the source of the problem, and perhaps even viewing the child as being plain bad.

Unfortunately, at one time, this was the designation of many conditions now seen as merely unhealthy, such as a poor choice of adult attachments or various learning difficulties or behavioral problems. Failure to attain an adequate job or education is still often viewed negatively, instead of being seen as a personality or learning disorder. The pain attached to an adult child's failure can be so great to all concerned that clear thinking is put on hold and old refrains of disrespect, such as, "I always told you that he was no good," come to the fore, even though the parents themselves may realize that this is not the true picture. Pain may defeat reason and thwart inquiry into the real problem, thus preventing real solutions in the areas of learning and personality problems.

Parents such as Anthony and Theresa should be prepared to listen to repeated promises or declarations of change from their returning offspring. "I'm sorry, I've learned my lesson and I'll never do that again," is generally acknowledged as a lie and a prelude to departing from the parents with pecuniary gain, setting a pattern of continuous taking followed by repentance. A verbal declaration of repentance – a promise to refrain from eating cake, to finish school, to get a different job – is not true repentance. *True "repentance" is measured by actual changes in behavior.* When a child says "I'm sorry," the behavior often does change, but when an adult child utters exactly the same words, the parents must be prepared that a recurring transgression might be imminent. For the child, the words often refer to an isolated incident, while for the adult child the words generally refer to a repeated pattern of behavior.

The parent should not chastise the adult child by pointing out false statements in a crude manner. Instead, he or she must translate those insights into positive precepts in order to encourage the wayward child to engage in critical behavior that the parent knows would be beneficial. *When an adult child asks for help, he or she cannot choose the preferred form of assistance alone, but must settle for the help that the parent is willing to proffer.* By the very act of asking for help, the adult child has reverted to dependency; the issue is whether it is temporary or permanent. Children do not make the decision to visit the dentist or to go to unpleasant school situations on their own; they may sometimes be sent to them for their own good, regardless of their objections. The parent's goal is not to punish the child, but to encourage correct behavior that will lead to a positive outcome for all.

SAINT THERESA

The parenting paradigm deals with the quality of the interaction between parents and adult children when the parents' awareness of the child's lack of perfection can no longer be ignored. This is likely to come to the fore in the build-up to a crisis. Initially, Theresa could help improve Tony's self-image by showing acceptance of him in the wake of the emotional trauma of rejection by his girlfriend. Sometimes small gifts can serve to reduce the inevitable narcissistic pain of rejection, which has intensified Tony's lack of self-worth. Buying a sports shirt for Tony – as opposed to going overboard and buying a whole wardrobe – could trigger a renewal of confidence in his looks. The emotional support generated by small and timely gifts could make him feel better about himself in the short-term.

Moderate steps of this sort help to prevent the arousal of child-like narcissism. Buying a whole wardrobe would convey to Tony the message that he is back home for the duration and that his excessive weight is acceptable. Mommy will heal his wounds as in the past, and he will not have to cope with the harshness of his situation. But parents' giving as in the past, without moderation, would weaken the adult child instead of strengthening him. Spending time facing minor choices such as rearranging ties, shirts and shoes can feel so regressively comfortable that there could be less incentive to move out again and re-face the external world of work and adult love.

Parents like Anthony and Theresa have deep eternal love for their children, and yet they have also achieved a certain degree of maturity for themselves. At the other end of the emotional spectrum are those parents who are totally non-supportive and who would tell their child to go buy shirts alone. Such behavior is psychological abandonment, which may often result in the child's turning to a cult or to drink or drugs as a substitute for the absent parental support. Anthony and Theresa's attitude towards their children is the opposite of that of those parents who dwell in the psychologically non-nurturing zone of emotional and educational neglect of their children.

Theresa should not create too many expectations by making facile promises that may later not be backed by actions. Parents lose credibility when they say, "Oh, don't worry. We'll take care of you," because often they cannot follow through. Furthermore, such promises feed the fantasy that mommy and daddy will make everything all right again. When their childish needs are not met, the disappointment and anger and sadness suffered by children can be devastating. Tony does not need to be totally taken care of since he is not totally incompetent.

In the past Theresa has made her men feel good by feeding them, but now she is facing a grotesquely overweight son. Her natural tendency would be to support her deprived adult child in his feeding frenzy. Over-eating is a socially acceptable disease for so many stressed-out adults who prefer a quality restaurant to simple home cooking. Apparently, the term "quality" refers to the restaurant's skill at successfully concealing cholesterol and sugar, which make a meal taste good. Obesity leads to heart conditions and diabetes, diseases of epidemic proportions in the Western world generated by the availability and affordability of food. Diabetes is a bitter disease leading to loss of autonomy and premature dependence on doctors. In addition to the issue of physical health, an obese son or daughter conveys a message of unavailability to a potential mate. If a person cannot take care of his own physical body, how could he meet another person's physical and emotional needs?

Anthony and Theresa cannot rationalize a health issue because they themselves grew up on meat and potatoes, milk and cookies, and peanut butter and jelly sandwiches. They might think to themselves: "We over-ate as children or adults and we turned out okay. How bad can it be? Besides, he is comforted by food more than by what we say." They may be naturally sympathetic to Tony's eating excesses, but they must intervene when the pattern becomes dangerous and insist that he take appropriate action, such as signing up for a weight-loss program or joining a gym. Giving good and obvious advice increases Tony's faith in his parents, strengthens the bond between them, and touches the primal belief in wise and all-knowing adults that Tony needs at this moment of crisis.

Theresa will have to shift her focus from being as accepting as a saint to becoming demanding like a rehabilitation counselor, otherwise the home situation will be so comfortable for Tony that he will never want to leave again to try to set up a home of his own with another woman. Theresa realized that Tony felt better at home than in Bridgeport. In spirit Tony had already returned home long before his physical return, due to the stress created by the girlfriend situation and by his job. Tony returned home physically only after many attempts to maintain his autonomy, even partially, in his own home. Numerous long-distance telephone calls and e-mails had preceded Tony's actually coming home, and the length of the phone calls had suggested to her that Tony was edging towards a crisis.

FROM CHAOS TO COMMUNICATION

Cultures differ greatly in the way its members cope with major insults, such as rejection and abandonment. The Anglo-Saxon tradition seems to urge clamming up and encourages bearing one's pain in stoic silence – as exemplified in the classical British "stiff upper lip." More volatile cultures such as the Italian one seem to sanction verbal and physical expression of emotions. When someone like Tony – who grew up in an Italian culture – comes home he is not likely simply to ask for help or to enter into a painful and unapproachable silence. He is more likely to scream out his frustration, hurt, anger and sense of devaluation, thereby involving others in his plight. Unfortunately, shouting is a painful screaming match that is the opposite of a healing dialogue, as can be attested to by every person who has ever been a participant in a monologue. Yelling and screaming stem from a source of inner pain; this pain is expressed as anger so overwhelming that it suppresses all other emotions. Screams can be as unnerving as an artillery barrage in combat with its endless rounds of senseless shelling. Not only is the screamer out of touch with his or her feelings, but the listeners also behave the same way by disconnecting from the yeller, digging in and closing their ears to the noise in a totally defensive stance.

Parents should not join their son's inner burning or permit the shouting to continue endlessly. They should be patient and calm, for example, by sitting with their son over coffee and a sandwich. Parents confronted with an angry yelling or crying child at any age should bring their child's emotional temperature down by speaking slowly and softly. A parent can gradually bring the child out of an active mode of venting anger. By straining to listen, the adult child relaxes, listens, and begins to feel not so terrible. Once in a receptive or listening state, the child will start to swallow and digest the sandwich, as well as any good palatable advice offered by the parent. Once the adult child's brain is engaged, emotionality and impulsivity recede in favor of intelligent and quiet thinking. The adult child then becomes emotionally available to the parent. The process of getting the child to accept a different view on a given problem is a gradual one that begins with having the adult child relax and then listen; otherwise, parents confronted with a screaming adult offspring may find themselves agreeing to their child's unreasonable stance merely to escape the verbal onslaught.

The parental home should be a haven of quiet, a place where voices can be heard. Home is the place desperate adult children choose when no one else will have them. Theresa should try to change the obvious condition of discomfort to an emotional state approaching comfort by hugging Tony and soothing him verbally with non-committal assurances that matters can be worked out. As he is offered simple food and drink, his own perspective should be listened to non-judgmentally. Theresa should validate her son as a person by attending to whatever story he tells. The parent who hopes to help a child find peace should pursue the goal of the child's emotional comfort tirelessly and endlessly until this near impossible task is fulfilled.

Patience is a virtue of the mature parent. When a parent like Anthony tries to get a message across, he often does not succeed the first time. It is incumbent upon Anthony to continue to send the same message many times, using different terms each time. The parent, becoming irritated at not being heard, can easily slip into the negative mode by saying, "You shouldn't do that!" rather than the positive, less emotionally laden statement, "This is what you ought to do." A critical statement to a dependent child in distress is often heard as a needless rebuke instead of a constructive comment as intended. A parent must make every effort to have the child listen. An effort is called for to make the advice proffered palatable to him or her.

THE WHOLE FAMILY COUNTS

The discerning parent should try to determine which meaningful figure in the family is "accompanying" their returning child – an absent spouse, a long-gone grandmother, the memory of a family godfather or even the memory of a younger version of the parents themselves. To melt the ice of sullen anger or heated shouting a parent may refer to a relative who is perceived as important, as in, "I'm glad Ma isn't alive to hear you talk this way. You know how she felt about profanity." Ancestors count when a troubled son or daughter returns home. Family figures interjected between parent and adult offspring can serve as mediators and a common source of authority, when used with the right amount of tact. If the family figure is perceived emotionally in a positive manner, the feeling can be transferred to the current situation, allowing both parents and adult children to smile and relax, as if the family figure were present. As the adult child smiles and visibly relaxes when the important family figure is evoked, there is an indication that the intermediary figure is perceived as a positive force. This positive feeling tone can indicate a readiness to listen to the parents. They can serve as judges whose jurisdiction in family disputes is recognized by family members.

Anthony, Theresa and Tony visited the cemetery where Theresa's sainted mother was buried. All three stood around her grave, recounting stories about her. Recollections of Tony's grandmother – a loving, nurturing, and loyal soul – offered the same comfort to her descendants after her untimely death as before. On the way home from the cemetery, Tony and his parents were relatively relaxed and smiling.

The search for the critical influencing family member can be an objective, rational process. A thoughtful, comprehensive examination will usually result in identification of that one intermediary family figure generally acknowledged by all to be the crucial person. Although the process can begin merely as an intellectual exercise, it may result in an emotional response and a change in the "feeling tone" of the returning child, thus opening up the lines of communication between the parent and the returning child. The parents should talk to each other and cull their collective memory and their own powers of reasoning to identify the influencing family member. Not a soul should be overlooked, for a child may be influenced by a figure from the past in an unexpected manner. For example, it may be easy to identify the grandparents' long-term positive influences, but sometimes an overlooked aunt or cousin or child caregiver may be crucial. Moreover, the child may be influenced not by the grandmother or the grandfather alone, but by the interaction between them. Then it is the task of the parents to discover the identity and emotional impact of these figures. Other members of the extended family and old friends beyond the immediate family view may offer a different valuable perspective to identify the critical intermediary ancestor.

Problems arise when the identity of the figure is unknown. Just as the memory of a beloved ancestor may make one feel good, the memories of ancestors who served as negative role models tend to be overlooked and suppressed on a conscious level. Such ancestors are more difficult to identify as intermediaries, and their negative influence is hard to detect and counteract. To illustrate this point, consider an extreme but not unfamiliar example. A woman's marriage was in trouble because of sexual problems with her husband. She did not respond appropriately to his overtures in bed, and both husband and wife were frustrated because of her inability to achieve orgasm. A friend of the wife knew that her father had been sexually abusive and had forced himself continually upon the wife's older sister. In fact, the wife had married early in order to escape her sister's fate. The wife's mother had condoned her husband's sexual abuse of the elder daughter by explaining to both her girls, "All men are pigs. That's just the way they are!"

While the wife's father was clearly in the wrong for having broken a powerful incest taboo with his older daughter, the more negative hidden role model was the mother who had failed to intervene to save her eldest daughter from incest. Her message about the "true" nature of men was the most psychologically damaging factor in her younger daughter's subsequent relations with her husband. Even within the context of marriage to a caring man very different from her father, the daughter could not turn off the incest taboo because she had internalized her mother's message. The daughter had cut herself off from normal sexual pleasure because of the real threat from her father, reinforced by her own mother's peculiar outlook on men. This combination of circumstances played havoc with her sex life. The influence of the negative intermediaries was so strong that the friend's insight alone into the cause of the wife's problem was not sufficient to resolve it. Eventually, at the friend's urging, the wife and husband went to a sex therapist who was instrumental in helping them solve their problems by shifting the focus from her own father's violation of the incest taboo to what really hurt her – her mother's betrayal of her and her sister in a crucial area of life. Once she understood that she distrusted her own mother, she was open to listening to objective information from the Masters and Johnson school of sex therapy on how to have satisfying sex. Once again, the crucial step is identifying the key family member as a precondition to resolving the problem.

The parent must try to determine the real problem. A positive intermediary can be a powerful instrument for parents to employ in their search for the source of their child's troubles. Positive intermediaries evoke shared emotional and visual memories for parents and their children. As a rule, positive intermediary figures tend to generate light, understanding and good results, whereas negative intermediary figures generate heat, noise, anger, arguments, fear and results that do not promote healing. Positive intermediary figures can be used to help bring the presenting problem out in the open. The parent should help the offspring tap into those memories in order to breach that dam of silence and shame that prevents the adult child from talking freely. The obvious cause of the dilemma may not necessarily be the true source. Listening to the returning child verbalize his or her difficulties and standing back and letting the words flow may help the parents assess what is wrong.

One mother was able to tap into her own relationship with her mother to help resolve her daughter's problem. One winter's evening a distraught daughter showed up on her mother's doorstep. The daughter had been walking through a bitter snow-laden wind for most of the afternoon. She was blue from cold and would not look directly at her mother. The mother knew that something was seriously wrong because of her daughter's avoidance of eye contact. She resisted an impulse to scold the daughter for wandering around so long in such inclement weather. Instead, remembering her own childhood and her mother's rituals whenever she came in cold from the snow, she invited her daughter in, sat her down in front of a heater and made her hot cocoa.

The giving of food was the mother's attempt to make up in some way for the daughter's emotional deprivation. Then she got her daughter into an old flannel bathrobe. Finally, she rubbed her daughter's feet and slipped them into socks that she had placed on the radiator. The daughter, warmed as much by these visible demonstrations of love as by the hot drink and dry clothing, began to relax and to talk. The mother's actions gave the daughter a sense of well-being that allowed her to open up. By behaving easily and efficiently she served as a role model of competence for the daughter and created an expectation in the daughter that the problem could be dealt with before knowing the particulars. In short, she generated the expectation that a solution was available for any problem.

A parent should be especially careful not to join the child in a search for "the guilty party." For example, a woman's adult daughter had returned home with her marriage in shreds. The husband had run away with another woman. In this scenario the husband is the bad guy and the other woman the interloper, who is to blame for the dissolution of the marriage. The obvious candidate for the role of villain is "the other woman." Such stories, often stated by a couple in crisis, seldom lead to a resolution because they are hard to clarify, while the interaction between the parties involved and their parents speaks volumes about their habitual relationships.

However, a parent knows from experience that focusing on the alleged villain will lead the daughter nowhere. Marriages generally break up because of problems inherent in the relationship itself, rather than because of any external figure such as another woman. As the daughter opened up, a more common tale of the breakup of a marriage from the wife's perspective came to light. The husband wasn't nurturing enough and the wife wanted her mother's care. He wasn't as good a provider as her father, and he wasn't enough of a man sexually. The husband's version of the crisis might well be stated in reverse terms. She still wants her mother's love and is on the phone to her every day. She is turning out to be just like her mother, and who wants to be married to somebody like that? Her father provided wonderfully for her family when she was a child until he left the family when she was an adolescent; she never got over her father's abandonment of her mother and of her. She is still looking for her father to return to them with heaps of money. She is dissatisfied financially and sexually, and "no matter how hard I try in both these areas, I find that I can't meet those needs. So I found this other woman whose financial needs were reasonable. I have no trouble meeting her sexual needs and vice versa."

Our ancestral intermediaries play an essential role. Knowing the parents' intermediaries can make all the difference for a needy child. Wise parents know their own ghosts.

Chapter Twelve

HAVE A LITTLE FAITH

INTRODUCTION

Immigrant cultures usually have immediate figures available as role models. Their ancestral family role models have been left behind and deemed to have little utilitarian value to their current life. But if both immediate and ancestral role models are unavailable, some would have to be created.

In the following story, Cam's daughter's request for money presents him with an opportunity to behave pragmatically for once in his life – if only he can come to grips with the immediate and past family role models he has rejected for religious reasons. When he finds that his own religious forebears and ancestors can't help him with a pragmatic problem, the extremely intelligent intellectual and atheist Cam turns to the medieval philosopher and physician Maimonides to find psychological peace. The purpose of religious reconciliation is less the discovery of the truth than learning to find a common path and peace between generations to live together, irregardless of the religious views. Attempting to resolve his theoretical problem regarding atheism, he enters a dialogue that enables him to be a parent to a disturbed child.

Synopsis

Cameron, a rebel against his family's religious values, is a militant atheist, one who attacks religion at every opportunity. His children, in turn, rebel against his belligerent anti-religious outlook on life and walk in different paths of faith. He is particularly concerned about his daughter, who has joined a religious cult and has relinquished all control over her life. How is a parent to deal with these issues? Cameron must deal with the flaws in his extreme outlook on religion in order to tackle his children's problems.

THE DILEMMA

Cameron and Sally met in their mid-teens at a formal dance at Cameron's prep school. It was "like" at first sight. The two met again as undergraduates at Harvard University, and before the end of their freshman year "like" had turned into "love." Plumpish, blond-haired and blue-eyed, both possessed an aristocratic mien and manners, as well as heightened inclinations to attack religion at every opportunity. Cam and Sally could have been fraternal twins. Their well-to-do families held a big wedding upon their graduation, blessing their union with silver, china, and for their honeymoon, the keys to the ancestral home in the Barbados, built by a revered family ancestor.

Cam's ancestor, the Captain, had made the family fortune by trading manufactured goods from New England to Africa, transporting slaves to the Caribbean through shark-infested waters and returning with rum for sale. Down through the generations his descendants had become lawyers, thereby intimating that they had inherited the cold blood of the sharks rather than the warm blood of the great Captain. Some of the family, including Cam's father, had become Protestant preachers to protect their reputation as the deserving rich. The dining-room conversation at extended family gatherings invariably revolved around issues of using money wisely and discreetly, and behaving modestly so as not to appear nouveau riche like the immigrants.

Cam, Sally and the contents of a large moving van eventually found their way to Johns Hopkins University, where Cam completed his PhD. Sally was not idle during this period. She gave birth to their three children and opened a small flower shop. This business venture incurred the displeasure of her mother-in-law, who, as Sally learned shortly after her marriage, had a history of manic depression, fixed ideas about appropriate employment for upper-class women, and a strong disapproval of a family member being "in trade." She apparently overlooked the great Captain's profession.

Cameron began to teach philosophy at a local junior college, specializing in the philosophy of science, as befitted the family rebel and practicing atheist. An ardent non-believer, he held the view that organized religion impeded the development of science and technology, and that it was more concerned with abstruse details of theology than with the betterment of the human condition. Sally shared her husband's views on religion, but was not as disparaging and did not invest much time or energy contemplating the subject.

Teaching at the junior college had been intended as a temporary measure while Cameron finished his doctoral dissertation. Much to everyone's surprise he remained in that job for the rest of his working life, becoming the only eldest son in five generations to do nothing to increase his family's financial holdings. At sixty-one Cam and Sally, having spent most of what they had inherited from their own families, were nevertheless looking forward to continuing their comfortable lifestyle in retirement based on the sale of Sally's flower shop and an annuity from Cameron's retirement fund.

Cameron's views were well known around campus. He would make his personal position explicit early on in his course on the philosophy of science with withering comments about religion. "If there's one thing I can't fathom," he would say, "it's people who claim to be scientists yet believe in the existence of some supernatural power. It's one thing if you're an uneducated boor. But for the life of me I cannot understand how anybody who considers the pursuit of knowledge – and I mean objective knowledge – to be a meaningful endeavor," he would pronounce with fervor, "can believe in such hogwash."

Cam's militant views notwithstanding, Cam and Sally's first-born, Jonathan, married a born-again Christian and was fascinated by revivalism and the witnessing of the spirit of God in historical events. Because their salaries were not high, they delayed having children. To Cam and Sally's embarrassment and dismay, Jonathan went to work for the evangelical movement of the small southern community where they currently live. They live frugally and are saving to buy a home and start their family. The youngest of Cam and Sally's offspring, Edward, is in his early thirties and operates his own small hi-tech company which manufactures software for the pharmaceutical industry. His wife, who is not working, is pregnant with Cam and Sally's first grand-child. After this child is born, both parents plan to attend church more regularly. Edward is more moderate than Jonathan in his religious orientation. He seems to follow Sally's path of getting along with the religion at hand, and is careful not to state his religious position to Cameron for fear of a heated family argument. He enjoys the social aspect of religion and likes feeling part of a religious community. Edward maintains good relations with his brother and sister.

If the religious tendencies of his two sons weren't enough of a cross to bear for a militantly atheist father, Cameron has been even less fortunate with his daughter, Jocelyn. Her ongoing struggle with depression constitutes a major cloud on Cam and Sally's horizon. Now nearing forty, Jocelyn was diagnosed with clinical depression at fifteen after attempting suicide by overdosing on sleeping pills. Cameron and Sally had placed her in a private mental hospital and subsidized therapy after her release. Between the ages of twenty-eight and thirty-two years Jocelyn had enjoyed a remission. During that time she had been able for the first time to hold down a low-paying clerical position, and she married a man who was an apprentice to a cabinetmaker and later became a master carpenter.

When Jocelyn discovered she was unable to have children for medical reasons, a succession of depressive episodes ensued. This time, however, Jocelyn refused to return to therapy, and eventually she and her husband joined a religious cult in the hope of finding solace there. Upset about Cam's views on religion and opposed to his confrontational and antagonistic approach, she didn't want to talk with him about the topic. For several years, while the two resided in a Vermont religious commune and Jocelyn scrubbed suburban floors for a living, there was little contact with Cameron, although Jocelyn kept in touch with her worried mother.

One day Jocelyn informed her mother that she felt strong enough to leave the ashram. She explained that she needed a two-story house with a basement. The basement would be used as a workshop for her husband, the first floor would be converted into a shop to sell his goods, and the second story would comprise their living quarters. Jocelyn was confident that if she and her husband owned such a house, they would be able "to make it" on their own. Jocelyn intended to remain a member in good standing of her cult, but she promised her mother that the house would never become an extension of the ashram or the property of the cult. She wanted to know if her parents would help her buy her dream house. Sally readily agreed to put Jocelyn's request to Cameron. "We'll have to see," was his reply. "Come on," Sally protested. "This is our chance to set them up properly, once and for all. We can do this for them, can't we?" Cameron frowned. "Maybe," he said, "but they'll have to wait until I retire and you sell the shop. Our trust fund money is almost gone, and aside from what we're making now, no new money is coming in."

THE REASONING

In contrast to the general guideline that an adult child should be encouraged to assume responsibility for his life and choices, in some cases, like Jocelyn's, there might be a real danger that the child is incapable of taking charge of her own life and thus might be exploited. Cam and Sally have to help their daughter and her husband. If possible, Jocelyn and her husband should participate in the purchase of the house by contributing to the monthly mortgage payments. Once Jocelyn and her husband have their anticipated regular income, maintenance and taxes on the property should be their responsibility.

To ensure that the house does not fall into the hands of the cult, Cameron and Sally will have to be the sole legal owners of their daughter's home. Jocelyn and her husband will have the right to remain there as long as no change in anyone's status takes place. In the event that Cam and Sally pass on, Cam and Sally's wills should state the conditions for Jocelyn's continued living in the home, particularly with regard to the cult. Since they are concerned about her mental status, they might decide to appoint Edward as executor of their estate because of his balanced religious outlook. If Jocelyn at some point wants to take out a second mortgage, her parents must first approve this action. If the house is sold, the profit from the sale would revert to Cameron and Sally's estate and be kept in trust for Jocelyn and her husband. Should Jocelyn elect to adopt, her children would also benefit from the sale of the house.

Cameron is justifiably reluctant to give money to a religious group of which he heartily disapproves. Cameron's suggestion that the purchase of a home for Jocelyn and her spouse should be delayed until the parents' retirement for financial reasons may be a way of showing opposition to the cult, but it is counter-productive. Cam and Sally should instead provide the younger couple with housing as soon as possible, even if this means belt-tightening for the parents. A smaller house in a less-than-ideal location is one way Cam can demonstrate his lack of enthusiasm for giving the money, but an outright refusal might permanently end any chance of family reconciliation.

Although the solution described above appears to be concerned merely with money and property ownership, the real issues involved here have little to do with fiscal matters. The underlying issue is religion – or the lack thereof. It is not mere chance that two of Cameron and Sally's three offspring chose religion as a way of defining their lives and rebelling against their father. Cameron's atheism did not satisfy the emotional and spiritual needs of his elder son or his daughter. In terms of rebellion, Cameron himself unwittingly served as a role model. He had refused to go into the business of making money, as his family had expected him to do. Instead of wheeling and dealing, he had spent his life thinking, a course he was able to pursue because his parents and in-laws had given their financial backing. No wonder Cameron's children have expressed their rebellion in a religious manner, for Cameron's anti-religious fervor has all the zeal of a devout religious preacher, like his father.

Religious differences and Cameron's lack of respect for his daughter's and son-in-law's religious beliefs turned out to be disastrous for his family. "Christianity is bad enough as an anaesthetic to the human mind," he thundered, "but this cult has put them into a coma of their own making. The ashram looks no better than the closed ward in Jocelyn's hospital." This insult to Jocelyn's religious choices caused a permanent breach in the family. It never bodes well when parents and children stop talking to each another. Moreover, as is often the case, the ensuing silence bred both emotional detachment and physical distancing. Jocelyn and her older brother both left the Baltimore area; only their younger brother, whose religious affiliation was marginal, continued to live and work in the same city as his parents.

For Jocelyn there were issues of autonomy as well. The unsuccessful struggle to make ends meet while her husband was learning his trade, coupled with her serious emotional problems, generated a sense of inability to cope. It was this lack of control over her life that triggered Jocelyn's move into the ashram, where she surrendered her autonomy to the cult, attaining in return a sense of belonging.

By providing help with housing for their offspring – at no small cost to themselves – Cameron and Sally can set a number of positive steps in motion for their family. First, the ball of communication will begin rolling again: neighborhoods have to be scouted, houses scrutinized and money transferred. Once the lines of communication are reopened, with some effort on Cameron's part and encouragement from Sally, perhaps they will remain open. Of course, all decisions pertaining to the choice of a house – its size, location and the conditions under which it is acquired and sold – must be discussed and negotiated by Jocelyn, her husband and her parents. The couples should sit down at the negotiating table as equals, and when they leave the table they should do so still feeling as equals. Cameron and Sally should try to work out any differences of opinion with their offspring without juvenilizing the younger couple, striving for a warm and business-like atmosphere.

Second, Cameron and Sally should explicitly demonstrate their love by giving their daughter a roof over her head that belongs to her, not her cult. The help is contingent, because Sally and Cameron do not have unlimited resources. Nevertheless, by showing Jocelyn that what they do have they are willing to share, Cameron is conveying the implicit message: "You have your religious beliefs and I have mine. They're different, but that doesn't mean that I don't love you or that I won't support you when you need my support." This is a message that a child always needs to hear.

Finally, although Cameron and Sally would be required to budget their savings carefully, their previous lifestyle would remain more or less intact. The reward for such generosity would be a dual one. They would be drawing closer to their daughter and to one another, thus strengthening their family emotionally. Most of all, they would be giving her the ultimate parental gift: the opportunity to reach and sustain genuine autonomy.

AT THE CENTER OF THE UNIVERSE: GOD OR MAN?

Cameron is truly a "modern man." He is devoted to science and views religion as a collection of superstitious beliefs that, by their very nature, are not amenable to scientific verification. What is more, he clings to his belief in the importance of objectivity and the supremacy of the scientific approach with all the zeal and fervor that is often associated with religious belief. His extreme position on religion has had a serious impact on his family. One of his children has become an evangelical Christian, another is mildly positive toward organized religion, and the third has chosen a different path altogether: a religiously motivated cult which is potentially a more serious deviation from social norms. In their choices his children have responded, each in his own way, to the rigidity of Cameron's position. Their choices are indicative of the uneasy state of Cameron's soul.

Cameron is the prototypical modern man who believes that Man rather than God is at the center of the universe. He is the beneficiary of the Copernican outlook on the world that was set into motion with the scientific proof that the earth revolved around the sun, not vice versa. In the pre-Copernican world the finger of God, in the form of divine intervention, constituted the prime mover or controller of world events. After Copernicus, however, the locus of control shifted from the finger of God to the hand of Man and no longer assumed divine intervention.

Cameron clearly had much on his mind as he pondered how to deal with his daughter's predicament, but this did not affect his last lecture of the semester on the progress of science and technology since the medieval period. The class applauded at the end of the lecture and a smiling girl came up to him and complimented him on his stimulating lectures, to which Cameron mumbled some agreeable answer.

The class left and Cameron gathered up his notes and went home to sit in his basement library, and pondered, somewhat bemused, on the student's compliment. It was not new, because he had been the smartest boy in the class for as long as he could remember. Still, a compliment went a long way to making one feel good, especially when a black hole is threatening to engulf one's being – a feeling Cam has been living with for as long as he can remember.

He was tired at the end of the day and slouched into the chair, wishing for a teacher who could argue with his position of atheism and science versus religion. He often used to have imaginary debates with imaginary teachers or philosophers so as not to feel so alone in the world. He imagined that he saw a shadowy figure of a man who identified himself as Maimonides. Cameron spoke to him. "I would like to consult with you more as a physician than as a philosopher, because I have an appointment with a psychiatrist for my daughter next week and I need to prepare for the meeting. Would you suggest that I read Scripture?" "Not at all," replied Maimonides, waving his finger in his face as he spoke, "Scripture is for the healing of the soul, but for your daughter's depression, you should go to a good doctor, for his wisdom also comes from God."

"But I don't believe in God as an all-powerful being," responds the worried father. "Besides, I generally find people who do believe to be characterized by arrogance and hypocrisy." "Not at all," replied Maimonides cheerfully. "Belief is just a special way of knowing something deep inside one's self and as such is a source of truth not dissimilar to external proof of a hypothesis. And as for your argument that all religious people are hypocrites, how come it took you as late as the third grade to realize that people are hypocritical? It is widespread and certainly not confined only to believers. It extends to include skeptics such as yourself, for a person who says that he doesn't believe in God is generally a skeptic who must be educated in the deeper levels of knowledge until belief is attained. That can take a long time – decades, jubilees, centuries. External evidence is not required, unlike in medicine. Faith in God's universe means that man is not central to the scheme of life and thus need not be egocentric. I am sure that most modern people, just like most medieval people, still subscribe to a vague belief in a higher force or God – with the exception of the committed and practicing atheists who are always but a few in each generation."

Cameron warmed to the task and waved his two index fingers back in Maimonides' face. "The world has progressed immensely since your time. For your information, Copernicus proved way back in the fourteenth century, about two centuries after your time, that the earth revolves around the sun, not the other way around. Indeed, God is no longer at the center of the universe, and man is better off because of it."

Maimonides countered, "Man is only partially better off since he placed himself at the center of the universe. By the way, the idea that the earth revolved around the sun was around even in my time even though it was not proven scientifically. Indeed, man's material world has progressed rapidly since Copernicus – but man's spiritual state has not proceeded at the same pace. Modern man has lost contact with the original purpose of life as it was perceived in the centuries preceding Copernicus. The centrality of man in the quest for happiness has not proven sufficient for the modern egocentric person who perceives himself as the center of all being. Despite scientific progress, there remains a wistful longing for the pre-Copernican God who cared deeply about people, and man's purpose in this world was closeness to and knowledge of God."

Although he was reluctant to admit it to himself, Cameron had an uneasy feeling that Maimonides was right about one thing: modern man's soul is not satisfied by the belief that Man is the measure of all things. This mitigation of the importance of knowing or believing in God results in a constant mild dissatisfaction within the self. Indulging in extravagances is an attempt, usually unsuccessful, to alleviate one's unhappiness. Maimonides' point that acquiring a belief in God may result in true internal happiness is well taken. By contrast, the acquisition of external material goods often leaves one with a sense of dissatisfaction. In this process, modern man first becomes dissatisfied with the defects of others and eventually becomes devastatingly critical of himself. Because of this focus on others instead of on God, the pain of the ills inflicted is attributed to external sources, such as an unfaithful spouse, a mean boss, fate or plain bad luck.

Cam might attribute his bad luck to his rapacious pirate ancestors or his religiously rigid extended family. In truth, the bad fortune of men like Cam generally comes from their own vices, not from an external source. When good health or material wealth does not come to them or their family, instead of taking stock of their own faith they blame God. Cam is a troubled adult who lacks faith in God in those moments of distress concerning his children. Cam has not internalized God and become an athiest. This lack of commitment makes Cam want to defer examining Jocelyn's request fairly.

Cameron's militant atheism leads to a sense of emptiness and a concomitant lack of closeness with his children. In order to reach out to his children in their time of need, he must look within himself to filling that void. By doing so, Cameron must reach the point where he is able to change his assessment of his adult offspring's problems. The family still has not lost the desire to be close to each other. Each is a dignified human being who can look forward to reaching a unique conception of where their life is heading. This family togetherness means that the indignities that they must inevitably suffer are but painful stones in one's shoes on a rough trip. Thus, problems can be dealt with in a balanced and proportional manner.

A fervent atheist like Cameron and his children – who may have faith or be profoundly skeptical or doubting about God – all have their own goals to reach. *Life is a journey – and it is often a hard trip.* Each person should look at his traveling companions on the trip through life and learn to enjoy the company of spouses and children. The purpose of the journey is to get to know the people close to oneself.

Obligations and "doing the right thing" make the trip possible. The focus on individual rights and on freedom of choice highlights the modern characteristic of personal decision-making, with little concern for the family context or closeness of friends. Freedom with no limits is irresponsible. The parents might have been responsible in the past for having raised their children's expectations of nearly endless entitlement, but they now must become responsible for setting limits. The endless entitlement of adult children is no longer possible as the family tries to do the "right thing" to solve a family problem, like that of Jocelyn, and to find the right balance between obligations and freedom. The judicious application of these principles can serve as a guide through the perplexing paradigm of the needy adult child.

Jocelyn's request for money for housing has provoked a relatively mild crisis but has also provided a great opportunity for a family plagued by religious differences. Her request for help was made after a long process of separating from the cult. She was taking her parents' position into account to the point that she was willing to have another psychiatric evaluation. Jocelyn's spiritual reassessment requires that her parents must also reevaluate their view of her situation if the family is to go forward.

The mature parent should prepare to give up the fantasy that the parenting task has been completed when the adult child marries and leaves home. Cameron and Sally had led their lives commensurate with their social and intellectual background and were self-centered enough to assume that their children would follow in their footsteps without too much effort. Clearly, a practical and theoretical reconsideration is necessary. Parents who see their child in a shaky marriage or an unhealthy personal or religious situation must evaluate their child's predicament as objectively as possible. Parents should use their empathy with their adult children for extensive planning and rehearsal for both the worst-case scenario and also for that moment when the adult child is willing to leave his or her protected environment and is no longer willing to "pay" with his or her autonomy for the spiritual protection of the cult.

Jocelyn's parents must replace their fantasy of what they would have wanted for Jocelyn with the reality of likely outcomes. Planning strategies that will help them achieve a socially desirable outcome – like having their child live in a decent place – must be adopted. Parents have to prepare themselves for all eventualities, including the possibility that their children might not go in the paths laid out for them. Parents must be ready for the next shock to their ordered lives by working on themselves, as well as evaluating the possible positive or negative outcomes for their children.

The tendency to seek fault in the offending party is ubiquitous, and leaders of the cult are often vigorously opposed by families because of their perception that they are harming the adult child. Anyone who could hurt one's adult child must clearly be evil. Parents may empathize with their child in considering the "evil nature" of the source of sorrow, be it a cult or a person. But the parent's job is to alleviate the adult child's frustration and anger and to think clearly with the child about the problem. The parent must strive to reduce the child's bitterness as a prelude to examining, together with the child, the pressing interpersonal crisis. Once the bitterness of separation has diminished, wise parents can balance the extreme views of their adult child with either their own more reasonable views or those of some expert.

Cameron must prepare himself for the personal differences between his daughter and himself when it comes to religion, as well as for the burden upon his purse. Failure to prepare and rehearse one's emotional reactions is as immature as not preparing for an important class, seminar or business deal. Constant examination of one's strengths and weaknesses is the prerequisite of successful change in interpersonal family relations. This examination should include consultations with people near and far, according to one's individual preferences.

Maimonides, who dealt with religion and science, saw Moses as the role model of closeness to God. He argued that knowledge of God is an internal state of mind, a highly personalized experience, rather than an external matter. He asserted – in his own unique language – in the first sentence of his major religious essay, Mishneh Torah, "Know ye that there is a God." A consideration of the word "know" in the context of the religious thinking of his time suggests that belief is an especially deep way of knowing.

A self-contained person such as Cameron may feel more comfortable discussing his issues with a respected person many centuries away from his time, such as Maimonides, instead of a contemporary "doctor of the soul," such as a psychologist or psychiatrist. Cameron is painfully aware that the fervent adherents of atheism are indeed "but a few in each generation."

Cameron – in his imaginary conversation with his unlikely interlocutor, Maimonides – reasoned that if his daughter was willing to reassess her views on religion for the sake of family unity, surely he should be prepared to do the same. Possessing a scientific bent, he could acknowledge that his fervently held hypothesis regarding the existence of God might be wrong. He didn't like being in a minority as a fervent adherent of atheism, but maybe he could become a solid skeptic as a compromise. That would go over well with Jocelyn. Then, perhaps, he could eventually reconcile with her.

Chapter Thirteen

COGNITIVE IMPAIRMENT: THE ROAD TO AUTONOMY

INTRODUCTION

Cam's needs led him to create for himself an imaginary parent to solve his own parenting problem. While a highly intelligent philosopher such as Cam can create for himself a source of parental support for a difficult moment, most individuals need continual parenting, and some young adults such as Ernie require neverending parenting. Ernie, who is intellectually impaired, is not concerned with abstract matters of faith as Cam is. He has faith in his parents. They will never abandon him. Ernie cannot conceptualize his aging parents leaving him for any reason. He has neither the intention nor the capability of leaving them. Most young adults plan to leave their parents at some time in order to grow up, but Ernie must gradually be taught that his parents have the right to separate from him.

Parents of the mentally retarded must overcome long-standing guilt as they maintain stability and gradually introduce steps and techniques that do not feel right to have an effect on the inevitability of separation. They must do this for Ernie and themselves, for the goal of parenting is autonomy both for their intellectually handicapped child and themselves. Mental retardation should not be confused with emotional retardation induced by the fantasies of contemporary culture. One purpose of parenting is to replace fantasy with reality, and Ernie's limited fantasy life focuses on the movie seen in his home of his parents' love and support. Ernie wants love and a steady job. He knows that trying to be normal requires hard work. He can be normal as long as his parents never leave him, age or die in the fullness of time. While the job of raising a retarded adult child is harder than regular parenting, it can be done successfully.

Synopsis

Fred and Dinah became neverending parents at the moment of their son's birth when they were informed that Ernie had Down Syndrome and they realized that they would have to take care of him from that day onward. Now, so many years later, the inevitability of aging, the threat of illness and reminders of their own mortality have led to their decision to separate from their intellectually handicapped adult son. They want to enjoy their twilight years knowing that Ernie is being cared for, and they need to assert their "selfish" right to their own autonomy. But Ernie doesn't see it that way and objects strenuously. Fred and Dinah overcome their guilt and assert their rights without causing Ernie to feel abandoned. They are comforted by their ability to find a humane and realistic solution for their "eternal child" who is, in fact, able to live a fuller emotional life than many "normal" adults his age. Because of society's support for the handicapped, many of the working poor who are physically and mentally healthy live with greater financial insecurity than the retarded.

THE DILEMMA

Fred at age forty-three and Dinah at thirty-eight met at a church function in the small Ohio town where they both grew up. Fred was an accountant for an auto parts manufacturing plant and Dinah a librarian. Neither had been married before and their relationship, which blossomed out of their mutual devotion to the church, led to their marriage at a mature age. Dinah soon became pregnant and bore a baby with Down Syndrome. The doctors, explaining that the mother's age was a factor in such cases, told her, "We just don't know as much about these things as we should." Fred and Dinah never once considered institutionalizing their baby or giving him up for adoption. Ernie was their "special child" and they felt fortunate that the Lord had given them the task of bringing him up. Their lives together were enriched by Ernie. His childish ways kept them young.

Their common concern for the child created an even stronger bond between Fred and Dinah. They became central figures in their local church. Together with the Ohio Mental Retardation Association they were instrumental in establishing a nursery school for both normal and intellectually handicapped children in the basement of their church. These were happy years for everyone. Ernie was quiet and somewhat passive in comparison to the other children in the nursery school, but he seemed to enjoy the company of his schoolmates.

When Ernie finished nursery school he attended special education classes in a school for the mentally retarded in a nearby city. His parents had to get him up at 5:30 A.M. to get him ready for the hour-long bus ride into the city. His school day began at 8 A.M. and ended at 4 P.M. Ernie usually took the bus home, but on occasion his parents would pick him up from school and go shopping in the city. Things continued this way for Ernie, who eventually finished his special high school in Grade 14 at the age of twenty. He had attained the level of education and the social skills of an average fourteen-year-old.

The company that employed Fred had a long-standing connection with the Ohio Electric Company. Fred, with backing from the Ohio Mental Retardation Association, opened a sheltered workshop close to his home for assembling small parts for the electric company. The workshop prospered, and each of the adults who worked in it earned 80 percent of the minimum wage. The remaining 20 percent was covered by the State of Ohio, as were the professional expenses and wages for the workshop's administrators, therapists and other personnel.

Fred and Dinah realized, from the moment their son was born, that Ernie was always going to need parenting. Because his parents understood this, there were no shocks or surprises for them during the years of Ernie's childhood or adolescence. Ernie grew into a sociable, friendly, open young adult. Moreover, he did not suffer from excess weight, a problem to which many Down Syndrome youth are prone.

As the years went by, some of Fred's friends developed health problems, died or retired to Florida. At about this time Dinah started having trouble with her back, the result of having to lift Ernie in earlier years. Eventually there came a time when the couple wanted to fly to Florida alone, particularly during the bitter winters, to be with their remaining close friends in a sunny clime. They couldn't do so easily because they couldn't leave Ernie. In the course of Ernie's childhood Fred and Dinah had done little traveling, and the trips they had managed had always been with Ernie. Ernie could not leave because of his job at the workshop and the importance of his social support system. Nevertheless, they had a "selfish" desire: they wanted to enjoy what was left of their life together. For them that meant retiring to Florida, just as their friends had done.

Fred and Dinah were proud of the way they had raised their special child and realized that Ernie's home was now the workshop. He was happy and secure in his home environment. Ernie had a hold on their hearts and consciences, and his desires had always come first. Ernie's needs were great, and his parents had always been the focus of his support system. Guilt was, therefore, the most acute problem for Fred and Dinah. How could Fred and Dinah meet their own requirements and, at the same time, make sure their son's needs were met as well?

At this point, external circumstances took a hand. Fred's employer was bought out by a larger concern and Fred was offered an excellent retirement package. Shortly after, his best friend died. It was unexpected and for Fred it was a warning bell. He was not afraid for himself but for his son. What would happen to Ernie if he or his wife died suddenly? Both parents together contributed to his welfare, and either one alone could not continue to safeguard their son.

THE REASONING

Fred and Dinah are the aging parents of a son who will always require supervision. Ernie is by definition a dependent adult, regardless of his age. At a meeting of the parents of workshop participants, a social worker suggested that Fred and Dinah talk to Ohio's Department of Mental Retardation, which is always interested in acquiring group homes for people in Ernie's situation. The deal generally struck between the state and the parents of handicapped adults is to name the State of Ohio the inheritor of the family home. In return for deeding the house to the state, the intellectually handicapped adult is guaranteed a place in the group home for the rest of his natural life. Fred and Dinah realized that if their son could reside in his own group home, he would be well provided for after they were gone, even if the workshop should close its doors. This solved the practical issues. But separating from Ernie was the real challenge.

Separation is an extended process, and parents of intellectually impaired adults should prepare for it well in advance. With the help of the state, for example, Ernie had taken short trips away from home in his younger days to summer camp or to the Special Olympics for the Retarded. But Fred and Dinah had not taken the further step of going away for weekends, leaving Ernie at home under adult supervision. By having him deal with short-term separations they could gradually accustom Ernie to become more capable of handling the inevitable long-term separation.

Another option to consider is that when Fred and Dinah relocate to Florida they could take Ernie and have him stay until he asks to go home. This is the usual scenario for developmentally challenged adults in stable surroundings. If they do this, in due course Ernie will miss his friends, his job and his old home. When he returns to Ohio, phone calls and letters will enable the family to maintain contact and sustain the supportive relationship between Ernie and his parents.

Fred and Dinah, by opting for the group home solution, are continuing to act as the loving parents they have been since Ernie's birth. They have always helped their son. The quality of his life has always been high, because it has been defined by stability rather than change. Security for intellectually impaired adults lies in having daily contact with surroundings and friends they have known all along. This is especially true for Ernie, who, thanks to Fred and Dinah's efforts, can remain in the neighborhood he knows and loves. The laundry, the supermarket, the movies, the mall – all facilities are within long walking distance of his home. *Ernie's universe may be limited, but it is safe and secure.*

When parents separate from their cognitively impaired offspring, emotional stress is generated. Ernie has sensed for some time that his parents wanted change. He knows they look forward to going on short vacations by themselves. Ernie has no desire to negotiate the issue of separation from Fred and Dinah; after all, his parents' wish for short vacations means potentially permanent abandonment in the future. This must be resisted at all costs. He resists their efforts at parting from him in every way at his disposal. His pleading manner – coupled with various subtle guilt-inducing ploys, often-unconscious maneuvers on his part – has been instrumental in bending his parents to his will for years. It is difficult for parents in Fred and Dinah's situation not to succumb to their children's emotional demands. But a changing reality for his parents means that Ernie can no longer own them exclusively. All three members of this close-knit nuclear family are being driven toward the goal of mutual autonomy by the inevitability of advancing age.

Although Fred and Dinah have raised Ernie well, separation will be wrenching and painful for their son. Ernie is aware that his parents want what is best for him, even if he doesn't understand how this can be achieved. Ernie lives his moments to the fullest without the awareness of a person's inevitable decay and death. In Ernie's mind, his parents will live forever and will always care for him. However, the reality is that Ernie will probably outlive his parents. His parents cannot allow themselves to leave this world worrying about Ernie's future. They should prepare him for that ultimate separation by a less catastrophic separation. Of course, it is not only Ernie who will feel the pain of loss; Fred and Dinah will feel it too. But they must endure it, because autonomy is right for Ernie and for themselves.

EMOTIONAL STRENGTHS OF THE COGNITIVELY IMPAIRED

Children learn primarily from the models with whom they grow up, namely, their parents. Children raised within healthy marriages generally develop positive modes of interaction themselves. By serving as good role models, Fred and Dinah have taught Ernie vital lessons as to the kind of person one should strive to be. Ernie has been blessed with stable parents and reliable mates in school and in the sheltered workshop.

Despite the fact that Ernie has been impaired from birth, he is better off emotionally than many non-handicapped children and adults who are exposed throughout their lives to poor examples of relationships. Many people have problems of attachment and separation. Their incorrect interpretation of social relationships renders them unable to connect and develop satisfactory social relations.

Ernie doesn't interpret relations. He thinks concretely, not abstractly, and deals with what he sees and feels in front of him.

Separation will be difficult for him, but objectively it will be less difficult than for others. Ernie can be expected to rigidly refuse to separate from his parents just as he will resist any change in relationships. Other people with a poor history of relationships may react even more rigidly and stubbornly and behave like "superglue," unable to accept the notion of separation. Such people often interpret filing for divorce not as an intention to separate, but as a form of communication designed to reconcile the couple. They interpret beating one's spouse not as a pathological outburst, but as an expression of frustration prior to an inevitable romantic reunion. To them, the manifest rejection represents underlying acceptance. Thus, Ernie is more fortunate than many other individuals.

Children, whether they think abstractly or concretely, should be able to learn the authenticity of love from their real-life models and hopefully understand that the Hollywood version of love is make-believe. The products of stable marriages, regardless of their intellectual level, know that serious domestic crises are rarely identified and resolved within the hour, with time-out for commercial breaks. But those whose real-life role models are deficient may get stuck in the Hollywood fantasy. How can parents counter the unrealistic images and expectations of love that one's young and impressionable children gain from movies and television? The answer is, of course, that the most important movie children will ever see is the one continuously playing in their own home. Most children, regardless of intellectual level, learn to distinguish between their own parents' deep personal relationships and the pervasive cultural messages that espouse a shallow conception of relationships.

Ernie had two years of schooling after high school and in his twenties has reached a mental age of fourteen years, which is enough to get by in life as long as he has emotional support. In contrast, people who buy into the Hollywood myth of romance are those whose mental or emotional age does not go much beyond eight or ten years. These people may graduate from high school and even go on to college and continue to develop their intellect according to their abilities, but if they have not matured enough to substitute reality for the Hollywood fantasy, they remain emotionally pre-adolescent in their conception of close relationships.

Many people reach adulthood with adolescent ideas about love. They are likely to harbor illusions about relationships and to believe in fantasy stereotypes that inevitably lead to disappointment. For example, she may be looking for a thoughtful man with a pipe, but finds that the smell of the pipe tobacco and slovenly habits of the philosopher are offensive. He may be looking for a quiet, intelligent girl to talk with, but eventually discovers that the reason she was so quiet was that she had nothing worthwhile to say.

Thus, the first job of a parent is to point out the disparity between fantasy and reality, in order to divest the offspring of such illusions. This message should be communicated continuously, since the illusion of Hollywood relationships is so pervasively extolled as a real possibility. Some individuals go to a movie, suspend their disbelief until the final credits roll, and then step out of the theater and back into their lives. Others live as though they were still in the movie, behaving like stars of a long-running melodrama by cultivating the wisecrack and the one-liner. Some individuals tend to make dramatic entrances and exits, as if they were in a film. During domestic arguments they utilize the clinching argument of a movie, such as, "If I had a woman at home I wouldn't look for one somewhere else," "A real man does what it takes to be a good provider," "Leave my parents out of this," or the ever-popular, "I'll see you in court." No adequate counter to such a cliché is possible because the purpose of such a low level of dialogue is not to enhance communication, but rather to "have the last word."

The emotional shallowness promoted by Hollywood ill equips one to deal with the real problems that inevitably crop up in intense relationships, including marriage; it does little to show that dialogue, rather than final-statement one-liners, provide the key to resolving conflict. Ernie, who is a candidate for marriage at some time, has already learned the basic lessons of dialogue in intimate situations through discussions about sex in regular group sessions at the workshop. He has learned that the most common reason for couples to refrain from engaging in sex is that one of the partners is angry at the other for real or imaginary reasons. The responses that Fred and Dinah provided to his questions about being married in the future were simple and standard, but not shallow. When he asked them if it was "okay to do it when I'm married," they answered in the affirmative and asked, "Anything else you want to know?" Ernie answered, "I already know. I should be nice and shouldn't fight and should talk about how I feel, even if it's hard, and everything will turn out all right. They said that at the workshop."

Ernie's level of intellectual and emotional maturity does not include the wisecrack or one-liner. He understands that both members of any couple should calmly state their reasons for dissatisfaction and talk it out with their partner. Using sex against the other person can only worsen an existing problem or can indicate just how far gone the relationship is. Although Ernie cannot articulate this, he knows that having sex in marriage is permitted and that having sex when he's not married is not allowed. He sees himself as a good boy and does what he is supposed to do.

Fred and Dinah's job since Ernie's infancy has been to help him grow to become independent of them. If a good parent is always working to put himself out of a job, and if he is doing such a good job, why does it never end? The reason that parenting is neverending is that offspring, intellectually impaired or not, mature or immature, always need their parents to some extent. Young children, in contrast to grown-up ones, are seen as legitimate dependents on their parents. They have bored deeply into the souls of their parents and sit within their parents' hearts securely with no desire or ability to leave. But parents like Fred and Dinah have to both accept their child and make life uncomfortable enough so that their offspring wants to leave and not come back.

Dinah always used to tell Ernie when he was hurt physically or emotionally, "Don't worry. If the beginning is bitter, it will be sweet in the end." She reinforced this verbal measure by giving him cookies and milk to tide him over the hardship. Ernie was comforted and overcame obstacles and thrived, continually repeating his mother's words of wisdom to himself and drawing sustenance from these words. His mother probably overlooked the reality of bitterness begetting more bitterness as well, but Ernie did not think about such things. He was a good boy and listened to his mother. His mother's simple statement made a greater impression on his life than any movie. Ernie could learn.

But cookies and milk are no longer the stable comforts needed when children become adults. The parents' continual deep emotional investment means that they should now provide adult love as distinct from the unconditional love they were expected to give when their children were small. Adult love has boundaries and obligations. Adult love provides stability when conditions are met. Stability is the major reason a limited adult child will terminate many short encounters with the opposite sex in favor of marriage. Marriage is the most serious long-term commitment an adult can make, and Ernie wants it for himself. After all, his parents and other people he has met seem to be in favor of it, so it must be okay.

EMPLOYMENT FOR THE RETARDED

By some twist of irony, Ernie is "fortunate" to be limited mentally because he works in the old economy at near subsistence wages with family and state support sufficient for his immediate needs. Ernie enjoys sheltered employment, in contrast to well-educated, intelligent and capable university graduates, who flounder in the insecurity of the employment market. Since Ernie's birth, his family has always known that he had to be protected to a certain degree from the harshness of market reality. His intelligent, well-educated counterparts are not so fortunate. Living in times when unemployment is rampant, they are often accused of being idle and living off the state welfare system. In the age of globalization, the middle-class population that always felt itself to be immune to the financial vagaries of the market has now crossed a boundary into the land of insecurity.

Many young, middle-class adults in the prime of their life and at the height of their prowess are the unemployed or under-employed in the new economy. They are called "stupid" for having studied subjects that do not lead to steady employment and for not working up to their potential. Ernie, on the other hand, may have been called "retard" or "dummy," perhaps, by an assortment of callow individuals, but he doesn't think much about it and enjoys self-respect for doing what he can in his controlled work environment. While Ernie does live partially off the state, he is considered a legitimate dependent person, while normal educated people suffer considerable degradation in a system that blames the unemployed for being unable to work. Ernie is, indeed, fortunate that he will always have a job, and is thus more secure financially than his non-handicapped counterpart.

By their acceptance of Ernie, his parents, his co-workers and society as a whole provide him with a positive view of himself. Ernie does not have a self-definition of being mentally retarded. That is a label imposed on him by society, one that does not affect his self-image. He's just Ernie, with nice parents and friends at work, and he is all right because everybody says that he is fine. He doesn't make a lot of differentiations between himself and others, and he feels himself to be an integral part of an ongoing system. By contrast, his well-educated counterparts try to differentiate between themselves and others, constantly evaluating themselves according to some socially determined standard. Ernie does not learn well and this, it turns out, is a blessing in disguise: he does not internalize negative lessons, like his more intelligent counterparts.

Separation from his parents will be difficult for Ernie. His parents have devised his universe. Ernie will not understand the separation because he wants his world to stay the same. Fred and

Dinah want the regular gradual changes of normal living and they must separate from Ernie without abandoning him in order to enhance growth for all. Ernie will have to work through the pain and fear of abandonment, perhaps with the help of counselors. His emotional stability and his guaranteed place in the sheltered workshop may cushion the gradual process of separation, and his positive self-image, stemming from his steady job, will be of great help.

Chapter Fourteen

AMAZING GRACE

INTRODUCTION

The story of Ernie placed great emphasis on emotional stability, good human relations, cultural values, love, work and the desirability of living a normal life. The psychological normality of a handicapped adult child like Ernie should be treasured. Ernie was intellectually handicapped with good parents. Only when normality is missing, as with individuals who are mentally ill, do we fully appreciate the ordinariness and order allotted to most people.

The following story is about the relationships among Joe, a schizophrenic adult, his mentally healthy daughter Naomi and the family psychologist, Mark. Joe's illness was permanent, so that normal life events were seen through the prism of mental illness. The relationship between the father and daughter had elements of normal family life mixed up with wide-ranging severe psychopathology. Naomi was a healthy person in a sick family, but she was a no-parent child. The inability to parent heightens the strains between a person with a normal life and a person with a severe mental illness. The lack of adequate parenting can evolve into unexpected emotional frangibility. One learns about one's parents by positive as well as by negative example. The bonds of trust are at the base of all human and parent relationships; as long as that bond isn't violated life continues.

The life ending of all the protagonists was determined less by their personality or intelligence and more by their parents. Mark knew that crises come to all families, including his own family of origin, and expose their strengths and weaknesses. He learned that education, professional training and even connection to positive role models sometimes cannot help with an overwhelming situation. He was left with a task worthy of Sisyphus: the endless search for the cause and cure of mental illness, thinking about the lives of the mentally ill and their families, hoping for the future, thankful that he and Naomi grew together for a while, and reconciling himself to becoming older and wiser. Mostly, he learned about the profound satisfaction of emotional involvement with people.

Synopsis

This final story deals with the relationships among Joe, who was diagnosed by psychiatrists as a chronic schizophrenic, his relatively mentally healthy daughter, Naomi, and their psychologist, Mark, who, together with many other caregivers, grapples with the issue of mental illness. Following pragmatic rules is generally sufficient to resolve immediate issues, but at other times, no matter what one does, the issues are beyond one's capacity and control. At such moments, one must learn to be thankful for amazing grace.

MENTAL ILLNESS

Joe and Celia met in the hospital, fell in love and got married. Joe had obsessive-compulsive personality traits; he was closed, withdrawn, suspicious, unfriendly, intellectual, distant and academically ambitious. He was nicknamed "the professor" in his routine job at the Archives of General Biology. Celia was an emotional and care-taking kind of person, garrulous, and always serving coffee and cake to anyone near her. She was used to "putting out" for many people and was generally considered a nice, friendly girl who "just couldn't keep her knickers on." Celia interpreted Joe's asexual orientation positively as respect for women, and she found his "braininess" sexually arousing. Unfortunately, the hospital where they met was a psychiatric hospital in the State of Indiana. Joe and Celia were both schizophrenics. The bizarre behavior of numerous family members included wild outbursts, lack of self care, public masturbation and arrests that led directly to the hospital instead of to jail.

Fortunately, Mark, their psychologist, was able to relate to them as individuals who were suffering from a particular state of mental illness, and he would not allow their dignity as people to be compromised because of their grim diagnosis. He had met them when he was a young psychologist in the closed ward of a huge mental hospital on the bank of the Wabash River that runs through Indiana. He instituted a peaceful socialization program in his ward, and personally served espresso coffee to his patients in an effort to enhance their appreciation of general civilization. His only curious side was his interest in schools of fish. He could spend hours looking into the murky river water, waiting for a bite. He believed that sitting on the bank of the river was mentally healthier than staring at the blank walls of the ward, and this belief was conveyed to his patients, especially to Joe, who became an expert in the fine art of fly fishing. Mark's best ideas came to him as he was contemplating fish and imagining the pain they must experience when they get hooked in the mouth. "The pain probably lasts only for a short time," he thought. "But here sitting quietly next to me is a man with an illness called schizophrenia which represents a pain so eternal that it is inconceivable."

After many weeks of sitting silently side by side, waiting for the catfish to bite, Joe felt secure enough to ask Mark how he had gone into this line of work. Mark told him that he had been studying out East when his cousin Lee died suddenly of "unknown causes" and that he had been astounded when the doctors couldn't answer his simple questions. He then returned to his native state of Indiana to become a doctor himself in an effort to determine the meaning of an "unknown cause." What he discovered was that some of the most important things in life were "unknown" but not necessarily "unknowable" if one could think clearly and persevere in pursuit of answers.

"No, no," said Joe, " you didn't understand my question. I want to know the real reason that you personally got into this line of work." Mark thought for a while, then said that it was because he had been Uncle Albert's favorite. Uncle Albert had been his extended family's godfather, responsible for the family's physical and mental health before modern science and psychiatry co-opted diagnosis and treatment for themselves. When a family member lost her first baby to Sudden Infant Death Syndrome (SIDS – now thought to be perhaps caused by insufficient lung development of the infant), the other mothers felt personally threatened by such a horrific occurrence, and her immediate community blamed her for not having been a good mother. Uncle Albert had been unable to dismiss the death as an Act of God. When Mark, a young child at the time, had asked him what had caused the death if not an Act of God, Uncle Albert had sadly shaken his head, saying, "I don't know. I just don't know." Albert, a non-judgmental and caring person, had visited the young mother on a daily basis for one year until she resumed the natural course of her life. Mark, turning to Joe, added that if it was okay for Uncle Albert to say that he didn't know something, then he figured it was okay for him to spend his life searching for the cause of "the unknown cause" of an illness, like the one that took his cousin Lee or the one with which Joe is afflicted.

Mark had felt a sense of kinship with his role model when he studied SIDS. The model of involvement in family matters is something that Mark carried over into his daily life when dealing with the "unknown causes" of illness. Mark decided that due to the changing times he would do well to clothe his natural abilities in the scientific knowledge of the day. Mark knew that he could not base his decisions only on the wisdom of his ancestor, but that he must acquire professional knowledge to resolve the emotional problems of his clients.

Taking stock of his abilities and their roots, Mark realized that his own family background was not unique, that many people in fact have the ability to "connect" with the emotional leader of their family – that ancestor who can serve as a role model. This is what parenting is all about. A parent facing a problem should be able to take stock of the issue with his family, asking what his own "Uncle Albert" would have advised.

Unfortunately, this in itself is not always enough. The wisdom of the critical ancestor, though crucial to parenting, is not always sufficient. In extreme cases the crisis or problem of the adult child is of such magnitude that the parent is powerless to help. In these cases the intuitive ability with which the parent is endowed should be complemented by modern scientific knowledge. This is where a professional like Mark comes in. The professional knowledge that Mark acquired in the course of his studies and his work gave him those additional tools to help resolve the emotional problems of his clients, but in the final analysis he knew that he was really still no wiser than his family godfather.

Mark never worried if he did not possess the professional knowledge necessary to grapple with a particular problem. He had been an extraordinarily calm student, confident that while plenty of smart people in the world could supply knowledgeable solutions to problems, he would tackle the problem armed with healthy instincts. Although Mark routinely asked colleagues for a second opinion about any problem he faced professionally, the second opinion he valued most was the role model within himself.

Mark trained at the University of Chicago with Prof. Sidney, a major researcher in the genetics of mental illness. This was the job he had coveted: it enabled him to study and help people like Joe and Celia. He had learned from his mentor, Prof. Sidney, that thinking was a worthwhile activity unto itself and that he, Mark, had the capacity to think rationally about patients and analyze their problems, while at the same time becoming positively involved with them.

Mark felt comfortable with Joe's cold intellectualism, which was emotionally akin to that of many of his teachers at university who had developed lack of involvement down to a fine art. These teachers had little difficulty preaching the virtues of boundaries and borders between doctors and patients because they seldom acted as practitioners. They had taught Mark that a human being needs at least one healthy parent to grow up to be a relatively healthy person. But unfortunately, as Mark was well aware, that is not always the reality of the world. After all, the mentally ill are people, too. They fall in love, marry and have children whom they cannot raise properly. Mark had reached a realization that would shape the course of his life: that while some parents are blessed by being able to help their children find solutions to their problems, others – such as schizophrenics – are doomed not to be able to help their children. Mark wondered whether he should take up the slack in the line of parenting, perhaps by becoming an "adoptive" parent to the children of the schizophrenics in his care. "It's not much of a job," he thought to himself as he strung his bait, "but somebody's got to do it."

Joe's next question penetrated his thoughts. "But what did you *really* learn at the University of Chicago?" he asked professorially, his growing confidence lending a more personal and penetrating air to his line of questioning. Mark answered: "I learned to stop speaking in psychiatric jargon and to put together a declarative sentence that made sense. My professors were so impressed by this that they recommended me for this job."

Joe was finally satisfied with Mark's answer. He started to make declarative statements that made sense to doctors at the hospital and he taught Celia to be quiet and cooperative with one female doctor who disapproved of Celia's "hysterical sexual activity." Soon they were both discharged with the stamp of "vastly improved" on their hospital records. Joe, in effect, had taken a sugar-coated verbal pill containing some unique, unknown ingredient that activated him to change his behavior and modify his relationships with his family and with Mark. Trying to ascertain the active ingredient is extremely difficult, perhaps impossible. Joe became vastly improved for a reason unknown to either of them. Joe said to Mark, "I don't know if this really helps, but I feel that people like me need people like you, so I keep on coming." Joe agreed to continue to participate in Mark's research endeavor, especially since a "real" professor from the University of Chicago was involved. Mark felt good about sharing his feelings with a patient as if he were a regular person with just another disease to be treated, and he wondered whether his conversations with patients constituted "real" therapy.

THE FAMILY OF THE MENTALLY ILL

Mark subsequently became godfather to the couple's two girls, Naomi and Abby, and followed their biological, psychological and social development from birth until their early twenties. He was engaged in longitudinal research that attempted to determine early markers of schizophrenia. Because of this long-standing relationship, he often felt like an anthropologist attached to an American Indian family.

Naomi was the "mothering child" in the family and became the family's minister of education, as she bossed her younger sister around and told her what and where to study. She was the cultural carrier of her mother's social acceptability and her father's achievement level. Abby was the "perfect little girl," whose personality could be characterized as "eternally pink," but unfortunately she displayed the early markers of schizophrenia from birth onward and led a limited and restricted childhood designed, for her own protection, to minimize stressful interactions.

The family was the darling of the social services; they met so frequently in group therapy at the outpatient clinic that they were awarded a designated parking spot. Both Celia and Joe were committed to the marriage and to educating their children properly.

Celia expressed feelings of jealousy toward her daughters, whom she viewed as beautiful. She tended to be resentful of her more passive, introverted and reserved husband, while at the same time appreciating his ability to work and support her. Joe was viewed by the clinic staff as a troubled person who worked hard at keeping his hallucinations and other psychotic features from interfering with his daily life, which he described as "a dream." The atmosphere in the home was characterized by passivity, lack of emotional involvement, and a kind of floating purposelessness reminiscent of a psychiatric ward. In fact, on one occasion when the children visited one of their parents in the psychiatric ward, Naomi mentioned that she felt "right at home."

Naomi and Abby were able to function in both the normal and psychotic worlds. Naomi was fluent in two languages, the one used by the normal people she encountered in school and in the neighborhood and the one used by her psychotic mother and father. After listening to Joe's ramblings and obsessive thinking, Mark would suggest a practical step for him to take in his complex relationship with his family. Joe would comment, "That sounds fine, but I don't know what you are talking about." At this point, Mark would ask Naomi to explain what he had just said. She would repeat Mark's suggestion but in terms understandable in the family context, and Joe would say that he now understood what had been said. In effect, the family interpretation – conveyed by Naomi – was more effective than the professional one. Perhaps this is the way it should be; after all, a professional is like the wall in a squash court against which the players locked in battle constantly bounce the ball. The family players give the professional's words dynamic and positive meaning with a life of its own.

Naomi appeared to be a "healthy" person, coping successfully despite the fact that she grew up in a "sick" family. Naomi was six years old when she first attended family therapy sessions. The psychiatric service that treated the family reasoned that the children must be at risk growing up in a "sick" family and should therefore receive some preventative care to allow for normal development.

Naomi was reported to be "perfectly normal," showing no sign of motor, perceptual, cognitive or affective problems. She was characterized as a "parentified child" – a child who takes on the role of the parent – and was described as calm, clean and orderly. She was close to her mother.

When Naomi was fourteen, she was described as having an athletic build and as being relaxed and alert during examination. Her motor, perceptual and cognitive functioning skills were all superior. She had an excellent attention span and was above average in reading and mathematics. She did not easily become frustrated. She was considered a leader and organizer both at school and at home. She had a strong will, was quietly assertive, and always tried "to do the right thing." Her tenth-grade teacher volunteered the observation that "this girl is the type about whom one says, 'still waters run deep,'" as if to suggest the possibility of some unseen emotional process taking place underneath a pleasant and placid surface. Naomi and Abby had parents with limited parenting capacity, and they would need a continuous support network of good-hearted adults, teachers and other professionals to complement their parents' deficiencies.

Naomi, now fifteen, showed up at the local baseball field as Mark was coaching Little League. She related easily to him, was free and open, and showed a warm and spontaneous expression of feelings. She seemed an intelligent, diligent and sociable adolescent. She discussed her friends and her relationship with her boyfriend with humor and sensitivity. She talked of her desire to achieve, but also wanted to have some fun. Then suddenly she changed the topic. "Do you believe that when people die they go to heaven? I mean, are you an observant person?" "Where did that question come from?" responded Mark in surprise. "I don't know, really. But my father said that I should ask you personal, penetrating questions so that you would think that I'm smart like he is. That's important to me, too."

"Okay," began Mark, "I'll do my best to answer. First, no one who has died has ever come back to tell us if they have been to heaven, so no evidence exists on the topic. Second, I presume you mean religiously observant." Then Mark stopped in his tracks, just short of continuing his pat answer. He was a therapist, not a philosopher of religion. His job was to listen carefully. "That really is a good question and you are smart for asking it. Actually, I'm not very observant of what goes on in the daily world. My family used to say about me, 'Imagine, he's been living in the house for seven years now, and he hasn't noticed that the cat doesn't have a tail.' Apparently I was a non-observant person who didn't notice the obvious. Since then I've learned that dysfunctional parents such as yours, an exceptionally neurotic dog, a mean canary or a mild-mannered bisexual cat for that matter, can all have sudden and unpredictable effects on a family member, particularly one in need. So, I would say that the answer to your question is that it is important to pay attention and observe what goes on in the house."

Mark fell silent for a minute, contemplating what he had just said. Naomi, too, was silent. Mark continued, "I came to grips with my own lack of perceptual sharpness by assuming that other people like me might be the same way. I sent a stream of volunteers to houses in the community to say, 'Ma'am, we at the church have been given a government grant to open a nursery school for the intellectually impaired and we're running a little short of children for the grant. Do you have a special retarded child in the house who you could lend us for the school?' The woman would answer, 'I'm sorry that we can't help you out, but we don't have a special retarded child in the house.' The volunteer would say, 'Not even one in the back room or the basement?' The person would answer immediately, 'Oh, that one! Sure you can have her for your school if that will help you out. Would you like a cup of tea?'" Mark paused for dramatic effect and then said: "Why am I telling you this story? Well, apparently, many people fail to notice that the cat doesn't have a tail or that there is an intellectually impaired child or a schizophrenic adult in the family."

"What the hell is he talking about?" Naomi thought to herself. But then she remembered what her father used to say, that sometimes one feels confused and that that is the way one generally feels in the presence of a smart person. "I guess my father would be proud of me for asking hard questions, even if I don't understand the answer," she said to herself. "I'm glad you think I'm smart," Naomi said out loud. "I like animals and children too. Maybe I'll be a vet."

Naomi had been taught to not pay attention to the sick members of her family and to refer to them euphemistically as people "who everybody knows are like that." Naomi and Abby sensed that Celia was the more emotionally available parent because of her involvement with them, but it was Joe, the parent they didn't pay attention to, who could return to disrupt their life plans. Naomi and Abby had been taught to suppress their disappointment in Joe's parenting by their mother's saying, "Don't pay any attention to him. That's the way he is. That's just the way he really is." This reckless recommendation to ignore a particularly disturbed parent, coming from an emotionally involved but equally unbalanced parent, teaches the child to mistrust her own feelings and perceptions.

Although Naomi seems an emotionally robust, normal child who has everything going for her, the hidden influence of the emotionally vacant parent might restrict her chances of success in life. She has to have that internal navigation instrument of turning to the right parent in times of need to steer her through life's turbulences. The existence of deficient parents means that a professional must be endowed with an emotional depth analogous to that of an adoptive parent who knows to be well prepared for trouble with the adopted children. Mark was prepared to assume this role for Joe and Celia's children without interfering with their authority, and he assumed this role with amazing grace.

DIALOGUES WITH NAOMI

One year later Naomi called Mark in crisis. Celia had been diagnosed as having breast cancer and was receiving radiation therapy. Naomi began to feel overwhelmed with tension and anxiety when she saw her mother falling apart. She realized that Celia was in danger with a potentially fatal illness and was beginning to fear the impending loss of her mother. She began to cry, but continued to talk about her feelings of closeness to her mother. She wanted some help for herself. She described the hours when the whole family was together as being "like organizational meetings" over which she presided. She didn't want to be in charge. She didn't want to continue to be the parent in the family. She wanted the job slot of a child. She wanted to tell the others how she felt.

She told Mark that she became angry with the therapists in the clinic when her mother had to take pills for her psychiatric illness, and she blamed the medications for causing her mother's state of deterioration. She quickly corrected herself by saying that she didn't mean that her mother should stop taking the pills. At times she denied that her mother was mentally ill. She empathized with her and wished that she could take her mother's "emotional pain" upon herself. Mark responded by reassuring her that she could not be "sick" like her mother and that she was a strong, realistic and competent adolescent who needed professional help in coping with this terrible situation. Mark told her that he would help by talking with her without the use of any medication.

Celia died from complications of cancer a few years later. Her husband and her two children had been well prepared by the psychiatric staff and were with her at the very end. Joe was moved by her death and was thankful to the staff. Still, he was disappointed with people who had wished him well during his wife's illness because she didn't get better. He could now no longer trust them.

A few years later Naomi, now married and almost twenty, turned to Mark for a letter of recommendation to college. She was still looking after her sister, but let it be known that she wanted a life of her own. She broke down crying and said to Mark, "I don't want people like you growing me up. I don't want to have to be a parent to my family. I want to have a regular family and raise my children myself and not have to turn to people like you all the time. You are really okay, but I want to raise my own family as soon as my sister gets settled." Mark pointed out that it was a good thing for her to fulfill her mother's "moral will" to look after her sister, but that she was also one of her mother's children and she needed to make time for herself and her needs. She smiled amidst her tears and said, "That's what my husband keeps saying. There must be something to it." While she had become used to the idea that she had been supported by forces external to the home, she intended to build internal strength with the help of her husband and to have a normal family life, finally freeing herself from dependence on complementary external parenting.

Mark lapsed into thinking out loud. "You are really a lucky person because your problems are so obvious and undisguised. Many people feel rotten much of the time and don't even know why. You're a lucky person because you are fully aware of why you're feeling so miserable." Naomi laughed ironically and continued laughing and crying at the same time. When she told her husband about the meeting with Mark, she laughed and cried again and was comforted.

Naomi still needed parenting despite her desire for independence. For financial and emotional reasons, Naomi and her husband lived with his warm, supportive, achievement-oriented, lower-middle-class family. After her first child she went into postpartum depression, was treated by a psychiatric social worker at the clinic, and snapped out of it. She was seen by the same social worker during her second pregnancy to prevent her from going into another depression. She was seen by Mark on a routine follow-up two weeks before giving birth and was found by him to be in good spirits. Both professionals agreed that she was not expected to go into a depression.

Nevertheless, she did suffer another post-partum depression after the second birth. She longed for the warmth and emotionality of her mother and thought about how much she missed her. The bond of trust between Naomi and her father had become deeply eroded since Celia's death. Naomi was reaching for the internal bond within herself to lift herself out of the post-partum depression. She came home to grasp at that rope of trust – unrealistically, it seems – to pull herself out of the pit of depression. However, despite the fact that the ties between Joe and Naomi had become frayed over the years, they did not break, though Naomi felt she was just managing to hang on. Naomi believed in parenthood because of her mother and expected that her surviving parent would continue to be committed to that bond between parents and children that survives the deepest disappointments. She turned to her father for support. His response was: "Don't bother me. I've got problems of my own." At 5:00 A.M. Naomi drove her car to the railroad crossing, and waited for the train before putting her foot to the gas. She missed her mother terribly.

WHOM SHOULD YOU TRUST: A PARENT OR A PROFESSIONAL?

Problems of mental illness may not be eased with age or maturity of the parent or the adult child. Naomi sought a temporary refuge from her pain when she turned to her father – who, tragically, was so locked up in his own emotional isolation that he was unable to balance his desire to help his daughter with his necessity to be continually focused on his mental illness. Joe was not capable of restoring any equilibrium to his daughter in distress because he himself was psychologically unbalanced. Unfortunately, in extreme cases of mental illness, an internalized sense of balance is precisely the missing factor. Naomi lacked a sustaining relationship with her father and couldn't wait patiently to be reunited with her mother, the figure who could provide that permanent sense of internal balance that allows one to deal with crisis. Naomi had succeeded in balancing her rights as a child with her responsibilities to her disturbed family as long as her mother was there to provide unconditional support and trust.

Joe had positive social and educational goals for his and Celia's children and, in the unfair game of life, sought to stack the cards in their favor. Joe's projection of his intellectual ambitions for his children lacked the emotional involvement necessary for success. He could not stack the cards in his children's favor because of his mental illness. Card players know that one should play cards with reliable and trustworthy people. Even so, one should cut the deck and shuffle before playing, just in case. Both Naomi and Joe needed to understand that trust is a precondition both in asking for help and in giving it. The live volcano of mental illness can be calmed, but not necessarily brought under enough control to warrant trust. Joe as parent, the mental illness always present within him, and Naomi were like three players in a two-player card game. Naomi trusted her father, but because of his mental illness, she was obliged to continuously cut the cards and juggle her relationship between her father and his mental illness. She had to remember at all times with whom she was dealing. Unqualified trust in her parent was never a realistic option for her, so she looked for trust in a reliable professional.

Naomi was not blessed with parents with normal and healthy capacities to raise children. She probably did not need parents capable of behaving like parental "super-heroes." Her surviving parent was not capable of becoming a better parent than he had been in the past and she had the bad luck to lose her nurturing parent. Naomi really didn't have a fair chance in life. The clinic staff's fears that she might be at risk turned out to be well-founded. Naomi was a seemingly normal young woman who played life and cards with the hand she was dealt. Joe played his game with a few missing mental and emotional cards. Naomi overlooked the obvious: Joe did not have a full deck.

A wise parent is generally preferable to a competent professional in solving an adult child's problem. A parent, unlike a professional, is more available. Joe is the exception that proves the rule. He was not available because of his mental illness. Further, Naomi's inner mental state may have escaped the critical notice of skilled mental health professionals. Naomi's fate might have been different if she had not continued to dwell in the "cave of mental illness" and, by contrast, lived with a nurturing mentally healthy parent.

Competent professionals must be involved to provide an optimal outcome. Professionals usually help substantively to cope with emotionally ineffective parenting but for multiple reasons cannot take on the role of actual parenting, not to mention time constraints. Mark's multiple professional obligations did not allow him to make the required effort to help Naomi through all the critical points in her life. Her best chance of surviving depended on continuous connections with people endowed with positive and healthy values, be it a parent or a professional.

THE PROFESSIONAL'S PERSPECTIVE

The true cause of Naomi's death may never be known. Maybe it was God's finger or some unknown biochemical change that touched Naomi's brain or soul at a crucial moment. Further, the unknown magnitude and depth of her problem may have been undefeatable due to genetic overdetermination. Responsible professional intervention is no substitute for good luck or divine intervention at critical moments. Moreover, Naomi was a grown-up responsible for seeking help for herself. Because she was followed so closely from birth to maturity, the tendency persists to think of her as a child rather than as an adult. Lest we forget, Naomi was the mother of two small children at the time of her death.

Mark reviewed the relationship. He realized that when she had asked him whether he was religiously observant she had been trying to establish an intellectually elevated dialogue with him as a fifteen-year-old girl trying to live up to her father's expectation for her to be smart. Mark also realized that perhaps she had been trying to establish a connection with a normal grown-up. He hadn't answered her question about religion, but instead had focused on the general importance of being observant. He had used authentic elements from his own background in a mildly mocking self-deprecatory manner to warn Naomi to be observant about her relationships. Unfortunately, his explanation had gone over her head and the warning had not been properly grasped. Naomi had understood the tale literally in a manner appropriate to her age and development, but had not extrapolated to her own circumstances, as intended by Mark. Mark could not warn Naomi directly about her father, and had hoped that she would get the message conveyed by the story. Further, when Naomi turned to Mark at the age of twenty, she may have been asking him for more than a recommendation for college. She was asking for a normal life.

THE PSYCHOLOGIST'S PERSPECTIVE

Mark tried to live a balanced life of his own in order to be a constant role model for others in their daily life. He was interested in people in general, including the mentally ill and their families, and was able to relate to them normally, as well as coping with their abnormalities. He could study Joe and fish with him. He had communicated well enough with Joe so that he and his wife were discharged from the hospital "vastly improved," but he had failed to communicate an essential cognitive and emotional message to Naomi.

Mark learned from the critical incident when Naomi turned to Joe for comfort that the sharpness of the tongue can be as fatal as the slice of a knife in life's critical moments. Fortunately, Mark was aware that his profession needs defence mechanisms similar to a surgeon's gloves to keep infections at bay. Sometimes problems can be so overwhelming for parents or professionals that even a careful following of the rules of parenting isn't enough.

Mark and Naomi went together and grew together for a time. His trip, like that of most mature people, was long and hard and filled with difficulties. One of these was Naomi's suicide. Mark is sure that he will meet God face to face at the end of his days. He would like to know why God didn't extend his hand to Naomi in that vital second between life and death. Perhaps if Naomi had had enough belief within her, the divine finger of God could have reached into her mind and saved her. Perhaps Mark should have been aware of the beginnings of a pattern of illness in her and found the genetic markers of mental illness. Perhaps his communication skills with both Joe and Naomi were not sufficient for the task at hand.

Living on the edge of life makes a man watchful and a little lonely. Mark gave up fishing on the banks of the Wabash River and became connected to his roots in baseball. He threw himself into Little League with all his energy. When a colleague asked why he took baseball so seriously, he said, "When you think that baseball is merely a game and that psychology is reality, you've really lost contact with your internal values."

Mark maintained a relatively balanced life, especially when compared to his patients. He had his quirks, but he could be a regular guy coaching Little League. He knew that baseball wasn't only a game, but a metaphor for life. One day Naomi's son showed up for batting practice, and with his first swing touched the bat to the ball with amazing grace.

Epilogue

Parents and children at any age are linked together – for better or for worse. To succeed at becoming a mature parent, the parent must constantly develop and strengthen essential characteristics and skills. A connection to one's intuitive people skills and maintaining faith in the importance of one's cause may ultimately help the parent succor his adult offspring. The parent must be willing to make major changes in his own life in order to become a positive role model for his child. In order to do so, he must seek a new dialogue in psychological or philosophical matters of importance to each of them. The dialogue might be fundamentally different from previous times, for each of them may change with time and events. When faced with the task of raising his adult child again parents should utilize the crisis to convey practical wisdom gained through age and life's experience. They can hope for a favorable outcome when previous wisdom is supplemented by modern knowledge. Even if the adult child has great difficulty in overcoming life's crises because of circumstances beyond one's control, one can still hope for amazing grace and a favorable outcome.

The parents' desire to achieve that internal sense of closeness to one's own being and to one's family will motivate them to cultivate the essential traits of mature parenting. Such an effort can make the trip up the mountain worthwhile for oneself and successful for the adult child. Ultimately, everyone has a personal mountain to scale. Life is a journey for most people; it is often hard, entailing much effort. One can stop in one's tracks and ask critical questions about why one is in pain. Pebbles in one's shoes may be painful and boulders blocking the path toward goals must be moved aside, often with great exertion. Sometimes the journey is through a desert or over the sea or in the air, but mostly it is an internal journey. The purpose of the journey is not to reach the end too quickly, but to form a relationship with the people close by who go together on the journey. Most of those people are your children and your parents.

A HEALTHY VALUE SYSTEM

A troubled adult child's best chance of thriving depends on connections with people endowed with positive and healthy values. A high level of commitment is expected from mature parents, but they do not have to reach "super-hero" status. Healthy value systems are often sufficient to help get an adult child's life back on track, but sometimes the mere possession of positive values is not enough. Naomi's parents, for example, had positive educational values, but lacked the normal and healthy capacities to raise children. Most parents instinctively say the right thing at the right time. Naomi's father said the wrong thing at the wrong time. He is the exception that proves the rule.

Such negative examples with unfavorable outcomes occupy a unique position in teaching one to become a mature parent, for it alerts the parent to the good fortune on his or her own road through life that keeps him or her away from the dangerous edge of the mountain. The lodestone of failure is often a more profound teacher than the accolade of success. Hopefully, highly motivated normal parents will become increasingly aware of the child's needs and have the capacity to develop the necessary skills and characteristics to succeed. Naomi's surviving parent, unlike most parents, was not capable of becoming a better parent than he had been in the past.

Modern man has lost contact with the original purpose of life, which was closeness to and knowledge of God, as in the example of Moses on the mountaintop seeing God face to face – or perhaps feeling the living God within him. Faith in God, in God's universe or in a higher force means that man is not the center of the universe, that he is not particularly important in the greater scheme of life.

The belief that man is not important in the journey of life means that God does not exist to heal the narcissistic injuries of humans and that man should look forward to reaching God on the metaphorical mountaintop. Mark is sure that he will meet God face to face at the end of his days, and he would like to know why God didn't extend his hand to Naomi. Perhaps Mark should have been aware of the beginnings of a pattern of illness in her.

Despite the belief in a higher power, people remain responsible for their own destiny. Neither parent nor child should wait for divine intervention. A healthy value system cannot be forced on a sick system. Mark's system could not be imposed on this family, for the problem was not sufficiently understood. Each family member is ultimately responsible for his or her own destiny and cannot rely on human or even divine intervention for solutions. Perhaps being aware of a pattern of illness would have helped. Perhaps if Naomi had had enough belief within her or more mental health herself, someone could have reached into her mind and saved her in that critical split second in her life. Parents have to look deep within themselves for their own sources of strength and health rather than rely primarily on an outside source, for a good enough pair of parents is often more effective than a competent doctor whose time constraints and emotional and scientific distancing mechanisms may not bring him close enough to the problem.

AN INTERNAL SENSE OF BALANCE AND STABILITY

An internal sense of balance between opposing forces, such as obligation to family and individual rights, is necessary for a stable family life. The adult child's sense of entitlement must be weighed against the rights of other members to prevent a family imbalance. Freedom without limits for anybody is irresponsible. The joint deliberation about mutual obligations renders problems manageable. *The parent must find a balanced guide through the perplexing paradigm of grown-up children returning home with the expectations that their dinner, laundry and allowance will resume as if nothing had happened in the meantime.* The parents, having raised their child's expectations of near endless entitlement, are now responsible for restoring an internal sense of balance by setting limits.

Unfortunately, in extreme cases an internalized sense of balance is precisely the missing factor. Naomi's father Joe was not capable of restoring any equilibrium to his daughter in distress because he himself was psychologically unbalanced. Naomi lacked a sustaining relationship with her father and couldn't wait patiently to be reunited with her mother. Naomi was an excellent juggler – since childhood she had been balancing her rights as a child with her responsibilities to her disturbed family – but she lacked a figure who could provide that permanent sense of internal balance.

Mark tried to live a balanced life of his own. He tried to strike a balance between psychology and baseball. He knew that baseball wasn't only a game but a metaphor for life. Perhaps something of his relationship with Naomi was transmitted to her son. Perhaps something of Naomi's relationship with her son was passed on through Mark's coaching of her son. Although he had failed Naomi, he now had a second chance.

Parents have often seen observable imbalances being righted through simple communication. Pointing out noticeable imbalances, not interpreting them, allows the child to focus on them. For example, a parent might help the child get his priorities straight by pointing out that people who are trying to maintain a relationship shouldn't behave in a particular manner, as when the adult child is working or spending all his time with his friends instead of investing sufficient time with his wife. Her reactive responses to his behavior may in turn make her seem imbalanced in her views on his work. The couple can easily drift apart as she wants to talk about relations while he wants to relax after a day's work. Eventually, they may develop different maps of reality itself with the attendant claim that one of them is living an illusion. When simple communication has broken down, a professional should probably be consulted.

Mature parents should try to do the right thing and be capable of repeating home truths. Mature parents need patience to exert their influence on their adult children, as well as reasonable wisdom and intelligence and adequate resources. Their patience may be the only way to erode the imbalanced positions of the adult children. Imbalances and disturbances abound in life, but no one person can take care of them all, so it falls to the parents to take care of those problems closest to them, for a parent – unlike a professional – is always available. Parents willing to devote themselves to the task of helping their children can generate resources of wisdom that no individual professional can muster.

MAINTAINING AN ORDERLY AND STRUCTURED LIFE PATTERN

The parent must concentrate on being a positive role model for the adult child. Being cheerful, content, connected to work, studious and thoughtful about relationships helps to provide an alternative model to the angry, quarrelsome, discontented relationships of a child in distress.

The parent engaged in a structured life pattern with little pain and good personal habits, including a good relationship with a partner, can provide a positive model of how to avoid pitfalls. By contrast, an adult child besieged in a disturbed relationship is frequently in psychic pain and often in physical distress, sometimes even neglecting personal hygiene and proper eating habits. Children in distress may neglect their appearance and look slovenly and dirty. They often put on excessive weight. Their anger may prevent them from maintaining a regular sexual relationship with their partners. If the relationship is especially bad, habits conducive to physical and mental health may deteriorate. Worse still, developing extra-marital relationships – a common response in the face of a dysfunctional relationship – is liable to make them feel even worse about themselves, especially these days when fear of a sexually transmitted disease such as AIDS can threaten them with death and dishonor. Adult children facing these issues do not need parents to berate them for their irregular life patterns, or constantly "nag" them to change their habits and life-styles. If mature parents are focused on their own lives, ultimately the children will look to their parents' ordered and structured life pattern for liberation.

THE IMPORTANCE OF DIALOGUE

The parents' first response is to deny the thought that their adult child is in trouble. Parents may rationalize this tendency by saying that the child should handle his or her problems alone because talking about them can only cause embarrassment and distress to others. How many of us are familiar with the mother's cry of outrage: "How could you do this to me?" "What will the neighbors think?" The continual denial of a problem is often a veiled way of telling the child in distress to go away and not bother anyone, as in, "Of course I would help my adult child, but he's doing fine. Just a minor matter with his wife." When it becomes clear that the problem will not go away simply by being ignored, the parent then reluctantly acknowledges that it may be discussed *within* the family. Not a word, however, should be breathed outside the walls of the home. The number of people who are "in the know" expands, but only within the family itself. After all, what would the neighbors think?

The tendency to "keep to a lid on problems" can be an impediment to progress. Even when a problem is acknowledged, help is generally sought within the family alone, and proper professional sources of help are not engaged. But no matter how self-sufficient the family unit is, there may come a time when external help is the appropriate choice. Modern man does not live in primordial caves or tents, but in urban or suburban environments in houses with hot running water, indoor toilets, access to doctors, psychologists, social workers, churches or synagogues, schools, financial services and courts. The amenities of civilization enable a person in trouble to seek help from sources outside the family, such as professionals and self-help books. Modern man is not required to handle all problems alone or with his close family in the cave or tent of their choice. He is civilized and can seek help from books and professionals who shun gossip and who respect his privacy. Personal problems must not be denied, and turning to the right person at a moment of crisis is both acceptable and permitted and, indeed, should be encouraged.

No parent is perfect and no one can meet all of society's expectations. In an ideal modern world man is taught to love his fellow man or neighbor as himself and to love God and strangers. He must constantly take into account other people in the urban environment. He is taught about guilt, transgressions, rebuke, repentance and forgiveness. He is expected to prevent wrongdoing by others, to be a good citizen and to vote for the worthier candidate. He is expected to respect the dignity of others and not shame them. Modern man is taught to be good to widows and orphans. Modern man is also expected to help his adult child in difficulty.

PARENTING IN TIMES OF CRISIS

When a young couple has been living together for a few months, or even a few years, parental involvement is generally minimal. Involvement increases somewhat when marriage is in the air and also when grandchildren begin to arrive. Under catastrophic conditions, such as an impending divorce, involvement may become total and all-consuming. What degree of involvement is appropriate under what circumstances? *The degree of involvement with one's adult child is generally a function of the child's emotional circumstances.*

Loneliness may bring adult children home in need of a temporary haven to lick their wounds. The operative word here is "temporary." The parent should encourage the returning adult child to deal with the pain of separation, offering tea and sympathy as a prelude to being assertive about re-attachment.

Mature parents know that in even the most carefully crafted scenarios, total acceptance of children as if they were infants is uncalled for. The rules of emotional acceptance change with circumstances. The acceptance of a person in a temporary state of dependence should be coupled with a willingness to place demands on the adult child. Parents should first give reassurance, approval and attention to the returning child. Then they must clarify whether the child has instrumental dependency needs, such as a debit or an accumulated credit card debt. Such issues must be dealt with immediately, perhaps by paying off the credit card debt, canceling the card, and giving the adult child only cash. After all, cash, unlike credit, is self-limiting.

After the acute practical issues have been addressed, parents should determine whether their adult child is still in a state of stress and requires additional reassurance or approval. In that case the parents must try to contain their anxiety and strive to achieve and maintain a level of calm detachment, the optimal state when dealing with any crisis, including – or especially – one related to a beloved child. Optimally, the parents will combine emotional acceptance with objective demands, with the ultimate goal of encouraging the child to regain his or her normal life and become autonomous once again. "You don't have to be in a party mood to go to a party!" can be a positive and supportive message to a distressed adult child reluctant to leave the security of the parental home.

ACCEPTING FINANCIAL ADVICE

Adult children who ask for help may be signaling their inability to handle freedom and independence. They may be seeking instead the security of parental restrictions because they feel better with boundaries. *The most important boundary for adolescents and adults of any age is money.* In many cases of crisis adult children find themselves financially worse off than they were before. This is obviously true when one is fired or loses one's business, and it is no less true in the event of divorce and the establishment of new fiscal realities. Under these circumstances mature parents may find themselves dispensing not only advice, but also financial assistance. Parents have to ask themselves, "How much and for how long?"

Financial matters should be discussed at length with the adult child in a private setting, otherwise those decisions made on the spur of the moment of need often result in the parent feeling a victim "hit on" for money. Mature parents must be confident they are making the desired statement when they give money, because a financial commitment may become a defining statement for the relationship between the parent and the child. The meaning of financial requests is often not clearly understood between both parties because one party may be defensive while the other is certainly anxious.

A modicum of humility may prevent the parent from jumping head-on into the adult child's tragic maelstrom and then being swept away and drowning in the storm of emotions and debt. For example, when an adult child comes to the parents with a problem relating to education, the parents may assume that he or she only wants them to pay for whatever course he or she fancies. He or she, on the other hand, may be seeking their input in a broader sense, including the "street smarts" that they acquired over the years about money, as well as the value of a particular degree. The adult child may need a lesson in fiscal reality more than the money itself.

Middle-class adult children of today's generation never expected to be poor like their parents or grandparents. Their affluence was promised to them as a birthright, and someone should be held accountable for that. It could be a spouse. It could be an employer. But in fact, it usually ends up being the parent. By contrast, people growing up poor have always known that the way a person deals with money defines them as a person. The middle-class adult child may know this on a theoretical level but has never had the opportunity to put theory into practice. A crisis will give him or her this opportunity at last. There have always been many people who have had to cope with endless poverty, but the modern "downsized" adult child has now the opportunity to develop new ego strengths by overcoming the insult of rejection by spouse or employer with the inevitable accompanying impoverishment.

The parent can prepare to deal with the emotional outbursts and financial onslaught of a distressed child by not being isolated in making financial decisions. Consultation with others can help in working through negative traits such as instant anger or excessive generosity or stinginess, which may handicap a positive resolution. The parent would be wise to routinely seek a second opinion about a contemplated financial transaction, in order to minimize the danger of sending an incorrect message. A considered second opinion about a contemplated financial act could be beneficial because the subsequent relationship may be unchangeable once a financial statement has been made. The mature parent should engage in preparing various alternative positions since the first batch of suggestions are often unpalatable to the upset adult child. Constant self-examination of one's strengths and weaknesses in financial matters is a prerequisite for success in interpersonal family relations.

HUMILITY

People have a natural tendency to use crises to show off how "good" they are at handling such situations, but in the process generally fail to make the prerequisite emotional contact with the adult child. Such behavior is commonly found among dominant relatives who lay claim to the ability to save situations at the last moment and frequently point to a successful track record of crisis management. Unfortunately, they often violate the rules of human problem solving by introducing egocentric thinking.

The mature parent walks in the middle way between financial, political and moral extremes. Techniques employed at the office to cope with interpersonal conflicts are not appropriate for personal problems at home. People may "act out" politically conservative or liberal biases, which may be largely irrelevant to the issue at hand. A politically conservative father may think that saying "no" allows him to keep the "tough guy" image he developed at the office even though it doesn't help his adult child. A liberal easy-going father may be tempted to maintain his "nice guy" image at the cost of becoming an ineffective parent. A superior or elitist, morally inclined mother may dispense advice that sounds good but misses the point. She has the unshakable belief that her recommendation is the only correct answer. This mother superior may be respected for her advice – despite the fact that it goes unheeded. She creates a portfolio of good advice never taken although widely circulated, thus enhancing her moral reputation. Parents must try to develop a comfort zone for their adult child. They should strive to be like the baby bear's bed in the well-known fairy tale: not too hard, not too soft but just right.

AN ABILITY TO CONTROL ONE'S ANGER

The parent should not explode in rage at the inappropriate behavior of adult offspring. For the mature parent who has mastered his or her anger, it is merely energy to be harnessed to achieve desired consequences. Controlled anger leads to a controlled outcome. Laser-sharp thinking can focus anger to solve the problem and thus facilitate a change in both the parent and the adult child. Keeping anger under control is necessary to prevent the parent from losing the ability to direct troubled offspring. Furthermore, since the adult child may be in a sensitive and vulnerable state, the parent must be careful to refrain from reproaching the child or escalating his or her feelings of insult or shame. Generating defensiveness can render the adult child non-receptive to the parent's suggestions. When the emotional climate of the discussion is kept under control, more pragmatic issues – where the grandchildren will attend school, which parent should leave the house in a divorce or which educational program the adult offspring should pursue – can be dealt with calmly and without outbursts. The mature parent knows that *anger shadows the mind and prevents clarity of thought.*

A WELL-DEVELOPED CAPACITY TO LISTEN

In addition to staying balanced and controlling anger, the parent must make a major effort to listen to an adult offspring. Parents begin by listening to their young children in order to establish a healthy friendship and to be confident that their children will turn to them in times of crisis. If there has been no family history of the elder generation listening to the younger one, the parent should make a conscious and concerted effort to begin to do so, for parents who have not been in the habit of truly listening to their children in childhood are not likely to do so later. This advice is hard to follow if the parents become agitated themselves, because listening is an active process requiring focus and a quiet mind. For offspring in any circumstances the knowledge that their parents listen to them – indeed, that they are worth being listened to – often gives them the underlying strength that enables them to resolve their own problems. *Listening in times of crisis is an active, not a passive process.* Active listening with one's entire consciousness in times of crisis provides insights that ultimately lead to the resolution of the problem.

The ability to maintain silence while listening in a crisis guards wisdom. Maintaining silence prevents one from having to retract hasty statements containing errors in judgment. Silence guards the parent from words later regretted. A well-preserved silence allows the parent to recover from the initial shock when he or she first hears of a misfortune occurring to a beloved son or daughter.

The mature parent serves as a friend to the adult child in crisis. Friends listen. A person in crisis vents emotions to a friend and comes away feeling better in the knowledge that someone has been listening intently, even if no external factor has changed. Parents should be secure in the knowledge that active silent listening is beneficial to the child. They must patiently listen to their child's angry verbalizations, to his or her ranting and raving. Eventually some substance will emerge from the pain and chaos. The parent's role is to pick up on that substance and to verbalize and elaborate on it.

What comes from the mouth should stem from the heart. Showing emotional support through financial gestures, such as paying for trips, is positive only if the offer comes from the heart without any signs of the cold cleverness of enticement. Speaking with honesty and integrity shows respect and friendship for the child at his or her moment of crisis. Mature parents should try to recall relationships of mutual attentiveness that were experienced in different times in their lives in an effort to draw a parallel. If the parents were not listened to as children by their parents, listening will not come naturally and will require a sincere effort on their part. Hopefully, they will succeed even though old habits and responses die hard.

When the adult child turns to the mature parent for help, his or her anguish should not be belittled. The parent should stick to the essentials, resisting any temptation to mock, cajole or reprimand the child. "How could you do something like that?" is an exclamation best avoided. Nobody likes to hear, "I told you so." Making wisecracks may relieve the immediate tension, but in the long run will lose points. Nobody really pays attention to a wise guy – however witty – and nobody really listens.

Conversely, parents must not join their adult children in the depths of their despair. Parents should listen to their adult offspring's misery in whatever form it takes. Offspring may be angry, petty, jealous, contemptuous or disrespectful toward the people whom they believe to be the architects of their personal or professional disasters – spouses, employers, judges, etc. The experience of being "down-sized" at a job is painful, even for an emotionally healthy adult with a successful work history; it is even more devastating for someone with a poor history.

For parents who had parents who listened to them, listening to their adult offspring comes naturally. Almost everybody has somebody in their past – a teacher, a doctor, a friend – who at some point listened deeply and made a difference in their lives. The parent should speak softly. Speaking softly is a sign that you are used to being listened to and expect others to be attentive and to hang onto your words. In contrast, people not used to this often speak loudly, as if in a non-responsive echo chamber.

Listening skills can be developed by practicing alone without the distraction of real people. One can develop listening techniques by having dialogues with verbally non-responsive objects or animals. For example, one often asks plants questions without expecting answers, as in, "Are you thirsty? Would you like some water? Are you getting enough sun? Would you like to be moved to a different spot in the morning?" One often talks to flowers in endearing terms, as in, "Gee, you're really pretty and smell good." One may practice empathy by looking into a dog's eyes and saying, "Yes, I know how you feel. You need a friend. Let's go out for our evening walk. We'll both feel better." One practices coping with frustration and ingratitude by petting and raising a cat, as in, "I know it feels nice to be petted. We all like that. But why are you so demanding and standoffish? You come to me only when you need something and not when I need some affection from you."

No amount of practice, however, can prepare one sufficiently for the difficult task of listening to a distressed adult child. The best preparation is belief in one's own value system, an internal sense of balance and stability, and the maintenance of a reasonable lifestyle to serve as a model for the adult child. The wise use of dialogue and care in the dispensation of money, coupled with the ability to control one's anger, should be sufficient to raise one's adult child successfully.

A Message for Society

The main goal for parents is to maintain emotional involvement with their young children and adult children throughout their lives as long as they are physically, financially and mentally capable. The argument that the children are now grown up, have moved away and that their troubles are of their own making is a shallow, passive, evasive ploy designed to absolve immature parents of responsibility. Adult children continue to need parental care in a new way in order to thrive. Harsh limit setting, withdrawal of love or money, or an unwelcoming and forbidding attitude deliver a message of emotional distancing, not supportive emotional involvement. Parenting ends when one of you is called to God.

Some people have hearts inclusive of other people's children as their own, but some do not. Some people are self selected to working with children and parents at any age – nurses, doctors, psychologists, teachers, etc. – and some are not. Some people do not relinquish value-based parental authority, while some abandon their emotional involvement with the undeserving needy as not being worthy of their association. The fantasy behind such immature thinking about long-term needy children and adults seems to be that the problems will disappear when services are no longer available, privatized or disappear from view.

The reality is that little problems neglected and untreated become big problems. Failure to help parents of the mentally ill, the mentally retarded or the learning disabled to solve their children's problems at all ages means that those adults return for parenting in the absence of socially available treatment. The systematic cutting back of public services for other people's children throws problems upon the backs of overburdened parents. The resulting strain on the aging parents may shorten their life span as society perpetuates neverending parenthood. An immature society is not fulfilling its duty to help parents raise socialized children and adults when it withholds emotional or financial support from the only group with an eternal willingness to support needy children and adults – their parents.

About the Author

Aaron Auerbach was born in Boston in 1934. He obtained a BA in history at Brandeis University in 1956 where he was introduced to the writings of philosophers such as Maimonides. A master's degree in human development at Harvard University in 1963 was followed by a PhD in developmental psychology at Purdue University in 1967.

His professional career has included teaching various courses in psychology at a number of universities (Iowa State University, York University, the Hebrew University of Jerusalem, the University of Chicago, Wilfred Laurier University and Purdue University), as well as carrying out academic research and publishing approximately twenty articles (mainly in the fields of learning disabilities, mental retardation and mental illness).

His clinical career began as a military psychologist in the United States Army for two years, and he later served as a psychologist in the Israel Defense Forces reserves for sixteen years. He has served as director of psychological services for children in hospitals, clinics and schools in Israel and the United States, also working in drug rehabilitation. In private practice continuously since 1971, he has specialized in complex family interactions.

Aaron Auerbach is a neverending parent to three adult offspring who, although fully independent, remain in close touch.

He can be reached via e-mail at:
aaronauerbach@hotmail.com.